Hope on the River

An Unlikely Captain's 1700-mile Mississippi River Journey
on a Leaky Raft to Save his Nonprofit

by Erich E. Mische

A Mostly Optimistic But Totally True Tale with
A Splash of Near-Death Encounters

Hope on the River

Published by Spare Key
480 Broadway Street,
Saint Paul, MN 55101

ISBN: 978-1-7371398-0-5

Developmental edit by Amy Martin
Line edit by Sandy Sullivan, Ivywild Editing and Writing Services
Cover art by Maisie Mische
Chapter Icons by Erich Mische
Photo Credit: Riverboat Captain Michael Coyle, The Twyla Luhr Pg. 37

Publicity, Marketing and Communications by Sarah Putnam, Natalia Simonett, Velocity Public
Affairs, LS2 Group, Bridge Public Affairs, The Ingram Group, Run Switch Public Relations, &
Bellmont Partners

Title inspiration by Brooke Lee

Design: Erik Christopher
Ugly Dog Digital

First Edition 2021

Prologue

A few miles past Lock and Dam Number 21, I came upon a large towboat pushing barges up the river. Nothing unusual, and not a large enough entourage to cause me much concern.

I looked at my navigation app on my iPad and quickly determined that I had plenty of room on the port side of my raft, the SS Hail Mary, to exit the navigation channel and just let the towboat go by. For some reason, though, I got on the radio and asked the tow's captain for his opinion. I was quite sure his first set of instructions aligned with my thought: that I should go to my left and stay out of his way until he got by me.

However, his response was not clear, and I repeated my request for guidance from him.

He then said, "One whistle"—meaning that we should pass port to port—and instructed me to go by him on the green buoy side, my right.

I was skeptical, but he assured me that the water on my side was deep and we would get past one another uneventfully.

I should have stuck with my original plan.

The space from the shoreline to his rolling wake—with me in the middle—was not very wide at all. As I approached his port side, I regretted the decision immediately.

I could tell that I had extraordinarily little room to wiggle between him and the shoreline, so I picked up speed in the hope that I could ride past his wake quickly.

Unfortunately, that tactic didn't work this time.

The wake he created was not a simple chop; it was a rolling tsunami. I quickly assessed my options.

I couldn't go right, because I would go directly into the shoreline.

I couldn't go left, because he had not yet gotten far enough past me to allow me to get back into the navigation channel.

So instead I rode head-on into the first of several massive, rolling waves.

The raft pitched straight down into the river and stopped. I gasped as I felt myself being flung forward and down.

The water poured in and the motors labored under the brick wall of water I had hit.

It happened a second time, and this time the raft went down deeper and I nearly flew over the steering console.

I knew I wouldn't survive a third time.

I stopped the motors and let the third wave wash over the deck as I pushed myself to the front of the raft and desperately threw three sandbags off the front, into the river.

I then throttled up the motors, turned the nose sharply to port, and made my way back into the navigation channel. I decided that I would fight the roiling backwash and turbulence of the towboat in the channel rather than battle any more of the wake outside it. It took me a good fifteen minutes to ride out this roller-coaster. As the waves got smaller, they came faster, until finally I made it to calm water.

I was exhausted. Sweating. The raft was soaked. And I found myself shaking. Not from the cold but from the realization that the SS Hail Mary had nearly ended up seventeen feet down on the bottom of the river, with me in it.

Months earlier, when I had decided to take a raft down the Mississippi, I had envisioned myself going it alone. After all, how hard could it be, right?

My vision of a slow and leisurely drift, complete with time to read books, wax poetic in a journal, fish for the monster catfish I'd heard and read about, and chat with my fellow "river rats" was as vivid in my mind as a motion picture.

My mistake in how I had rearranged the weight on the raft that morning was multiplied by the error of not trusting my judgment about going to the left side of the channel. Had I done so, the encounter would never have happened. The near sinking would have been avoided. And I would have been in a better position a couple of hours later when the next catastrophe struck.

For Dudley

Contents

SECTION I
Trip Preparation

SECTION II
On the Water

Foreword
By Norm Coleman

The Mighty Mississippi evokes some powerful imagery. It's an artery that runs through the heart of America. And along the way, it pumps life into countless towns and cities from Minnesota to Louisiana.

In the fall of 2020, at the height of the Covid pandemic, Erich Mische journeyed down the Mighty Mississippi, from St. Paul, Minnesota, to Baton Rouge, Louisiana, in a homemade, makeshift raft. It was a journey in which he encountered big barges and high hopes. And although he had no nautical skills or experience, he survived to tell the tale!

Certainly, this excursion does not have the grandeur of Sir Edmond Hillary scaling the summit of Mount Everest, or William Peary being the first to reach the North Pole, or even Minnesota's own Charles "Lucky" Lindbergh soloing across the Atlantic. But in a time of Covid darkness, Mische encountered countless rays of hope—from the stories of those who lived and worked on the river to the timeless grandeur of the Mississippi itself. And Mische's retelling of this journey of hope will bring hope and optimism, which is so desperately needed today.

I have known Erich Mische for almost thirty years. He ran my successful campaign for Mayor of St. Paul in 1993. He was my chief of staff when I served in the United States Senate. He wrote countless speeches and press releases for me. He knows how to communicate, and that will be obvious to readers of *Hope on the River*.

In the fall of 2020, Erich took it upon himself to "conquer" the Mississippi by traversing it in his raft to raise money for the charity he has led for the past nine years, Spare Key. This organization helps families dealing with medical crises avoid adding financial crises to their lives by assisting them in paying their bills. Surely it was a noble effort—but at significant risk and a little crazy! Because the one thing Erich is not ... is a mariner. He is not skilled in sailing, nor river navigation, or nor boat-building.

But Erich is a storyteller.

And along the banks of the Mississippi, he encountered stories to tell. Stories that reflect the American spirit. Stories that reflect the power of that iconic river. Stories of individuals and communities staying afloat in the midst of Covid. And in times like this, we need those stories.

As so many struggle to get their lives back on course almost a year into the global pandemic, we should welcome Erich Mische's journey of hope.

For some, it will be an inspiration to do what others tell them can't be done. Those who live their lives on mighty rivers like the Mississippi will tell you they can be dangerous, particularly for someone unschooled in river currents, passing through locks and dams—and avoiding getting crushed or capsized by massive towboats. When Mische first discussed his proposed quest, I thought he was insane and that he was going to get himself killed. And as one reads his journals, there were numerous occasions where he must have thought those fears were going to be realized. But he persevered and made it to Baton Rouge. I hope this journey's story encourages folks to dream big, stay the course, and achieve what others tell you can't be done.

This chronicle's significant contribution is that it reminds us that the American spirit is alive and well—even in the midst of a Covid pandemic. This country made its way from sea to shining sea by folks with grit and perseverance. In these modern times, those attributes are still required for folks who live and work in the shadow of the Mighty Mississippi. And though many of the "normal" gathering spots, bars, and restaurants were shuttered by the pandemic, Mische was still able to connect with folks along the way—graced by their hospitality and now, as a storyteller, telling their story.

But most of all, this is Erich Mische's story. Motivated by his desire to keep helping sick kids and their families, he committed himself, both physically and emotionally, to challenge Mother Nature—and he persevered. This book is about hope—hoping that you didn't commit yourself to something that will kill you! Hope that your efforts would allow Spare Key to continue to help families focus on their loved ones and not their bills during a medical crisis. Hope that kept river towns alive during a terrible pandemic. Hope that keeps you going when reality tells you it's time to quit.

Hope is a powerful elixir. We need it now more than ever. And Erich Mische gives us a healthy dose in *Hope on the River*.

It's an American story. And it's worth telling.

It has been said that one light has the power to conquer all the darkness. This journey of hope is such a light.

—Norm Coleman, former United States Senator from Minnesota, February 2021

Hope on the River Launch Ceremony Speech, St. Paul, Minnesota, August 27, 2020 By Owen Mische

When my dad announced his intention to float down the Mississippi River on a homemade raft, I was skeptical, to say the least. This is a man who knows very little about sailing or being on the water, navigation, or boat construction. However, those are all technical skills. They can be learned by most anyone who attempts, with some effort, to learn them. The qualities that will determine the success of this venture are more intangible. Determination. Commitment. Flexibility. Many, many more. Anyone can learn to read a map. Not everyone can deliver results.

Our family has gotten used to my dad's rather uncanny ability to rapidly advance his schemes from the wishful thinking stage to the "I am standing in front of my raft about to set sail" stage. I have no reason not to believe that my dad will deliver results with this voyage. He is, to paraphrase the John Wick films, a man of focus, commitment, and sheer will.

My personal involvement in this enterprise, beyond jumping over the boxes of supplies and provisions that littered our home like a minefield, was as a part of the construction crew. Over a five-day period, my dad and I spent many hours with family and friends building the magnificent vessel that sits before you. I learned a little about construction, mostly that I am not good at it. It was hot, it was fly-infested, and several times I was convinced that we would never finish, but my time helping build the SS Hail Mary was easily the best time of my summer. It was a blast for a lot of reasons, but the foremost one is I got to spend time with my dad.

My dad does not undertake this voyage in any grand maritime tradition. He is certainly not a salt dog, a shellback, or an ancient mariner. He does, however, add his name to the rolls of several great American traditions. Traditions like service to others. Refusal to accept failure. Overcoming obstacles simply because they are there.

The significance of a trip down the Mississippi is not lost on me. The Mississippi has been hugely important to this country, as a means of transportation, trade, and identity. The image of steaming or floating down the Mississippi is a vivid and uniquely American one. He will be traveling across a huge swath of this nation. He will meet people who represent a far broader cross section of America than the Twin Cities. This journey of Hope on the River, much like the river itself, will bring people together. It already has, and I am confident that it will for the next two months and beyond.

Hope on the River is something special. It is going to be a great feat, a great service, and ultimately a great adventure. Not just for my dad, but everyone who is with him in spirit. And although this trip will almost certainly not place Erich Mische among American heroes like Dick Winters, Gene Kranz, or JFK, it will further cement my dad's status as a hero to me.

Good luck, Dad—fair winds and following seas.

Preface

The writing of this book seems, now, like a logical conclusion to my Hope on the River journey. It wasn't planned. Or imagined. And, for that matter, it has been as interesting, challenging, and frightening as the journey itself.

I've spent the better part of my adult life writing for myself and for others. I don't consider myself a particularly great writer, and my daughter, Maisie, will attest to the fact that I violate nearly every generally accepted rule of writing. Amy Martin, who has helped me bring this book to fruition, will also confirm that my unorthodox writing style belies easy editing, formatting, or for that matter literary structure. I write like I talk. Quickly. And often with fast, abbreviated sentences followed by what can be lengthy run-on commentary about things that capture my imagination. My writing style creates multiple paragraphs where they shouldn't exist. Something that drives my daughter nuts, annoyed Amy to no end, and yet has become as much a part of who I am as the wrinkles on my face and the gray in my increasingly thinning hair.

My ability to put words to paper, or to a word processor, could never have happened without learning the most important skill I have ever possessed in my life: the ability to type. This was perhaps the most important skill I ever learned at Fairmount High School. Without this ability I doubt my life would have ever taken the direction it did, or that I would have had anywhere near the adventures I've had in my life.

I consider myself to be a storyteller. Even in my role as Executive Director of Spare Key, my job is to tell the story of this nonprofit's mission. It's what I have been doing since 2012 when I took on the role, and every single day since then my job has been to tell the story of what it means to be committed to helping families facing medical crises avoid financial crises.

Spare Key will be the recipient of every dollar earned by the sale of this book. We will use the funds to continue supporting our program that assists families in all fifty states find the financial resources they need to help them pay their bills while dealing with medical emergencies.

This book is my chance to tell another story to help those very families. It is my privilege and my honor to be able to do so.

I spent a lot of time trying to figure out a way to capture the essence and meaning of my Hope on the River trip. To be sure, I was looking to raise money and awareness for Spare Key. But if all the trip was going to be about was fundraising, it wasn't going to embody what I felt was an important part of the message we have tried to convey as long as I have been Executive Director of Spare Key: that our mission, at its core, is about giving hope. From my first days leading the organization to the moment I got on the raft, I have always believed that my job, and the purpose of everything I do, is to work towards giving hope to families who far too often find themselves with far too little of it.

The more I planned the trip, the more I read about the river, the more I found a synergy between the river itself and the mission of Spare Key. The river has instilled a never-ending reservoir of hope to people who have lived on or near it for as long as human inhabitants have been in the land through which it flows. The water that begins the river in Itasca, Minnesota, finds its way into the Gulf of Mexico but the river never stops flowing.

Nor does the hope that people need during the darkest, most difficult times of their life.

I was looking to find hope for Spare Key. But I was also looking to share with people along the river that Spare Key was about bringing hope to those who needed to find it.

So, bringing and finding Hope on the River became the name, purpose, and meaning of my journey.

This book, like my journey, would never have been possible without the support, encouragement, and kindness of so many people that I fear the names themselves would result in an entire book on its own. Rather than forget anyone, I want to simply thank everyone involved for making it possible and for being with me on my little raft looking for Hope on the River.

This book is dedicated to:

Captain Michael Coyle, whose wisdom, advice, and kindness kept me alive.

The thousands of men and women who work, live, and raise their families on and along the Mississippi River. They are so much a part of the untold story of American Exceptionalism. They work the river. Move the goods. Create the jobs. Build the communities. And feed the world!

My brother, Fred, his daughter, Matilda, my son Owen, my friend John Apitz, my brother-in-law John Richter, and my buddy Ray VinZant for building me a raft that got me exactly as far as Baton Rouge and exactly no farther.

The Spare Key Board of Directors, Jason Haus, Cindy Koebele, Julie Peterson Klein, Rob Roe, and Wendy Pajor for their past, present and future leadership of the Spare Key Board of Directors. The dedicated staff of Abby Hunt, Sarah Putnam, Alexia Sebesta, and Kristi Beaudry, and the many sponsors of my journey.

My mom, Betty Mische, for being the inspiration for every adventure in my life.

Gus Gaspardo for believing I could do it and Lee Nelson making me believe I could do it.

Every stranger who became a friend along my journey on the river.

My brother Karl, without whom I would never have succeeded in reaching my goal.

My wife Mary-Helen, son Owen, and daughter Maisie, who keep me afloat in every mile I travel in my life.

SECTION 1
Trip Preparation

Chapter 1
The Idea

On August 27, 2020, I climbed aboard my makeshift vessel built from a fifty-year-old pontoon and an excessively modified Home Depot garden shed and began a trip down the Mississippi River. The goal: to save Spare Key, the nonprofit I lead, from financial disaster due to the Covid-19 pandemic.

My trip was envisioned as a way to raise funds and awareness, and make up for the significant revenue shortfalls we experienced due to fundraising events being cancelled when the pandemic hit. I traveled through ten states, nearly 1,700 miles, and my journey took two months to complete. The America I saw on this trip, the people I met, the stories I heard, and the communities I spent time in illustrated not the divided nation we hear about so often on the radio, see on the television, or read about in newspapers or on the internet. The America I saw is a hopeful America. An America where men and women reached out to a stranger on a raft with pontoons that leaked, a thirty-two-year-old boat motor that repeatedly threatened to quit, and a captain wholly unprepared for the trip. They gave me all they could to allow me to succeed. Nobody asked me which presidential candidate I was voting for, which political party I belonged to, or if I was liberal or conservative. They simply asked, "What can I do to help?"

The raft trip was more than just a fundraiser, of course. It's a metaphor for my life and work.

I've never been the smartest guy in any room. But nobody was ever going to outwork me, and I was never going to give up.

My genius isn't in my head.

It's in my heart.

I do what I do and what I can because I believe I will.

Spare Key started in 1997 as a nonprofit serving families in one state, Minnesota. In 2013, we expanded to three additional states. In

2018, we began to expand our presence in other states, and as of October 26, 2020, five days after I completed my journey down the Mississippi River, we had filed paperwork in Louisiana, allowing us to legally serve families in all fifty states and the District of Columbia.

When Covid-19 arrived in the United States, it hit Spare Key and every other nonprofit. Donations dropped precipitously from individual donors as people lost their jobs or were concerned about losing their jobs. Corporation and foundation gifts became scarce as some companies simply ceased to exist, and foundations, attempting to address social, economic, racial, and cultural inequities, restructured their mission and funding priorities. In early March of 2020, I closed our office and directed staff to work from home to avoid exposure to this virus we knew so little about. Except to secure critical equipment and materials, we haven't gone back to the office since then, nor is it likely we ever will again. The operations of Spare Key continue to be done remotely, and successfully so, because of our small but dedicated and passionate staff and an equally dedicated and passionate board of directors.

On June 16, 2020, as I biked back home from a birthday lunch with a friend, I rode along a windy stretch of the Mississippi River between South St. Paul and Inver Grove Heights. As had been the case since March, I was contemplating what Spare Key could and would do to keep our doors open, our mission intact, and our dreams alive of helping tens of thousands of Americans facing medical crises in a world in which a global pandemic threatened our very existence.

I thought about creating a fundraising event where I rode my bike down the river to New Orleans. That idea sounded like a lot of work for an out-of-shape fifty-seven-year-old man. I envisioned taking a kayak or a canoe down the river, despite the fact I possessed no skills in being able to operate either one of them. When I got home, I mused more about the river and whether I could travel down it in a way that would help raise funds and awareness for Spare Key.

Ultimately, I rejected the canoe and kayak because of my lack of training and because the notion of camping outside creeped me out beyond measure, since I am afraid of the dark and scared of wild animals.

The more I thought about it, researched it, and talked to others, it became obvious that my best means of conveyance would be some kind of raft. The type of raft would be important given my lack of experience and knowledge about the Mississippi River. I thought about building one similar to those that others have constructed and taken down the river, which use fifty-five-gallon barrels with a wood platform built on top and some type of primitive house constructed on top of that. I also had visions of myself leisurely drifting down the river without the use of power but relying on long poles to keep me inside of the navigation channel used by recreational and commercial vehicles alike.

I presented my wife, Mary-Helen, with a fifteen-page memo that outlined my thoughts about the trip, the rationale behind it, how long it would take, and the safety measures I intended to follow to make sure I made it down the river and back alive. While she reluctantly agreed with the premise, she made it clear that my initial intention to name the raft the "SS Hail Mary-Helen" was a no-go. With her permission, I moved forward with other elements of preparation for my trip so that I could be in a position to share my idea with the Spare Key staff and board of directors, to get their approval and support.

I knew who I needed to lead the effort to build the raft—my brother Fred. Fred, who was given the responsibility by our mother of making sure I kept my mittens and hat on in the winter when we were children, is handy, has built things, and has a creative, problem-solving mind. I figured he had enough invested in keeping me alive when we were kids that he might have a similar investment in keeping me alive as an adult.

We talked a bit and ruled out the notion of the fifty-five-gallon barrels. They weren't efficient in terms of moving through the water and they were likely subject to falling off the raft. Given that I would be on this trip by myself, figuring out how to grab hold of wayward barrels drifting down the river and reinstalling them seemed to me impossible. Next the discussion turned to building something on top of a pontoon, and that is when we decided the basic infrastructure would, indeed, be a pontoon.

For the next couple hours we talked about all sorts of things, specifically how to steer the vessel given that I envisioned not having any kind of propulsion. This is where my knowledge, or I should say my lack of knowledge, moved front and center.

As Fred pointed out, in order to have any kind of rudder system you need to have some amount of speed to make the rudder work. Given that the current speed on the Upper Mississippi River is barely two miles per hour, it didn't seem that a simple rudder on the back of the raft would prove worthy. Additionally, while the U.S. Army Corps of Engineers is required to keep the channel itself at least nine feet deep, there were likely places on the river that were deeper than that, and what would happen if the push-poles I intended to use weren't long enough to steer me? The more we talked, the more anxious I became about how one would successfully drift down the river.

After meeting with Fred, I had a meeting arranged by my longtime friend John Apitz with Lee Nelson, President of Upper River Services, a company that operates barge and fleeting services. Lee has worked the river for decades and knows nearly everyone and everything on the Mississippi from St. Paul down to the Gulf of Mexico. When I shared with him my idea for the trip, including my vision of drifting to Baton Rouge, his immediate reaction wasn't positive. While I am not quoting him verbatim it went something like this: "You're crazy. Don't do it. You don't know what you're doing. You're going to get yourself killed."

This wouldn't be the first time, or the last time, someone would say this to me. The truth was, aside from the comment about me being crazy, he was absolutely right that I didn't know what I was doing. And if I didn't learn more about what I was doing, there was a decent chance I might, indeed, get myself killed.

After we chatted more, and I emphasized that I was aware of my limitations but that I was intent on doing this trip because Spare Key and its mission were important to me, he relented and said, "Okay, if you're going to do it, then I am going to make sure you know everything you can know before you go so you have the best chance possible to succeed." He made it clear that drifting down the river was never going to happen. He also made it clear he believed I needed two motors—one that would be the workhouse and one as a backup in case that one failed.

While he referenced large barges and towboats and how they were much bigger on the lower river than on the upper river, I have to admit it all seemed abstract to me. What I knew of barges and towboats is what I saw in St. Paul and, to be honest, they just looked like big boats.

He also said that I needed to understand the rules of navigation, plus have a series of electronic and paper charts and a host of other items.

That's what I was looking for! Someone who understood the river, knew the people, and most of all was willing to share their knowledge of how to give myself the best possible chance of success. I thanked him for his time and proceeded to continue to talk to others about the trip.

Even before talking with Lee, I had spoken with two other people who would be essential to this trip's ultimate success. The first was Captain Jim Kosmo. I remembered Jim from my days in politics and government in St. Paul, and in particular during my time with Mayor Norm Coleman and Mayor Randy Kelly. At the time, Captain Bill Bowell ruled the river in St. Paul and ran the Padelford Riverboat Company. Bill was one of the most high-energy individuals I had ever met. He was unphased by obstacles of any kind and, as I learned later from someone else, had himself traveled down the Mississippi River in an unconventional way years earlier in a small speedboat. I shared my plan with Jim and he in turn shared his thoughts about how one should prepare for such a trip. He also offered to connect me with people who would be good sources of information and resources to ensure that I would have the best chance possible to make it down the river safely and successfully.

One of those people was Gus Gaspardo, who had purchased the Padelford Riverboat Company from Jim, who himself had purchased it some years earlier from the Bowell Family.

With Jim's promise to do what he could fresh in my mind, I felt that he, along with Lee Nelson, were two important resources; they were only giving me greater confidence that I could put together a trip that would be successful.

A couple days later I sent an email to Gus, who I admit I did not remember having met over the years despite my proximity to St. Paul and connection with Captain Bowell and Jim Kosmo. Gus immediately responded and said he would be happy to sit down and talk. This conversation would likewise become one of the most critical ones I had on my way to making the journey a real possibility.

I met Gus in the Padelford Riverboat offices. Gus is tall, lean, and lanky. He is laid back, has piercing eyes, and is sharp as a tack with a quick laugh and a warm voice. He is an invaluable source of knowledge after decades of working on the river. This year, unlike in previous years, Mother Nature in the form of Covid-19 had thrown him back hard on his heels. The Padelford company had survived floods, but Covid-19 hit them harder than any flood ever did. While Gus expressed confidence that everything would be okay eventually, it was clear that he was worried for his company, his employees, and of course his family.

During the course of our conversation, Gus never told me not to take the trip. He did, however, make it clear that I needed to prepare myself as fully as I possibly could. He explained to me that the Upper Mississippi, with its lock and dam system, was almost serene and gentle compared to what I would experience once I got into the Lower Mississippi. He emphasized what others had, that I likely would not be able to drift down the river. He made it obvious to me that I had to re-evaluate some of my assumptions about the river, especially how I was going to navigate it. We spent more time talking, and before I left Gus let me know he was ready to support the trip in any way he could and that I shouldn't hesitate to reach out to him as I continued my preparations.

Everything was starting to come together, and soon I would be ready to approach my board and staff and outline my plan. But first I needed to find the materials for the raft.

And I needed a team to build it. I already had Fred and had a good idea of who else I wanted on the team. John Apitz, whom I have known since 1987, was one of the first people I asked to be on the build team. John is handy with tools and construction, and a problem solver. He also knows a ton of people, like Lee Nelson, and has collaborated with me on many of my crazy ideas over the years.

The next person was Ray VinZant. Ray is a contractor, carpenter, and plumber. He is no-nonsense and just gets things done. I knew that Ray, a dear friend for years, would be uncowed by any obstacles to building this raft.

My brother-in-law John Richter was also an important part of the build team. John is someone who asks tons of questions, has boundless optimism, and is willing to be a team player. I trusted John to also be honest about his thoughts, and I needed people who would be straight-forward with me.

John Vruno, someone I had known for the shortest amount of time, was skilled at building and understood construction. Unfortunately, early on in the process he contracted Covid-19 and was not able to be with us as we began the project in earnest. However, he was an important early member of the team and helped us with our vision of what kind of vessel to build.

The other two who would be critical members of the build team were my brother Fred's daughter Matilda and my son Owen. Matilda is bright, energetic, earnest, and capable. She dove right in and was with us every step of the way on the project, and I owe her a debt of gratitude for her participation in making the trip possible. Owen is the smartest and most honest person I know. I also knew that Owen would be brutally hon-est with me about what he thought we should or shouldn't be doing with the raft. It gave me great comfort having my son involved with this effort. And it would make me proud to take the raft down the river knowing that my son had played a critical role in its success.

With my build team complete, it was now time to focus on the next step: sharing the idea with the Spare Key staff.

Chapter 2
Selling the Idea, and a Titanic Story

I knew I was going to need the buy-in and support of the Spare Key staff. So one morning, on the lawn outside my townhome, we gathered as a team to talk about how we were going to move forward in the age of Covid-19.

I spelled out the challenges facing the organization. While we'd been fortunate to have held our major annual fundraising event, the Groove Gala, just weeks before the onslaught of the pandemic, there were other fundamental challenges facing the organization. From March through the middle of June, we had seen donations crater dramatically. While some of that was due to the nature of our revenue cycle, there was no mistaking the fact that a global economy shutting down nearly overnight was jeopardizing our future.

As we sat outside, I shared with the team the nascent plan I had to get on some kind of raft and ride it down the Mississippi River as a way to raise funds and awareness for Spare Key. In my mind, I felt we could raise money through sponsorships, asking people to make pledges per every mile I traveled, and making online appeals through social media and by doing a Livestream of the journey each day. I didn't have all the details figured out, but in each passing moment I thought about the trip I convinced myself we could raise enough to keep Spare Key afloat. Any hope of an enthusiastic response from my staff was quickly abandoned, as they had a load of questions and concerns ranging from doubts about my personal safety to hesitation about the logistics.

In hindsight, their response is precisely what I should have expected and wanted from the group. It was vital that they had the space to challenge the idea. After all, not only was the future of the organization at stake, but so was their livelihood. They, like millions of Americans, were scared, nervous, and uncertain about the future. And the idea that their executive director might end up at the bottom of the Mississippi River, further jeopardizing their own futures, certainly had to be in the back of their minds. Reasonable, too, were their questions about whether the trip would work, how it would raise money, and whether it would be of any benefit to the organization at all. I didn't have answers to all their questions, but I promised I would try my best to get them.

The fact is, I had run out of good ideas and options at that point. I had been the executive director of the organization long enough to have a clear understanding of the challenges—and opportunities—we faced and would continue to face. The longer the economic uncertainty of the pandemic existed, the more difficult and challenging it was going to be to keep Spare Key afloat—and the more unlikely it was that we were going to be able to keep everyone employed. The possibility that we would need to shut the doors and discontinue our work was very, very real.

Sitting on folding chairs at plastic tables in my yard, eating McDonald's with the young staff who represented the future of Spare Key and its mission, I was grateful for their concern and their willingness to challenge me. In the end, though, no matter how crazy my idea sounded, they committed to doing what was needed to make it work if it went forward.

As I talked with my team, I recalled a similar situation I found myself in back in 1998, when the company I worked for, Media Rare, was in the early stages of opening our "Titanic: The Exhibition" event at the St. Paul Union Depot. This massive undertaking and the improbable success we had in bringing the Exhibition to St. Paul, not to mention in getting the United States Postal Service to allow us to use a venue that had been boarded up for decades, was impressive. Yet it hadn't been cheap, and the company had a lot riding on the success or failure of the Exhibition. More than a million dollars had been committed to the project, which included the construction of a building to house a massive chunk of the Titanic, not to mention the costs associated with bringing the relics of the Titanic to St. Paul and storing them safely and securely.

We had high hopes for the Exhibition, and projections for attendance promised that our hard work and effort would be returned in significant profits to Media Rare. Within a few weeks, however, it was apparent that our optimism was misplaced.

With the excitement and interest in the *Titanic* movie long gone, and despite a massive amount of marketing and advertising to promote the Exhibition, it was failing. And failing fast. Expected attendance of 5,000 to 10,000 people a day, with significant crowds on weekends, did not materialize. In fact, we were barely getting anyone to attend, and the school groups that we expected to arrive were slow to book. Unexpected costs for security, logistics, traffic control, and the like continued to pile up while crowds did not.

Everything that could be done had been done to assure the Exhibition's success, but we had hit a point in which demand for the product simply no longer existed.

At the time, I had worked myself up to smoking four packs of cigarettes a day and spending too much time at one of the bars in the depot drinking Black Russians. I wasn't sleeping. I was exhausted. I would get home after a long day at the Exhibition and wake up early in the morning to see what the receipts for the previous day looked like. I then dealt with a myriad of challenges, problems, and issues ranging from volunteers not showing up to ongoing conflicts I had with the owner of Media Rare, who was both brilliant and mercurial. He had committed to the project and then disappeared from the company, leaving the rest of our business without guidance and direction and me with an event that was quickly spiraling into a financial disaster. We had gone over budget, so much of that was my fault. While I had spent so much of my time marketing and promoting the Exhibition, I hadn't spent enough time paying attention to the renovation and construction details associated with getting the facility ready. As the bills came in and then came due, it was clear that I had failed to manage the budget aggressively. On top of that, I had overestimated enthusiasm for the show and underestimated what it would cost to produce it.

Adding to the stress of my own shortcomings were the owners of the Exhibition, RMS Titanic; in particular, their attorney and the head of the company. The two principals I dealt with played Good Cop and Bad Cop so frequently that it was nearly impossible to figure out how to get answers and solutions to any of the challenges we faced. Furthermore, the contract we had signed with them guaranteed them money whether the Exhibition failed or not. There was little incentive for them to take any kind of risk. Additionally, representations they made relative to national partners and sponsorships were little more than fingers-crossed promises. We had counted on national sponsors to help promote the event and spark continued interest, but the sponsors had long since vanished, and more importantly, their interests had moved elsewhere to other projects.

It was against this backdrop that I found myself inside the cavernous Union Depot walking, literally in circles, throughout the exhibit at three o'clock in the morning. With a drink in one hand and a cigarette in the other, I paced around the Exhibition endlessly, trying to figure out what to do to save the show. There was no money left to market the event any more than we already had. Everything that could be said about it had been said, and the initial bursts of excitement and publicity had given way to the hard reality that the Exhibition was failing.

So was I.

I don't recall exactly the time or the moment, but I do vividly remember finding myself standing at the base of the Titanic's massive whistles. They were mounted high above me. There was a description of the whistles and of how loud they had been when the ship was still alive. I could see a few noticeable dents in them from their journey to the bottom of the ocean. Mainly, they just looked big.

How long I stood there, I don't know. But I kept staring intently at the whistles as though I expected them to make a sound, or talk to me, or say something. Finally, a straightforward question came from my lips to nobody but me: "I wonder if they work?"

I laughed out loud and repeated it a couple more times after that. Soon it was no longer "I wonder if they work?" but "I bet I could get them to work."

It didn't matter then, or now, that I knew nothing about whistles or whether they could work or would work.

What mattered was I had an idea.

And, in those early morning hours, I came the realization that if I was going to save the Exhibition, those whistles were going to be the key to turning it around.

Weeks later, with hundreds of thousands of people huddled around the whistles, we blew them in front of the Union Depot. While the promised sound didn't live up to the hype, they did make noise, and in doing so brought the Titanic back to life.

More importantly, they brought the Exhibition back to life. Weeks of global interest in the whistles and whether they would work had stirred the public's imagination. We went from a weekend attendance of a couple thousand visitors to 10,000-12,000 people a day on Saturdays and Sundays and thousands of people a day during the week. A simple idea had meant the difference between near-certain failure and, ultimately, some higher level of success.

Now, as our Spare Key front yard fundraising meeting broke up and I waved goodbye to the team, the Titanic Exhibition and my desperate plan to save it by blowing the whistles was definitely on my mind.

I didn't know how I was going to get down the river. I didn't know whether the trip would work or not, if I would make it or not, or even if it could raise money for our organization. Standing in my driveway, though, my thought no longer was "I wonder if it can work?" Instead, with my decision clearly made to take this trip, it was, "I bet I can make it work."

Now it was time to talk to my board of directors.

Throughout my nearly nine years of service to Spare Key, the Spare Key board has always been keen on taking bold and smart risks. But they expect details, and they want to know that ideas that I present to them have been thought through and, most importantly, that I have sought and heeded their expertise and ideas in any plans that impact the organization.

This would be no different.

They, like the Spare Key staff, understood the stakes and the situation we were facing. In fact, many of their own businesses and jobs were under significant stress due to the pandemic's impact on the economy. I didn't need to convince them that times were tough—they were living it.

One by one, I reached out and talked to each individual board member.

Not one told me not to do it.

Every single person had legitimate questions and concerns about what other options and alternatives existed, and what the risks were, both to the organization and to me.

I tried to give them as much information as I could. I made it clear I didn't know how it was all going to come together, but that we had a limited amount of time to make an impact on Spare Key's future. My window of opportunity to do the trip was limited as well; I had to factor in weather, because cold weather, even in the south, would start to become a reality. Furthermore, as Gus and Lee informed me, I would be heading down on the river during one of the busiest times of the year—harvest season—so time was becoming a precious commodity. While this trip and the planning around it would be accelerated beyond what most people would consider reasonable, waiting until the spring or summer of 2021 wasn't realistic if we wanted to have a fighting chance of keeping our doors open.

In the end, I wasn't looking for a vote or even unanimous approval, but I was hoping that the vast majority of my board would be onboard—so to speak—with the idea! I wasn't disappointed. With their support, along with the support of my staff and my family, I was able to start assembling a growing team of people who were prepared to mentor me and help build the raft.

It was now time to start turning my attention to other critical elements of the trip. We needed not only a build team but a team to help with media and public relations, and especially with sponsorships and social media. I needed someone who could help me understand how to navigate the river, establish connections with people and places down the river, and put together an inventory of materials and equipment I would need. The trip was officially a go, and now it was time to take real-world steps to move this idea from concept to reality.

Chapter 3
Building the SS Hail Mary

Isearched and I searched for pontoons online. It was my hope to find something cheap and, if possible, something someone would be willing to donate. The challenge, however, was that with Covid-19 the popularity of all things outdoors was surging throughout the country. And nowhere was that more evident than in the boating industry. There was literally no inventory anywhere, and the inventory that was available was expensive or simply not useful for what we were hoping to do. Finally, I spotted something on Craigslist: a twenty-four-foot 1970 Kayot pontoon that included a 1991 Nissan 60 HP (horsepower) motor. The Boat Doctor, in Montgomery, Minnesota, initially wanted $1,000 for it but were willing to part ways with it for $800. I shared photos of it with my build team and the consensus was that it was perfect for what we wanted to do.

The company agreed to rent me a scissor lift trailer for the day, but I still needed a place to store it and, more importantly, a place to build the raft.

For this I turned to Lee Nelson and asked if he had any ideas. As he would do many times in this process, he got back to me within a couple hours to share a dry-dock location near South St. Paul that he said would be perfect for us. He would permit us to build the raft there. It was becoming real!

I drove to Montgomery not quite expecting what I would see with the pontoon I had purchased. Over the phone, they told me that it was old, that the platform was in decent shape, and that the Nissan motor leaked oil but otherwise seemed to work fine. To be honest, I wouldn't have known any different. When I got to their location I sized up the pontoon and took pictures.

It clearly looked old. The pontoons had dents in them, but I was assured they were seaworthy. The motor looked old but beyond that I couldn't have told you anything about it other than it seemed to be in one

13

piece, as did the rest of the pontoon.

There was a metal frame on the top, under which, I assume, there were once chairs on the pontoon deck. To the port side of the raft, and about six feet from the stern, was a three-foot-high console with a worn steering wheel and the remote control to the Nissan motor.

The frame had three doors: a door in front, and one each on the port and starboard sides. (I chuckled as I wrote the previous sentence—my brother Fred, my son Owen, and anyone who knows me is aware that I knew nothing about the terms "port" or "starboard" prior to this adventure.) The plywood floor decking wasn't nearly as solid as they had told me it was, but I figured Fred and the build team would figure out how to mitigate any problems with that.

After sending everyone pictures of the pontoon, we concluded that it was as good a base as any for the raft and I completed the transaction. I had some help putting the pontoon on the scissor lift and was instructed on how to transport it on the road.

As I drove away, I realized that a scissor lift is not the most desirable way to transport a pontoon any length of distance. It wobbles and wiggles and feels, and probably is, unstable. Every time I went into a curve, or got to a certain speed, the trailer would bounce and the pontoon would lean from side to side. It wasn't an awe-inspiring introduction to the scissor lift, and later on, that same type of lift would prove to be an issue for the Build Team on two more occasions.

Finally, I got the pontoon to the location that Lee was allowing us to use, a huge warehouse that was perfect for our needs. It was secure, indoors, and had lights that would allow us to see at night, which was when most of us would be able to work on the raft. It also had tools available that we would need.

Unfortunately, one of the challenges of building this raft was scheduling. Between the build team's daytime schedules and the Fourth of July holiday, the pontoon was going to stay put for a week or two before any real work could be done on it. That would have a further impact on my timeline moving forward.

My original plan had me leaving mid-August, but this date left little room for all the other things that had to be done. Additionally, my family and I had a long-planned vacation to Mackinac Island scheduled that would essentially have me embarking on my river journey three days after we returned from our trip. I needed to re-evaluate my departure date based on these realities but wasn't yet ready to announce when it was going to be.

In any case, we still had the matter of what *kind* of raft would be built on the pontoon's deck. The build team went through a lot of conversations and iterations. Should it be a simple flat-roof structure? Would it have windows? How big would it be? What would it need to be capable of doing? Where would another motor go if we added one? How would I steer the second motor? And how would I steer the raft with a rudder if we had to add one?

On and on the questions came, and each time one question got answered, another one would come up.

I had to also take into consideration how I was going to monetize the raft. In my mind, I had to cover every inch of it with sponsor signage, so the construction of the raft was going to be vital to maximizing that part of the project.

There were also all sorts of variables that had to be considered, including how would the raft react to wind, rain, the current, and the never-ending issue of weight and balance. At one point we concluded that we would construct a peaked-roof structure using 2x2s as our framework and have a lot of screen windows all around the four sides of the raft. There was a kit that we could order that basically provided all the equipment we would need, and then we just had to cut the 2x2s to the kit description and that would be the base of the raft. Unfortunately, the kits got back-ordered and would have delayed our building another two weeks.

We talked about building the cabin from scratch, but no one had the time or a clear understanding of the construction specifications needed, such as how much it should weigh. I knew we were running out of time, and I knew I had to make some kind of decision just to close the discussion about the type of structure we would build on the top of the pontoon.

I got online and started looking at a variety of different garden shed kits, particularly those that came in a kit that had all the parts already. Kind of a garden shed in a box! Again, as with many things related to the outdoors, due to Covid-19 the inventory was slim everywhere.

The costs, not to mention the weights, of the sheds I was researching were starting to get pretty outrageous for what we needed. Finally, I found a garden shed at Home Depot that was in the price range I wanted. It fit the basic concept design of the plan we'd agreed to with the 2x2 construction. I thought about reaching out to the group to get their feedback but realized there was only one shed left within a 200-mile radius, so I simply bought it and figured we would make it work.

The next day I rented a pickup, had the shed loaded into the truck, and drove it to the dry dock. Once there, we were able to have it lifted out and set on the ground next to the pontoon, knowing we would wait until after the Fourth of July to open it up and figure out what we were going to do with it.

Once the holiday was over, we were finally in a position to begin opening up the box and seeing what the garden shed involved. Fred, Ray, Owen, Matilda, and I got it opened up and started to separate the pieces. Ray also brought his massive inventory of tools that same night. As we removed the shed parts, we began to talk about how things would need to be built, what parts we would do away with, and how the structure would ultimately need to be positioned on the pontoon deck.

The original size of the garden shed was eight feet tall, eight feet wide, and twelve feet long. The interior of the pontoon frame was less than eight feet wide, so we decided to first make sure the shed fit inside the existing frame and then provide some additional stability. I wanted to keep the pontoon frame because it was a perfect base for sponsorship signage. The frame of the pontoon was also only ten feet long, which meant we would need to cut two feet off the length of the shed.

Then came the conversation about the height.

The taller the shed, the more wind it would pick up, acting as a sail and creating any number of unknown variables for me down the river. We decided to reduce the height by about a foot. In hindsight, I think it would have been prudent to reduce it by another foot or two, but at the time none of us really knew what the conditions were going to be out on the river, so we felt good with the decision.

The next issue was reducing its weight. The total allowable weight for the pontoon was roughly 3,150 pounds, which needed to also include for the weight of the Nissan motor and any equipment and materials that I was going to bring with me—not to mention my own weight!

Using all the materials that came with the shed would result in nearly 1,200 pounds just with the shed. Furthermore, based on how the shed was going to be positioned, we were having trouble determining whether its weight was being appropriately distributed. So the decision was made to get rid of anything but the bare essentials and make sure that we had ample screens for a full 360-wraparound of the shed. This would enable me to see out at all times, it would reduce wind resistance, and it would make it easy for me to escape from the raft should something catastrophic occur.

Ultimately we were able to construct a cabin on top of the pontoon that weighed slightly under 800 pounds. It had three screen doors, allowing me to have ingress in the bow, on the starboard, and on the port. While the screens were all permanently attached on three of the four walls, the rear end of the raft had removable screens. Fred strongly believed that I needed to have full-time access to the stern, including another avenue of escape, so we custom-built screens for the rear.

This, like many decisions, would prove to be invaluable as I made my trip down the river.

We did make a grievous error when we failed to notice, before constructing the cabin, that the swinging doors on the pontoon frame were built to open inward—and now it was impossible for them to do so. Worse yet, the hinges were on the wrong side to be easily removed. But John Richter saved us. With the patience that only he has, my brother-in-law spent a considerable amount of time slowly cutting the screws out of the hinges and successfully repositioning the doors so they would swing outward!

My friend John Apitz then constructed two screen doors to fit the narrow space where the doors swung open, effectively allowing me to be able to access the outside. This would become critically important as I made my way down the upper river. I had to be able to secure moorings on docks at marinas and elsewhere. Additionally, being able to navigate through the lock and dam system necessitated having easy access to both the port and starboard sides of the raft from near the steering console.

The build team worked together extremely well. Everyone pitched in and had great ideas, and soon we were close to having completed the basic construction of the SS Hail Mary.

At some point we were going to need to put the raft in the water, and we all knew that once that happened, it was going to make it the prospect of this trip even more real.

In the meantime, however, we had to start getting other aspects of the raft ready. One item on the list was getting our signage arranged, and the other was figuring out the Nissan motor. The placement of the signage, and selling the placement to sponsors, was a priority. Luckily we had a company, ASI Signage Innovations, owned by Spare Key's board president Wendy Pajor, that would print all our signage for free. Meanwhile, the Nissan was causing me endless headaches. I didn't really know if it worked or not, and the folks at the Boat Doctor, after having original-ly told me it had an oil leak, then told me it didn't. Not only that, but still I didn't even know how to start the dang thing!

The one thing I did know was that before we put the raft in the water, I needed to be sure it worked. With Lee and Gus and their admo-nitions in my mind constantly, I also knew that I needed to figure out a second motor solution. But as with so many things on this project, I didn't have a clue as to how to approach that issue. How did one add another motor? Where would it go? How big did it need to be? How would I start it and steer it? I was flying blind and so was my build team. This wasn't their area of expertise any more than it was mine.

I bought a motor flusher that could be attached to a garden hose and clamped it on the Nissan to see if it worked, out of the water. I only knew of this because I had an old boat at my cabin and somebody once told me this is how mechanics work on boat motors when they are out of the water.

So, with the flushing device in hand and on the motor, I attempted to start the Nissan.

Of course, it wouldn't start.

And no matter what I did, I couldn't get it to work. The process of starting the motor involved a key attached to a device on the steering console inside the raft. Each time I turned the key, it would crank but wouldn't turn over. So I called the Boat Doctor and asked them to walk me through the process of successfully starting the motor. Finally, with their help and a bit of self-discovery on how the idle operated versus the choke, I got the motor to start.

I am not familiar with two-stroke motors except in the sense that I know there are such things. But the two-stroke Nissan was thirty years old, and I had no idea how old the fuel was in the tank that came with it. The thing smoked like a steel plant's chimney, and it chugged and chugged and constantly sounded like it was going to stop running. To be honest, it didn't impress me and made me wonder whether or not it was even capable of running once it was in the water. For now, though, it worked, and that felt like a victory for me.

The raft was almost substantially complete, the motor had started and even stayed running, and it was time to start working on signage. At this point, it was Wendy Pajor, Spare Key's Board President and owner of ASI Signage Innovations, and her team who came up big. Wendy, whose family have been long-time supporters of Spare Key, was the first board member I'd talked to about the trip. She hadn't even hesitated. Perhaps more than many of my board members, she understood the economic impact that Covid-19 was having on businesses. Furthermore, as a cancer survivor she knows what it means to take risks and what it takes to overcome obstacles and challenges. She was not only onboard but told me that whatever she and ASI could do, they would do to make the trip a success.

Two members of her team, led by Paul Benick, came over and took all sorts of measurements. We talked about how I envisioned the signage looking on the raft. The roof needed to have our website URL, www. hopeontheriver.com, and there should be plenty of options for sponsors on top and on all four sides. My message was that we wanted to sell every square inch of space we could to maximize revenue from the trip down the river.

The other issue we had was how to cover the screens during bad weather and at night. I had already made the decision that I would not be traveling in the evening on the raft, nor would I stay out on the river in the event of thunderstorms or other threatening weather. However, to keep things dry inside, including electronics, we needed some system to close up the raft during rain, and also at night since I would be sleeping on the raft. Our original plans included plastic on the screen windows, a pulley system involving isinglass, and any number of other schemes.

Finally, I asked Paul whether or not the same kind of material that is used to wrap buses, which has printing on the outside but people can see through from the inside, could be created to serve as storm windows on the raft, covering the screens. He thought this was possible but said they could print logos on one side of a sturdier plexiglass material, and I would be able to see out while people wouldn't generally be able to see in. It would also keep the elements at bay. And he felt they could build a channel system so these printed storm windows (aka signs) would easily slide in and out and I could put them on or off at my convenience.

That sounded perfect!

Everything related to the raft was coming together. Now I could start turning most of my attention to the sponsorships, media relations, putting together my travel schedule, and of course worrying about how I was going to address the matter of another motor.

Before then, though, Gus suggested we take a few hours on his company pontoon and go down the river, so that I could get a feel for it before I actually began my trip. That sounded like a brilliant idea and one that would ultimately pay dividends.

I'd been on pontoons many times in my life, but never on a river. My recollection of being on pontoons on lakes was that they are a great way to enjoy the company of others, relax, and all in all are kind of like being on a couch with a motor on the water.

I met up with Gus at the Padelford dock on Harriet Island, where he had a pontoon boat, and the two of us got onboard. As we began our journey down the river, the first thing Gus did was put the motor in neutral to give me a sense of how the pontoon would behave if I truly attempted to just drift. He emphasized that the current near the Wabasha Bridge up until the Robert Street Bridge in St. Paul was likely a bit faster than I would experience for much of the trip on the Upper Mississippi. He indicated that the current speed would often be less than two miles per hour and, to be honest, as we sat there and floated for a while, it was obvious to me that my initial idea of drifting down the river had in fact needed some serious adjustment.

Powering back up, Gus brought us down through a stretch of the river where there were barges on both sides of us, not moving. He cautioned me to stay inside the navigation channel marked by red buoys on one side and green buoys on the other and reminded me that the Army Corps of Engineers was expected to keep that channel at least nine feet deep. The buoys would be an important navigation tool for me as I traveled down the river. As you head downstream, the red buoys are always on your left while the green are on your right. This helps you keep your bearings, stay inside the navigation channel, and generally avoid underwater hazards that can cause damage to your vessel. Gus informed me that as one travels up the river, the process is the same but in reverse: the red buoys are on the right. The phrase "Red Right Return" (i.e., red on right when returning) is intended to remind mariners of this as they travel upstream on the Mississippi.

He also cautioned me about wing dams, structures built by the Army Corps that are used to help commercial traffic down the river. They're often hidden underwater, particularly on the river above the locks and dams, so a boat could find itself tearing off its motors and transom if it gets out of the navigation channel and hung up on one of these wing dams. Other dangers included submerged trees, flotsam that could appear out of nowhere, and of course pleasure craft and commercial boats.

We continued our leisurely travel down the river, and I asked Gus if he could show me how to bring a pontoon up on the shoreline. This was one of the skills I was going to need to learn, as there would not be many places to tie up the raft once I got past the Upper Mississippi into the lower section of the river.

Gus slid the pontoon into the shoreline with ease, and then with equal skill brought us off the shoreline. He stressed that it was important to come into the shoreline at a ninety-degree angle to shorten the distance to where you want to tie up. Failing to do so would take longer to reach the riverbank, increasing the chance one would catch some submerged structure in the river. He also emphasized that I needed to make sure that my motors were trimmed up as I came into the shoreline so they wouldn't get stuck on the bottom of the river.

The further down the river we went, the less calm the river became, giving me a small, and brief, glimpse of what I would be experiencing on my trip. Gus asked me if I would have a depth finder on the raft, and I told him that it never occurred to me I should have one. He strongly advised me to get one, then showed me how to use it and how it would be valuable on my journey. I made a mental note to purchase one as soon as possible.

We also talked a great deal about how I was going to add an additional motor to the raft, what size, and where it should be located. Options included putting a trolling motor at the front of the raft. The challenge with that was it would require me to physically be there to steer it and, with the heavier stern, would require some fancy work to keep the raft from spinning around on me. Furthermore, a trolling motor might not have the power needed to move the raft, particularly when it was fully equipped. The notion of a kicker motor on the back of the raft was discussed, but I wasn't sure that the platform that supported the Nissan would be big enough to add another motor. It was quite clear, however, that another motor of some kind and in some location was needed.

As Gus worked us back up the river, we came across a couple of small towboats that created some wake and bounced us around. At least, I thought they bounced us around. Gus chuckled and said that I would find myself dealing with significantly more chop as I came across large pleasure craft and towboats.

He asked me what kind of radios I would have, if I knew how to communicate to commercial boats, and what I should ask them when I contacted them. It was clear I still had much to learn before I got on the river, and the more Gus and I talked the more mental notes I made as to what additional questions I needed to ask him, and Lee, and others. We were on the river for a couple of hours, and in that time I learned even more about what I didn't know. As we came into the dock I thanked Gus for his time and his advice and wisdom, something I would continue to do many times over.

Driving home, my mind was racing. I was going to need to find some time to learn the basics of river navigation and how to communicate with commercial traffic, get a depth finder, maps, and charts, and gather so many other things. I had been so focused on getting the raft built and working on promotional aspects of the trip with my Spare Key staff—preparing sponsorship information with Abby, developing our communications strategy with Sarah, and managing Spare Key operational issues with Alexia—that I had spent precious little time actually thinking about the trip itself. Things weren't going to work out well for me if I didn't start spending some time getting myself smarter than I was.

But I still needed to solve the motor puzzle and begin putting together the equipment list for the trip. Trying to figure out the motor was keeping me awake at night. Once I did figure out how to get one, getting it installed and getting the Nissan tuned up was another project. I didn't have the cost of a boat motor built into any budget for the trip, much less the cost of installing it.

I reached out to the place I'd bought the pontoon, emailed boat companies throughout the state, posted on social media, emailed my board, asked friends and others if they had ideas, suggestions, or extra motors lying around, or if they could tune up my existing motor.

I wasn't having any luck at all.

Then I got a text from Cindy Taube, a former board member and, more importantly, a longtime and trusted friend who has never wavered in her support of Spare Key or, for that matter, my crazy ideas. Cindy said she had reached out to John Wooden, the owner and CEO of River Valley Power and Sport of Red Wing to see what, if anything, he might be able to do. She indicated that she had also talked to a guy named Mike Wilson, who knew the river very well and was connected to John Wooden, and that he wanted to help in any way he could.

I've known Cindy since my early days as Spare Key's Executive Director. Cindy handled public relations and public affairs at Treasure Island Resort and Casino, and when I became Executive Director I reached out to her to introduce myself. Treasure Island had long been a supporter of Spare Key, but as the new leader of the organization it was important for me to make a personal connection with them. Cindy, who undoubtedly got calls from nonprofit people like me all the time, was polite and indicated she was happy that Treasure Island was able to support Spare Key but didn't know that there was any more they could do. I then asked if it would be okay if I came down and had lunch with her at Treasure Island, to meet in person and share with her my thoughts about the direction I wanted to take Spare Key. I emphasized that I wasn't coming to ask for money but to get to know her and share who I was and my vision for the organization.

She seemed surprised that I wanted to drive down but agreed to have lunch with me.

Cindy is warm, kind, and generous in spirit and in words. She is also passionate about the work she does, the community she supports, and the causes she believes in. She was a powerful advocate for Treasure Island, and when we met she spent a great deal of time bringing me around the property and explaining how the organization was structured. She was very proud of the business that she had played a role in helping to build.

We sat down for lunch and I then spent my time introducing myself, my background, and what I believed the potential was for Spare Key to serve more families in the future. By the time we wrapped up our meeting, I felt I had proved to her that I wasn't a flake, and she had proved to me she was someone who could get things done.

And it was this person who can get things done who was now hot on the trail of finding me a motor for the raft!

Mike Wilson, who was a candidate for mayor of Red Wing, Minnesota, is another guy who gets things done. (I am pleased to report that Mike won his race!) He is someone well-known in the community for his civic involvement and passion for Red Wing, and he has connections nearly everywhere. I spoke to Mike on the phone and introduced myself. He indicated that he, along with Cindy, were talking with John Wooden and trying to figure out what they could do to help support my trip. He also told me he wanted me to talk to a friend of his, Matt Stokes.

Matt is intimately familiar with many things on the river, and in particular is well-versed in the safety, communications, and basic navigation issues that I needed to understand. I told Mike I would talk to Matt as soon as possible and added that to my list of things to do. A few days later I got a call from Cindy.

"I think we have your motor problem figured out," she said. "John Wooden has agreed to provide you with a brand-new kicker motor and brand-new 60 HP motor to replace the Nissan."

I nearly fell over!

I asked her to repeat that, and she said that the Mercury Marine Corporation had agreed to donate two motors for the trip, that River Valley Power and Sport of Red Wing would install them, and we would be good to go. While the trip would be underway from St. Paul we would need to make an overnight stop in Red Wing to install the new motor and make other updates. Ultimately, the Nissan would remain on the raft and be tuned up while the new kicker motor would be installed. Whatever the case, I was delirious with joy and thanked her profusely!

While there were a number of details that still needed to be worked out, the solution to my motor needs had now been achieved and I could stop worrying about that problem for the time being!

As the date for our family trip to Mackinac Island was creeping up, having the motor situation resolved was a huge relief for me. I could begin focusing my efforts on some of the navigation issues that were nagging at me. I reached out to Matt and we chatted a bit, and he said he had always wanted to do the trip I was planning on doing and wanted to be as helpful as possible. We agreed to find some time in the next couple of weeks to set up some Zoom calls, and he would provide a tutorial on all sorts of issues, including what kind of navigation and communication equipment I should be using. I thanked him and told him I was looking forward to our conversations.

Things were starting to tighten up. The next thing to do was figure out if the raft was going to float! One should feel reasonably confident that a pontoon boat built to be in the water should float when it is put into the water.

But given that our custom-designed shed on top of the pontoon had been neither envisioned by the pontoon manufacturers nor built by people who understood much about the impact of weight distribution on a boat, it was going to be an interesting process of discovery.

The original plan was to put the raft in the water, make sure it floated, and then return it to dry dock, finish putting signage and other equipment onboard, and then launch it from Padelford Landing.

The more I thought about it, however, the more concerned I became that putting the raft in the water, taking it out again, and repeating that process would make it potentially more likely that something bad would happen to the raft. I wasn't sure *what* would happen and given that I was planning on taking it down the river for two months, I guess I should have considered my unease to have been a warning signal. After all, if the SS Hail Mary couldn't sustain being put in and taken out of the water a couple of times, how was she going to hold up in the difficult environment of the Mississippi River?

Before we even got to the point of worrying about taking the raft out of the water, we needed to figure out where we were first going to put it into the water. The original thought was to use a ramp area right near the dry dock. However, because of the steep decline of the ramp along with low water, made that option not the best possible one for us. The next plan was to use a boat ramp in South St. Paul, barely two miles from where we had built the raft. Unfortunately, this would require us to go over a highway bridge for about a quarter of a mile—no easy task given that none of us had any experience in towing a pontoon with a garden shed on top of it!

The day before we intended to move the raft, I drove back down to Montgomery, Minnesota, to the Boat Doctors to get the scissor lift for the pontoon. While I was uneasy with this particular trailer, we didn't really have much choice, since we didn't have anything to actually lift the raft onto a more stable pontoon trailer.

The questionable stability of the scissor trailer with just the pontoon on it was enough to give me anxiety but adding the pontoon with the shed on top of it and then trailering it up onto a highway ramp, over a highway bridge, and then down a highway ramp was going to be a challenge.

When I arrived at the dry dock to load the pontoon onto the trailer, I proceeded with a great deal of caution. The first couple of times I attempted to lift the raft with the scissor lift, it literally looked like it was going to tip over to the side. I finally decided to lift only as far as I felt it needed to go to keep the raft from hitting the ground as we towed it. That, at least, reduced some of the wobbliness of the pontoon while it was on the trailer.

I then tied it all up with as much rope and chain as I could to keep the raft on the trailer, then used some tie-down straps to provide some— not much—side-to-side stability. We had alerted the media that we would be putting the raft in the water with the tease that we didn't know whether it would float or not. I figured if we suggested there was a chance it could sink, it might increase the likelihood we would get coverage. And to be honest, I had no idea what was going to happen.

If it did sink, I would not be surprised. Not because the build team didn't construct a solid raft, but because none of us knew whether our placement of the garden shed, or the condition of the pontoon itself, was going to result in a catastrophe!

I woke up early the next morning and made my way back to the dry dock and the raft. I double-checked everything, including starting the motor and letting it idle for a while. I got a call from John Apitz asking if I had arranged for any kind of police escort. I chuckled because I hadn't, but I knew that John was likely already trying to figure it out.

He was and he did. A short time later, he called me to say that he had spoken with the Dakota County Sheriff and we would shortly have a deputy joining us to provide us with a squad escort to the public access in South St. Paul where we would launch the raft.

A bit before nine o'clock, the deputy showed up, as did Fred and Matilda. John Apitz showed up to greet the deputy. Sarah Putnam and Abby Hunt from Spare Key were there as well, to film the endeavor and provide us with additional escorts along the way. We walked through the plan of how we were going to proceed to the ramp.

First, we were going to go very slowly. I didn't know how slowly, but I knew it was going to be just north of a crawl.

Second, Fred would be directly behind me, John and Abby ahead of me, and Sarah would be further ahead to grab video of our little entourage.

The deputy would start behind me, but then would likely go ahead of us to block any intersections we would need to go through to get to our location.

Before we left, I'd had a conversation with Gus regarding my concerns about putting the raft into the water and taking her out again. He suggested another option—simply driving the raft to the Padelford dock and parking it in between the shoreline and his maintenance shed. After all, we were going to launch the SS Hail Mary from that location in a few weeks, so why even return her to the dry dock?

I was enormously relieved at this offer and immediately accepted. This would relinquish any need for us to worry about getting the raft back up out of the water and back onto the trailer and back on the highway to where we started.

The challenge from the outset was simply getting the raft out of the area where it was built. The road in and out of the location was pockmarked, and some potholes were pretty deep and filled with water. I couldn't make any sharp turns, so it would require me to first navigate over a road that didn't provide any relief from deep potholes and then make a wide turn to the left. As I began to drive, I could see the raft slightly wobbling on the trailer behind me but there wasn't any way to avoid that. What we needed to avoid was it increasing its wobble frequency—I bet you never heard that phrase before!

The road outside the gate of the dry dock was heavily used by semi-trucks, and thankfully the deputy was able to block them from encroaching on us as we made our way onto the roadway. As we headed south, I could see through my sideview mirrors the semi-trucks starting to jam up behind me. The semi-trucks in front of me, for the most part, simply pulled over to the side, with the exception of one truck who decided, despite the flashing squad car lights, to make a break for it and speed by me, ignoring the obviously slow procession.

As we came upon a set of railroad tracks for our first turn I gritted my teeth and made my way slowly across them, watching the raft wobble to the left and right. I radioed Fred, who was behind me, to ask how it looked and he said it was pretty stable. I'm pretty sure he was lying so I wouldn't get nervous about just how much the raft looked like she was going to tip over!

Once we made the turn and got over the tracks, we had to proceed onto another road that had traffic at higher speeds. At this point, the deputy sped ahead, blocking the road and allowing me to slowly turn to the right. This meant there was one more right turn, which would put me onto the on-ramp to the highway and the highway bridge. The deputy sped forward, blocking access to the ramp, and allowed me and our contingent to make our way, slowly, up the ramp.

At this point I had kept the speed to under five miles per hour and I didn't intend to change that even when I got onto the highway.

With Abby and John in front of me, Fred behind me, the deputy drove ahead onto the highway with lights flashing to make cars slow down and switch to other lanes.

Finally we made it across the bridge and onto the off-ramp. I breathed a big sigh of relief because now it was simply a matter of a couple more right turns on little-traveled roads and then getting to the boat ramp.

Turning the trailer itself required being enormously careful too. I couldn't turn too sharply or it would create chaos with the trailer. I couldn't turn too wide or I would run up on top of center medians, creating even more of a threat to the stability of the raft.

Soon, however, we reached the public access ramp and were joined by John Richter, by my friend Ray VinZant, and also by reporters from KARE11 and KSTP television. The goal now was to figure out how exactly we were going to back the trailer up into the water and slide the SS Hail Mary into the river. Getting the trailer turned around and angled onto the ramp was no easy task. Again, it all had to be done very slowly and having two television cameras rolling while trying to do all this just added to the tension. I impressed upon my team that we wanted to "measure twice, cut once" and simply move cautiously.

I also made sure everyone understood that once the raft was in the water, assuming it didn't sink, it would remain in the water, and that any additional work that needed to be done would be done at Padelford Landing. John suggested we might want to review that issue again after the raft was in the water, but I told him that it wasn't open for debate. If the SS Hail Mary was in the water, she was staying in the water. I think everyone, including John, agreed it was the right decision. John wanted to keep our options open if for some reason we needed to re-evaluate. I appreciated his perspective but given everything, it was clear the best option was to keep the raft in the water.

Eventually it was time to back the trailer into the water. Slowly, we took all the straps off the raft. After a couple of false starts, we finally were able to lower the SS Hail Mary into the water. Now it was time to winch her down and see if she would stay afloat once the trailer was pulled out from under her. I drove the trailer forward hurriedly and got it several yards away. Putting my vehicle into park, I jumped out.

She was floating! She hadn't sunk!

All of us were thrilled!

We congratulated one another on our success of the raft staying afloat, then began the process of getting things ready to head out onto the river. I was able to get the motor started pretty quickly (which was good) and kept it in idle while we made sure there were life jackets on the raft and that all the other equipment we would need at Padelford Landing was loaded onto the raft.

I did interviews with the TV stations, talked with Fred and John Apitz about plans to meet up at Padelford, and then went and parked the car and the trailer to come back later to retrieve. Alec Bircher, of Bircher Films, had also showed up and was doing some videotaping of the event.

One of the television crews wanted to come out on the river for a few minutes while I made sure everything was running okay with the idea that he would use a portable camera and I would then bring him back to shore. After about ten minutes on the river, I brought the raft back to the public access dock and unloaded everybody but me.

I reconfirmed with John and Fred what the plan would be for going upriver to Padelford Landing. With that, I backed the raft out on the river and began the process of pointing her toward the navigation channel.

I was exhilarated!

The raft floated... the motor was working... and we were now that much closer to the trip being a reality.

I didn't have any idea what to expect with this trip up the river. All I knew was I needed to keep the red buoys to my right, the green to my left, and to keep a lookout for any boats or towboats coming down the river.

I also didn't really have much of a sense for how to run the Nissan or how fast I was going. So I set the throttle to what I suspected was about halfway and began to head up the river. I sent some text messages to Mary-Helen and others, letting them know the SS Hail Mary was underway. Fred and John Apitz and others sent me text messages and called me on my cell or on the walkie-talkies we had been using to check on my progress.

Given that I had no sense of where I was or how fast I was going, I didn't really have much of a clue how long it was going to take me to go seven miles—especially going against the current.

As I made my way, I encountered my first couple of pleasure boats. When they passed me they created wakes which sent the raft bobbing from side to side. Because the only weight in the raft was me—and the garden shed—the bobbing was pretty intense and gave me my first indication that I would need to learn how to approach these kinds of waves to avoid finding myself being tossed about like a bobber on the ocean.

A little while later, the first towboat I encountered made its way down the river. At this point I did not have a marine radio and I wasn't really sure what I was supposed to be doing, so I simply stayed on its port side.

The wake that the towboat created was, of course, even more intense than those created by the pleasure boats. Once again I was reminded that I needed to talk to someone about how I would approach this in the future.

Making my way up the river on this day felt amazing, and I was really starting to understand how close we were to getting the trip underway. There was still a ton of work that had to be done but we had now achieved proof of concept for the trip, and we had a fully functioning raft and a boat motor that, for now, was working.

As I came around the last bend before Padelford Landing, the City of St. Paul, the Robert Street bridge, and the Wabasha Street bridge came into full view. It was a sight to behold!

I had made it up the river, the motor hadn't stopped, I hadn't capsized yet, and the raft hadn't sunk (yet, anyway). John Apitz was there waiting for me to tie up the raft. This would be my second time bringing the raft back into some kind of dock. In this case, I would be tying the raft up between the shoreline and the Padelford machine shed. This would require me to go further upriver and then turn around to come back down the river to squeeze into the space.

And to do it with current pushing against me.

I was absolutely nervous about this, and since it was just John Apitz and myself there, there was a good chance I was going to mess it up! As I came around, John had made his way to the location we would be tying up the raft. I slowed down and tried to come in as slowly as I could. It wasn't slow enough.

I shoved the motor into reverse, just to try to resist the current and keep from slamming into the structures that were in front of me. Eventually John was able to grab the raft and the rope and somehow or other we figured out how to get the raft turned around again so that her bow was facing the river current. Once the SS Hail Mary was tied up, John and I celebrated a bit by patting one another on the back and making sure the raft was securely fastened.

Abby and Sarah showed up around that time. They were going to give me a ride back to my car. Before that, though, John and I went through the effort of securing plastic to the screen windows so that the raft was tied up snugly for the night. Then, satisfied she was tied up tight and secure, John and I left Padelford Landing. John was going home, and I was heading to my car and then home, to decompress for the rest of the day.

The day had been a great success. We had a lot more work to do, but as I took one last look at the raft, I was satisfied we had successfully completed some of the most challenging elements of our planning.

Chapter 4
Provisioning the Raft for Travel, Broadcast, and Sponsorships

Figuring out what to bring on the raft was exciting, nerve-wracking, and a chore. There were some basic things I knew I needed to have: safety equipment, some food, clothing, and navigation equipment. The only real questions were what kind, how much of it, and, once I got it, where would I put it on the raft?

Truth be told, the amount of equipment I thought I would need started out pretty minimal. I predicted that most of my time would be spent inside the raft's cabin, including time sleeping, and this required some basic equipment and necessities to sustain me and protect me—things like smoke and carbon monoxide detectors, fire extinguishers, lights for the cabin, and flashlights. I began my journey with an inflatable mattress but ultimately went through several of them before I landed on using a foldable cot. (Something I should have started with at the beginning!)

I packed a combination of clothes—for warm weather and cool weather—and later found that I had not only packed too much, but I didn't pack enough of the right combination of clothes. As my trip progressed, the days became colder in the morning and the afternoon warmth would recede more quickly. But most of the clothing I had was for warm weather, not cold. A Minnesota boy should have learned his lesson about "layers," but at fifty-seven years old I had failed, as I have many times before, to heed the basic lessons of life! There would be days on my journey where I wished I had warmer and dryer clothes, and others where I wished I had lighter and cooler clothing.

We had outfitted the cabin with a cushioned vinyl flooring that is often used on yachts—not to make it fancy but to allow me to walk around inside without slipping when it got wet. This would be one of the smartest construction choices we made early on, as the inside of the raft was often wet!

We also partnered with the Minnesota Renewable Energy Society (MRES) and in particular Doug Shoemaker, who had reached out during construction of the raft. They provided me with a rechargeable battery and a sixty-watt solar panel for the trip. I had hoped, initially, to be able to have a robust power source of power fueled by the sun. However, the need to balance construction design, weight, and sponsorship signage diminished our ability to use significant space on the roof to accommodate multiple panels. Furthermore, while solar power was something I really wanted to have as part of this trip, I had to weigh (literally) its cost/benefit to the trip against other needs.

It was my intention to bring a gas generator no matter what power source I would be using, and thankfully our good friends at the Minnesota Law Enforcement Memorial Association (LEMA) loaned me their immensely powerful and reliable Honda generator. The utilization of this generator became absolutely essential during the trip, particularly in keeping the raft afloat!

Another critical aspect of our power needs related directly to our use of technology, particularly our capacity to livestream. The success of the trip was going to rely heavily on constantly providing updates to social media followers, sponsors, donors and others following the trip. We felt that providing people a glimpse into my journey was an important part of the entire effort.

I reached out to our friends at EideCom, the virtual event company that had supported Spare Key's Groove Gala the past several years. The team that Charles Eide has assembled is impressive, particularly Kyle and Ryan Arndt, brothers who handled the production and technical end of our event. I spoke with Kyle and told him that we were hoping to have a near "Truman Show" presentation of my trip down the river. The key would be to have a reliable "always on" connection to a wireless signal that would allow us to share video. This would need to be coupled with a system that would be easy for me to operate, give us the capacity to do live feeds on social media platforms, and, if possible, also do live Zoom calls with donors, the press, and others.

The amount of energy consumption for this kind of endeavor was not something we had thought through very well or, to be honest, thought about much at all. The MRES combination of battery and solar panel would provide enough serviceable current to host steady low-power consumption, but it was not built to accommodate the high-power needs of the livestreaming we had in mind.

Kyle and Ryan, along with a guy named Mike Palazzola, came over to the raft and installed a system called "Buzz Buzz," envisioned and built by Mike. The concept was that it would pull a wireless signal from anywhere along the river, as long it was a signal we were subscribed to, and allow me to connect to social media platforms throughout my trip. They spent a couple hours on the raft installing the system, including a number of cameras. In theory, I would be able to share views in real time from the raft deck, as well as from inside the cabin. I would also be able to talk to people about various aspects of the expedition. (A downside was that Buzz Buzz could also broadcast things like me calling my credit card company to check on a charge, sharing the account number with all!) Kyle and Ryan also built an easy-to-use system with a laptop that had a number of pre-set camera shots that allowed me to simply press a button to change the camera view as I traveled down the river.

When all was said and done, I think we did a pretty amazing job communicating—often, and in real-time—with our supporters, giving them an inside look into my journey. The livestream worked as well as the technology and available cell towers allowed it to work. I was pleased with the efforts of EideCom and the Buzz Buzz system. Additionally, we were able to cobble together a multitude of different options to provide people with what I think was a neat insight into my trip.

In terms of the specifics of the power consumption, the Buzz Buzz system drew a TON of energy and would quickly draw down any power in the MRES powerpack—the solar panel, which did a nice job when it was sunny, wasn't so good when it wasn't, and even when there was full sun it couldn't charge the powerpack quickly enough or consistently enough for me to be able to run the cameras all the time. I would alternate the battery in the powerpack with the gas generator to keep the Buzz Buzz system operational but that meant, in addition to the sound of the boat motors, I also had the sound of the generator going. This, coupled with the fumes of the charger and the gas fumes of the Nissan, would often make me light-headed when I was sailing under power.

In the early days of the trip, I added two additional powerpacks. The first because the MRES powerpack loaned to me quit working, and the second because I wanted to have a backup to keep the livestream camera going as much as possible. As I got further down the river, my ability to keep it going became a challenge because the system often would not maintain the signal. This was frustrating! I compensated by using my phone and then trying to do a comprehensive update via livestream at the end of the day, sharing with people what I had gone through.

In hindsight, I realize I could have done more video and just uploaded it later. But, as you will discover throughout this book, the farther down the river I got, the more chaotic my journey became. It was increasingly difficult to do much more than simply get from Point A to Point B, particularly as I got into the lower part of the Mississippi River.

The livestream was just one (important) part of getting trip visibility. The other aspects included media, both traditional and social, and of course our sponsorships. We counted on our sponsors to communicate their participation with the trip to their employees, followers, and others on their respective social media channels.

We were pleased to have secured a number of sponsors. Some of them provided money, and others provided visibility. It was all enormously helpful to our cause. Our primary sponsor, Lend Smart Mortgage, was featured on the roof of the raft, along with our website for the trip, *www. hopeontheriver.com*. ASI Signage pulled all this together and made sure the signs fit on the raft and were as visible as possible.

Two sponsors that were critical to this project were the *St. Paul Pioneer Press* newspaper and Garage Logic, a podcast anchored by longtime *Pioneer Press* columnist Joe Soucheray. I've known Soucheray for years, not well and not in a highly personal way, but centered around things I have done in government, politics, and elsewhere in life. Joe has built a solid following with his podcast after his years with a radio show on KSTP came to an end. Those who listen to Garage Logic, mainly men, are extraordinarily loyal. On my trip, I joined Joe once a week from the raft to talk about my adventures, and invariably Joe begged people to donate money so I could end the trip early and come back home alive!

The *Pioneer Press*, thanks to Lori Swanson and Mike Burbach, offered me the chance to write a weekly column about the expedition. I've worked with Lori over the years on several projects, including the Titanic Exhibit, and Mike I got to know in relation to civic issues associated with the City of St. Paul. Both were fun to work with, and Mike implored me to share my story in a way that would resonate with people "who always wanted to do something like your trip and live vicariously through your journey." This opportunity was invaluable, and the column helped to serve as an additional "diary" of my trip.

The support of these partners, along with the work of our media team—led by long-time friend Carl Kuhl and others from the states I would travel through—was crucial in helping to tell the story of the journey and keeping people updated throughout the two months of my trip. Sarah Putnam, Spare Key's Chief Marketing Officer, participated heavily in this effort, as well as led a group of interns who provided frequent social media updates on the trip, gaining us additional invaluable exposure.

The final part of my pre-preparation for the trip included pulling together maps, digital maps, food, and other equipment. First I purchased two massive spiral-bound chartbooks produced by the Army Corps of Engineers; these books measured eleven inches by seventeen inches and, together, weighed about ten pounds. One covered the upper river from Minneapolis, Minnesota, to Cairo, Illinois. The other covered the lower river from Cairo, Illinois, to the Gulf of Mexico. Both would be the most important navigational tools I had with me.

I also brought a copy of *Quimby's Cruising Guide 2020*—a spiral bound book which included a list of all marinas in the area through which I was traveling. This proved to be an invaluable tool for me and Spare Key's chief administrative officer, Alexia Sebesta, during those times we could plan ahead to schedule where I might be able to moor the raft, particularly on the upper river.

Loaded onto my iPad were an assortment of navigational apps that would enable me to identify where any ships might be along my journey, the depth of the river, and the speed of the raft, plus an assortment of other indicators that would help me avoid getting hung up on submerged detritus and other river obstacles.

My material and equipment list was extensive and ranged from safety and security items, flashlights, and batteries to toilet paper and everything in between. I had two boxes of food, one of which was filled with MREs (military jargon for "Meals Ready to Eat"). These are prepackaged meals that come with a variety of entrees, sides, utensils, and, in the case of food that needs to be heated, a simple water-based "oven" system. Of all the meals I ate, these were the worst, while still being the most convenient and filling. The other foods I brought included a bunch of ramen and canned goods. This collection, along with a two-month supply of beef jerky from Jack Link's, would ultimately provide me with plenty of food for my journey.

I also secured plenty of safety equipment, from a flare gun to a first-aid kit to fishing equipment. The other thing I got, something I would appreciate much later, was a weapon.

Our family had moved to a suburb outside of St. Paul in December of 2020, after having spent more than a quarter of a century living in the city. In the townhome community we settled in, we met several wonderful neighbors, but perhaps none more incredible than O'Neal and Sarah Hampton. The two of them have become fast friends, and we are grateful for their kindness and appreciative of their tremendous love for their family. O'Neal is a former Army Paratrooper who served with the Green Beret, and he is proud of his family as he has every right to be. He is also an enthusiastic gun owner who knows everything there is to know, including how to own them responsibly and how to teach others to do so as well.

When he learned of my trip, he immediately communicated to me that he wanted to help in any way he could. One of those ways, he made clear, was to ensure that I was safe. It's important to note that I do not come from a family in which guns are a prevalent part of our lifestyle, nor do we hunt or do anything remotely associated with guns. My mom often tells the story of my dad, armed with a single-shot shotgun, taking our dog, Sigfried, out to go hunting one day and then coming back, putting the gun away, and never using it again.

My own life experience with guns is not particularly lengthy either. When we owned a cabin in Wisconsin, I purchased a shotgun and during the more-than-a-decade we owned the cabin, I fired it twice—once to make sure it worked and the other time to put an end to a red squirrel that was terrorizing our neighbors and their home.

Beyond that, I generally find myself in a cold sweat when it comes to being around guns. My own position on people owning guns typically runs along the line of it being none of my business as long as they do it responsibly and safely.

O'Neal is a seasoned owner and user of firearms and teaches a conceal and carry class. He offered to teach me at his house, and I readily took him up on the offer. We spent about three hours on the class and then several trips to the gun range, where he assured me that I was ready to obtain my permit.

Once I received my permit, I also secured two handguns for the trip. It was my hope I wouldn't need to use them in any way, shape, or form, but because I was undertaking this trip down the river alone, and planning to spend time sleeping on the river alone, I felt it was a prudent course of action to take.

As I mentioned above, later in the trip having these guns would prove to be important to me and my own safety.

Finally, the raft was provisioned and fitted out with everything I thought I might need, from navigation and tech equipment and gear to fuel, tools, food, and water. The sponsorships were in place and significant media coverage had been arranged. I checked and rechecked everything—over and over and over again—and then started from the beginning again!

The next step was the launch of the SS Hail Mary.

SECTION 11
On the Water

Chapter 5
Purpose, Peril and Pepin

On August 26, 2020, friends, family, and the curious gathered at Padelford Landing for a pre-launch event for the SS Hail Mary. Speeches, pictures, and jokes about whether I knew what I was doing abounded. Guests came onto the SS Hail Mary, which was tied to one of the Padelford riverboats, to see where I was going to live for the next two months. I gave short tours and assured people that I had plenty of safety equipment and gear. It felt, in a lot of ways, like the calm before the storm. Yet everyone was happy and excited, and I was anxious to get going.

At one point in the evening, Scott Flaherty, CEO of Lend Smart Mortgage, one of Spare Key's Board of Directors and the lead sponsor for the Hope on the River trip, came aboard the raft. I had met Scott a few years prior and have found him to be someone I admire a great deal. Scott is a hardscrabble Iron Range kid who has worked hard and built a successful mortgage company. He loves his family, he cares for his employees, and his faith guides in him all the things he does. Scott has been a strong supporter of Spare Key since reaching out to me a couple of years ago to say he wanted us to be the charity beneficiary of a golf tournament he hosts.

As Scott and I chatted about the trip, laughing at the absurdity of the situation the organization and the world found itself in, Scott handed me a little box. In it was a necklace with a Saint Christopher medal. Saint Christopher is the patron saint of travelers, and Scott hoped that he would be my guardian angel down the river. This generosity and kindness touched me. I took that Saint Christopher necklace and medal and attached it to the front of my raft, where I looked at it every day. In the midst of the most dangerous moments of the trip, I knew that Saint Christopher was watching over me and my journey.

While Scott had expressed concerns about my safety on the trip, he was also mindful of the sacrifice my family was making in having me gone for two months. He was concerned for them as much as he was for my survival, and I appreciated that sentiment then as I do now. More than any other board member during my trip down the river, Scott checked in on me nearly every week to make sure I was doing okay.

With the speeches done and the crowd gone, I went home for the evening to make the final preparations for my journey. The next morning I would get up early, load my car, and head to the Padelford Riverboats dock. What struck me, perhaps more than anything else, was how quickly this 1700-mile expedition had come to be a reality. My upcoming riverboat expedition, which had started as just a crazy idea while riding my bike on my birthday, had taken on a life of its own.

I could have waited for a better idea to come along. But the fact was that Spare Key was bleeding red ink because of canceled or postponed events and significant drop-offs in donor contributions. Waiting was akin to giving up.

I wasn't ready to give up.

So, that idea born out of desperation on my June birthday moved into reality after the Fourth of July when we hauled our rotted-out, fifty-year-old pontoon to the warehouse in South St. Paul. Upon this glorious beast, a raft was to be created. Crafted by Fred, Matilda, Owen, three friends named John and one named Ray. Together these seven people helped me plan, design, and build the vessel that would carry me down the Mighty Mississippi from St. Paul to Baton Rouge. Today was August 26. The next day I would embark on my journey. My Hope on the River adventure was about to get real.

On August 27, 2020, I gathered with the Spare Key team, several board members, Mary-Helen, Owen, and a lot of friends and family at Padelford Landing to make brief remarks. After that, I was to climb aboard the SS Hail Mary and be escorted away from the Padelford dock, pulled along the river to the Lafayette bridge in St. Paul, Minnesota.

O'Neal Hampton got us started with a powerful blessing of the raft, and of the person who would be boarding it and traveling down the river.

Gus Gaspardo and others offered their best wishes to me, as did Scott Flaherty. Matilda read the poem "Great River" by Barbara DeCoursey Roy.

The most powerful moment for me, and the one that made the tears flow, was a speech written by my son, Owen. It's reprinted at the beginning of this book, and each time I read it I can imagine the care and attention he put into crafting it. Even now I find my eyes watering when I look at it, and I remember his deep voice saying those words that morning.

With hugs to my friends and my family, I climbed onto the raft at about 11:00 a.m. Well-wishers, friends, and family climbed aboard the Padelford riverboat. Gus blew its awe-inspiring Kahlenberg horn and we departed Harriet Island.

As we proceeded slowly down the river, I chatted with those aboard the riverboat, who were laughing and taking pictures. I was preparing for the inevitable casting off from it once we neared the Robert Street Bridge.

With a few more waves, smiles, and best wishes, the Kahlenberg horn sounded again and I was given leave to begin the initial phase of my journey, accompanied by sheriff's deputies from Ramsey County. They were going to provide me an escort all the way to Red Wing, Minnesota, and make sure that my first hours out on the river didn't end my trip before it really got going. Ultimately, at different points on the river before arriving in Red Wing, we were joined by Pierce, Goodhue, and Dakota County sheriff boats as well. It was a pretty impressive sight and one that I am sure caused those on the shore, as well as on other boats, to wonder what I had done wrong to enjoy such an impressive entourage!

I was glad to finally be on my way down the river. I was nervous, anxious, excited, scared, and uncertain, but most of all determined. All of the planning and preparation notwithstanding, I had to admit I felt totally unprepared. I didn't know what to expect. At all. What I knew was that I would have to figure it out—every bit of it—as I went. (Even now, as I write this book, I shake my head at how little I actually knew about what I was getting into.) All I knew was that I had made a commitment to take the trip because I needed to do something to raise money and awareness for Spare Key. I felt I could figure it out along the way. Little did I know that I would need to figure out literally everything along the way.

As my sheriff deputy entourage and I continued to Red Wing, I pondered the work that still needed to be done on the raft before I could fully begin my journey. We needed to add the Mercury motor, tune up the Nissan, and add running lights, a depth-finder, anchors, a hard-wired VHF marine radio, and some other minor equipment.

The fact that I didn't know how to use most of this equipment, much less the motors, were things I kept pushing to the back of mind. As mentioned, I'd decided to figure it out along the way. If I had been seventeen, or twenty-seven or even thirty-seven, this kind of thought process would seem entirely reasonable. But, at fifty-seven-years old, it just seems completely dumb. In hindsight, it is as dumb now as it was then. Yet I had made the decision to go, so go I would.

I arrived safely in Red Wing about six hours later. I would be staying at the Ole Miss Marina and was met by my good friend, Cindy Taube. I got the SS Hail Mary tied up and we worked out the details with River Valley Power and Sport about what time I would be picked up in the morning. The plan was for the raft to be trailered from the water and driven to River Valley Power and Sport, where it would have its Nissan 60 HP motor tuned up and a 9.9 HP Mercury kicker motor installed, along with a depth finder, VHF marine radio, and running lights to keep me visible while I docked for the evening. Once this work was completed, the vessel would be returned to the water and my journey along the Mississippi River for 1,700 miles—two months through ten states—would start in earnest.

Cindy and I grabbed some dinner. We brought it back to the marina area and sat on a picnic table at Bay Point Park. Over burgers and fries, we talked about what the trip might be like and just how much work had taken place to even get us this far. I thanked Cindy for all her help. She told me to let her know if I needed anything else that night, and that she would be available the next day if needed.

I finally got to sleep, only to be awakened by a massive thunderstorm that had made its way into the region. Booming thunder and luminous, frequent lightning flashes got my attention quickly. So, too, did the winds that cascaded in and started blowing the raft from side to side.

As I nervously looked for weather reports for the next couple of hours, I withstood both the torrential rain and high winds that rattled the raft and its occupant. I contemplated what I would need to do should the storm get any closer and was prepared to run for shelter if necessary.

Thankfully, the storm passed. I relaxed and got ready for the transfer of the raft from the water to River Valley Power and Sport.

At 7:00 a.m., the SS Hail Mary was removed from the water and trailered to River Valley Power and Sport. Once I arrived at their facilities, they went to work like nobody's business. First things first, though—they had to let nearly all the air out of the tires of their pontoon trailer to get the boat into their workshop. It didn't faze them a bit. Then, like an expertly trained professional sports team—or better yet, a finely trained Indy 500 Pit Crew—they descended upon the SS Hail Mary.

Eight hours later, they had tuned up the Nissan and added the Mercury motor and the rest—and my American flagpole post. I am still amazed at the speed, skill, professionalism, and determination they demonstrated in simply getting the work done and done right.

I also had the opportunity to spend time with Mike Wilson. As well as running for mayor at the time, Mike is the founder and curator of the Red Wing Marine Museum. In the weeks leading up to the trip, Mike and his friend Matt Stokes were advisors and advocates for the Hope on the River journey. Both counseled me repeatedly to respect the river, be prepared, and ultimately do my best to enjoy the experience. Mike is someone who is not afraid to reach out to help. And help he did for Hope on the River.

I also had the opportunity to meet John Wooden, owner of River Valley Power and Sport of Red Wing Marine. Twenty-six years ago, he started out his company with a lawnmower. Today he has the largest marine company in Minnesota. I could see why. He is smart, passionate, driven, and generous. John was the one who had reached out to Mercury, securing their donation of the motor, and now had assembled his team to do the installations and put us on the water safe and sound. Simply put, this trip wouldn't have happened without his help!

Once the work was done, the SS Hail Mary was put back in the water and I headed to River Valley Power and Sport's marina. Unfortunately, the pontoon tube on the starboard side began to take on a ton of water, and by the time I arrived at the marina, I was listing heavily on the starboard quarter.

It was a pretty unnerving site.

Mary-Helen had driven to Red Wing to have dinner with me before I shoved off the next morning, but dinner would have to wait. The raft was sinking before our eyes. Clearly, the tube needed to be repaired before I could proceed any further.

A young man and four other helpful souls climbed onto a towboat and brought me back upriver to the Ole Miss Marina. As darkness descended, the raft was brought ashore and it was determined that the weld spots used to secure the Mercury motor to the pontoon had punctured holes in the starboard tube. The amount of water inside the tube was evident, and it was clear that I wasn't going anywhere until we resolved that problem.

The raft was driven to the welder's repair shop, and I spent the night in a local Red Wing Hotel. The next morning I got a text from Joe at River Valley Power and Sport that the SS Hail Mary was ready to go. Unfortunately, upon arriving, I was given the news that the condition of the pontoon tubes was worse than initially assumed. Fractures and cracks had been puttied up during the years, and some of that putty had gotten loose. The welder did the best he could do, but the situation was going to require constant attention on my part.

Joe gave me a pump with a hose, and instructions that any time I stopped it would be wise to pump out the tubes by attaching the cables to my boat battery and getting out as much water as possible. We put the hose down one of the pontoon tube openings, and it fit perfectly.

We then took the SS Hail Mary back to the Ole Miss Marina. And off I went down the Mississippi! My vessel floated and drifted magnificently.

I could not have had a better ride. The Nissan was in neutral the few times I needed to urge the raft back into the channel, but it was performing flawlessly.

It wasn't long, however, before I began to see signs of what the rest of the day was going to look like.

First, it's important I share some information about Lake Pepin. Twenty-two miles long and only two miles wide at its widest point, the lake is part of the Mississippi River as it flows along the border of Minnesota and Wisconsin. It was formed when the river was partially dammed by a delta from a tributary stream and spread out across the valley. It is considered the "birthplace" of water skiing and, in 1890, was the site of one of the worst maritime disasters on the Mississippi when the Sea Wing ferry capsized in a bad storm, killing ninety-eight people.

As one gets closer to the mouth of Lake Pepin, the river traffic picks up considerably. And the passage into the lake becomes narrower. The traffic from large pleasure boats becomes even more pronounced. As do the waves!

I eventually figured out how to weave in and out of the navigation channel leading to the mouth, thanks to my new depth finder. I waited out the large ships and then pointed my bow into the waves and managed to get through it. I felt pretty proud of myself about all of this—until I got into the lake itself.

Once out in the vast openness of Lake Pepin, the wind is startling and the waves are brutal. If you love to sail, it can be one of the most enjoyable places on Earth. If you are an idiot on a raft who knows nothing about what he is doing, it can be one of the most hellish experiences of your life.

As the next few hours would attest, I would find myself experiencing all of the latter and very little of the former. Hello! I am fifty-seven years old and I know nothing about steering a homemade raft on a lake with the wind and waves of Lake Pepin.

It was there I made my first real mistake of the day.

Instead of hugging the lake's far shoreline, which would have blocked much of the wind, I chose to hug the opposite side of the lake. This meant I took the full brunt of the wind as it came across the open water, creating big waves and shoving the raft around like a toy boat. Big mistake!

This only intensified the wind pushing me around like a bobber. It was brutal. Water began pushing up through the pontoon floor—which, thankfully, my build team had anticipated. The drain hole was built in the rear of the raft, so the water quickly departed.

But the waves were relentless. I bounced and weaved and turned and bounced and weaved some more. Sailboats were flying across the water and I was barely moving. My depth finder and iMarine app showed me plugging along at around eight miles an hour. Not fast, but at least I was moving.

Eventually I got lined up at an angle that allowed me to move back into the center of the lake and start escaping the worst of the wind and the waves.

At least three times, I was convinced the SS Hail Mary was going to capsize.

I am grateful for Scott Flaherty's gift of my Saint Christopher medal, because I'm pretty sure divine protection, along with the relentless grind of my Nissan, played a significant role in my navigating through Lake Pepin successfully.

I breathed a sigh of relief as it all came to an end.

Then—I made my second big mistake of the day.

As I was putting along, I knew I needed to tie up for the night. So, emboldened by my success in crossing the lake, I thought I would try my luck at tying up on a sandbank for the evening.

Yup. Not a good idea.

Not so much because I shouldn't have tried it. I just shouldn't have tried it on that day in that location. I was exhausted and not paying as much attention as I should have. And the current was much too fast in this particular spot.

And, for reasons I would learn shortly, I was too heavy, and the raft hit the sand before it hit the shoreline.

Ugghh!

Between surviving the pounding of Lake Pepin and now getting stuck fifty feet from shore, I was both frustrated and unsure about what I was supposed to do. Thankfully, a group of good souls came up and chatted with me for a while as I tried to figure things out. They said that they could push me off the sandbar, and once free I should back out with my motors, get back into the channel, and find somewhere else to tie up for the evening.

It sounded like a reasonable plan to me, and I thanked them for their assistance.

Sure enough, they got me off the sandbar.

But then, for the umpteenth time that day, disaster struck.

I got stuck again.

It was clear that I was deeper in the water than I had guessed, but the raft cleared one sandbar only to get stuck on another one. I pulled out the push-pole I had brought with me and managed to get myself free again.

At this point, though, the back end of the raft was pushing up against the river's southward current. That current was amplified by the amount of boat traffic coming up and down the navigation channel, which I was now about ten feet inside, and it was narrow.

Water rushed up and over the back of the raft as I tried desperately to get my motor started. Finally it caught, and I tried to accelerate forward to get out of the way of approaching boats.

Then the Nissan, flooded with water from the river, quit.

No worries, though. I had the kicker motor.

Of course, the kicker motor, swamped with water, wouldn't start.

I grabbed my anchor and threw it madly into the river, hoping it would find some kind of purchase.

It didn't.

Multiple throws later, the anchor stuck, but not before I asked myself repeatedly, "What the heck am I doing out here?"

John Wooden had purchased a river equivalent of AAA for me before I left Red Wing. The plan allowed for boaters who found themselves stranded to call a 1-800 number to ask for assistance. Here, in the middle of the navigation channel, it was clear I needed help.

Unfortunately, there were two real ships on Lake Pepin (not rafts with garden sheds) that were taking on water, and the tow company was trying to get them to safety.

I was on my own.

But, of course, I wasn't.

People came from every direction to ask if I needed help.

Two couples on a pontoon came up and told me what I already knew: I was in the navigation channel and I needed to get out of there before a towboat came and ran me over! Thankfully, they offered to tow me to the nearest marina, and I gladly accepted their assistance. Their kindness was one of many examples to come of people assisting me on my journey down the river.

The plan was to tow me to a place called Parkside Marina in Wabasha, Minnesota. This marina, which was about a mile or so away, was where I should have pulled in initially rather than attempting to beach the raft on the shoreline. This would serve as one of the many lessons I would learn on the river about planning ahead and having a backup plan every single day.

On that day, I had not planned ahead. I had figured I would just go as far as I could go and then tie up somewhere.

When that plan failed, I didn't have a backup plan.

Now, necessity was forcing me to have a backup plan, and as I expressed my gratitude to my Good Samaritans, I found myself replaying the day as I waited for us to reach our destination.

At one point in the towing journey, one of the women on the pontoon remarked that the raft appeared to be listing significantly on the starboard side. To be honest, I couldn't really tell much about listing at this point in my journey because I barely knew what "starboard" meant, much less "listing." However, I assured her that all was fine, I knew that the raft had a small leak in it, and I would be able to remedy the matter once I got tied up.

About forty-five minutes later, I got to Parkside Marina and thanked the folks who had towed me there. I latched onto an old gas dock in a gorgeous harbor. Once I was tied up and my Good Samaritans had gone, I assessed the condition of the raft.

The floor was wet. My feet were soaked.

Worse, though, the pontoon was clearly listing at the rear on the starboard pontoon again.

Worse yet, the access to the pontoon, a little spigot that was covered by a three-quarter inch cap that screwed on, was nearly underwater, too. If that spigot went under, there would be no way I could get the water out of the pontoon and the raft might literally sink before my eyes. With the raft tied up to the fuel dock, I quickly grabbed the pump and the attached hose, connected it to the battery, and began to unscrew the cap.

And discovered yet another problem.

When I was in Red Wing, we had tested the hose by putting it into the opening on the port side of the pontoon. It fit fine.

But clearly, it was not fitting into the starboard pontoon tube.

I shoved, cursed, and tried multiple ways to get the garden hose into the spigot shaft, but it simply would not go.

Failing to make any headway with this effort, I finally resorted to grabbing a small pump I had purchased to get drinking water from a five-gallon bottle of water I had aboard the raft. The pump had a thin, narrow plastic tube that I shoved into the spigot, and surprisingly it began to draw water. Not a lot, but at least it gave me comfort that I was making some progress as I tried to come up with another plan.

I tried putting engine oil on the garden hose, thinking that might get it to slide into the spigot.

That didn't work.

Then I thought maybe shaving some of the plastic coating off the garden hose could make it thin enough to slide in. All that did was have me cutting holes in the hose, as my knife-shaving skills aren't all that impressive.

I was quickly losing ground in this battle.

The pontoon was still perilously close to sliding under the water, pulling more water in with it and sinking the raft.

I had to get up and figure out a plan. So I put the cap back on the spigot and tried to catch my breath and ponder my options.

As I did, I walked by a little structure that was on top of the fuel dock. There, on the wall, was a long black hose hanging from a nail. I don't know what the hose was used for, but I could tell it was narrower than the garden hose I kept trying to shove into the spigot.

Looking around and seeing nobody to ask permission from to use the hose, or tell me that I couldn't, I grabbed my knife, cut off a two-foot section, and walked quickly back to the pump.

My good fortune that day was that the length of hose I had just taken fit perfectly and snugly inside the garden hose attached to the pump.

As I unscrewed the cap, I hoped to myself that this hose would fit inside the spigot.

It did!

I hooked up the pump to the battery, and with the hose inside the pontoon, suddenly water began to come out and gush into the river. *Success!*

For the next forty-five minutes, water continued to pour out of the tube.

Unfortunately, in all the excitement, I didn't calculate how long it took to remove that water, so I couldn't tell exactly how much was in the tube. But it was enough that the tube was noticeably higher after the pump finally spit and said it couldn't find any additional water.

So, that problem was solved! For now!

Somewhat spent, I took a break and sat down for a bit.

Soon the owner of the marina, Mark Wickersham, came up to chat and ask how I was.

When I recounted the day's events, he chuckled and indicated that when I had been stuck out on the river in the navigation channel, he had gotten a number of calls from people asking if he was going out to help me. Clearly, I didn't need to be helped off the river anymore, but I did need a place to stay for the night and collect my thoughts.

He told me to feel free to spend the evening there and not worry about it. I thanked him, and then decided I would give the motors a try to see if I could get them started.

I first tried the kicker motor.

It sputtered a bit but finally caught, and I let it idle for a while before I turned it off, satisfied that it had dried out and was functional.

Unfortunately, the Nissan wouldn't start.

Which would, of course, be a severe problem and setback for me if I couldn't get it started. My concern was whether or not my bonehead disaster on the sandbar had some way or another sucked sand into the motor.

If it had, I supposed that given my lack of knowledge about motors, I would need to have someone repair something in order to get back on the water. There wasn't much I could do at that point. The day was coming to an end.

I was grateful to be safe, off the river, and tied up to a sturdy dock.

I awoke on Sunday morning, and it was gorgeous. With the day before not yet a distant memory, I got up and had some coffee.

My plan was to try the Nissan again at 8:30a.m. and see whether it would start. If it did, my plan was to head out toward my next stop on the river. If it didn't, I really didn't know what I would do. Luckily the marina office would open at 10:00.

Promptly at 8:30, I tried to start the motor. No luck. It tried to fire but just couldn't and wouldn't catch. I was frustrated but clearly without any option at this point. When the office opened, I wandered over and told Mark how I wasn't having any luck.

He suggested that the Nissan was still wet and that I should consider removing the motor cover and letting it dry out in the warm sun. I was skeptical but also knew that I didn't know anything about boat motors, so I did as he suggested.

He also suggested I try removing the spark plugs and try some new ones. So he loaned me a wrench and a couple of plugs, and I went about doing that.

Mark explained that he didn't have any mechanics on Sunday, but that if Monday arrived and I still couldn't get the motor to work, we might want to pull it out of the water and let his mechanics work on it.

I was hoping that wouldn't be the case and told him that I appreciated his kindness in letting me stay an extra day.

Mark gave me a ride into town so I could pick up some supplies, as well as some sandbags to replace the extra ones I had left behind in St. Paul. A quick note about sandbags—because we hadn't really been sure about how well the raft was going to perform with the garden shed on top of it, we had added about 120 pounds of sandbags to the very front of the raft. The idea was that I would adjust the sandbags as necessary and, if required, tear them open and dump the sand in the water if I didn't need the additional weight and ballast. Frankly, I had no idea what to do with the sandbags. They were there, but I didn't actually understand what impact they had or didn't have on the performance of the raft. Yet for some reason I felt compelled to replace the ones I had left behind.

At the same time, I figured it would make sense for me to have some additional spark plugs and a spark plug wrench, so I picked those up at a local auto parts store. Sometime in the middle of the afternoon, with the motor having been in the hot sun for several hours, I decided to give the Nissan a try with new plugs in the engine. With my fingers crossed, I turned the key, and suddenly it sputtered.

I tried again, and it sputtered again, then finally caught and roared to life!

I could not have been more thrilled. I kept the motor running for nearly twenty minutes at a low idle to make sure that fuel was running through the line and that it would keep working. It was too late in the day for me to get underway, but at least I now had two fully functioning motors again.

The marina office was closed, but I wrote a quick note to Mark and left the wrench he had loaned me in his pickup truck along with a thank you note for his kindness and generosity. With the rest of the day ahead of me, I sat down and relaxed. My plan would be to get underway on Monday morning with two working motors, a pump I could now use to remove water from the pontoon, and a more positive feeling about where I was at in the journey.

Confident about the path ahead, I ended the day with gratitude for the kindness of strangers, and for the warm August sun and its healing properties on my aging Nissan motor.

Chapter 6
Remembering Not to Forget

I awoke early, made myself some coffee, and prepared to get underway. It was a bit breezy that morning, but nothing that seemed too threatening. After my adventures in Lake Pepin, I was quite sure that the morning wind wouldn't be nearly as challenging as the previous day's waves.

The day's trip would bring me a short distance of fifteen miles to Alma, Wisconsin, and the Great River Harbor Marina, where I would spend the night. I crossed my fingers as I started first the kicker motor, then the Nissan. I was pleased that both seemed to be running just fine.

Due to the wind, I had removed all of the acrylic signs from the raft except for the large "Hope on the River" logo sign on the back of the raft. I thought it would be nice to have our logo on display as I made my way down the river to boost visibility for the trip. I made sure that everything was fastened securely, then slowly turned the SS Hail Mary around to face the navigation channel's opening. Slowly throttling up, I nudged the raft's nose into the river and turned to starboard to begin my journey to Alma.

Almost immediately, I knew I had screwed up by underestimating just how much wind there was. Within seconds, the large "Hope on the River" sign flew off the raft, rose into the air, and blew away behind me into the river. I lost sight of it within seconds.

I contemplated turning back to try to find it. However, I didn't have much confidence that I could track its flight path and figured I would burn valuable time looking for something that had probably already sunk deep under the water.

Shaking my head, I throttled up the raft and began my trek to Alma with a mental note to send a message to Wendy Pajor, to see if she could replace the sign I had lost barely days into my trip!

Later I was to travel through Lock and Dam Number 4, which

would be roughly halfway to my final destination for the day. With only fifteen miles to go, I spent a fair amount of time drifting and motoring and enjoying the scenery as much as I could.

As I got further from St. Paul, my perception of the river changed with each mile I traveled. For twenty-five years, my impression of the Mississippi River had been formed mainly from the work I had done for the city, as well as from where I lived in St. Paul. My home was roughly a half-mile from the banks of the Mississippi River, and my family and I spent a great deal of time running, walking, and biking along the path that meanders for miles on both the St. Paul and Minneapolis sides of the river. Those hiking path views gave me the impression of a serene river that seems reasonably tame and welcoming, albeit wide in some areas. But as I had learned on Lake Pepin and was to discover again that day, the river is more complicated and unpredictable than what I have known.

The Mississippi doesn't always lie within easily identified banks, nor does it always resemble the winding bends of the friendly river I have known. In some areas, it is wide and spread out, like Lake Pepin, where the only way to understand where I was supposed to bring the raft was defined by the red and green buoys that mark the navigation channel. In other areas, there are relatively narrow channels, with long swaths of wooded islands on either side that serve as a natural windbreak and make for a gentle trip down the river.

One aspect of the river I needed to quickly learn about was the lock and dam system. Each of the nearly two dozen locks and dams I would be "locking" through are the creations of government public work projects from decades ago. They are massive structures and manage the ebb and flow of commercial and recreational traffic from north and south along the Upper Mississippi.

There is a process that one must go through on the locks and dams. On this particular day, as I approached Lock and Dam Number 4 that lies above the City of Alma, I got on my VHF radio and turned it to channel 14, which is used when one wishes to communicate to lock operators to let them know you will need to lock through at some point.

I radioed ahead when I was about a mile out from the lock and dam to let them know I was en route. Due to me not paying close enough attention, as well as my general lack of awareness of river protocols, I somehow got on the wrong side of a green buoy when I couldn't locate a red one. I wasn't even aware of this until a call came in on my radio saying, "Hey, the guy in the shed boat, if you don't get back in the center of the buoys you're going to rip your motor off on a wing dam!"

Moving with purpose, I turned my raft back into the channel that I thought I was supposed to be in, until I got in between clearly marked red and green buoys.

Unbeknownst to me until that helpful radio call, in a bay or harbor area off the main river channel, the red and green buoys are positioned on the *opposite* sides relative to their positions in the main channel. Who knew? I had taken "Red Right Return" to heart.

In this instance, as I had entered the bay, I thought I was continuing downriver and the green buoys would be on my right. However, the green buoy was on my left—and since there was no red buoy within view, I assumed I was on the wrong side of the green buoy. Nope! If I had continued, I would likely have ripped the pontoons off my raft on some submerged rocks or obstacle.

I eventually made it to my slip in Alma, where I unpacked, re-packed, and got myself situated for the night.

On Tuesday morning, I started my journey to Winona, Minnesota. I wasn't going to be stumped on my departure, so I dutifully followed the line of navigational buoys until I got into the big river again. I had no sooner started to relax when my cell phone rang. It was Alexia, Spare Key's Chief Administrative Officer, saying, "Say, I just got a call from the marina you left, and your gas generator is sitting on the gas dock. Do you need that?"

Ugh!

I turned around and proceeded slowly back *up* the river and through the channel to the gas dock, grabbed my generator, and then went back through the channel to begin my travel *down* the river.

I got my bearings once again and proceeded to drift towards Winona and Lock and Dam Number 5.

Now, I won't lie. The most anxiety-ridden part of the lock and dam process for me isn't inside the lock and dam. It's the process of getting myself into it.

I made sure to call at least one mile before I arrived to let the operator know who I was and what kind of vessel I was in, and to make sure there wasn't traffic tying up the lock. Once they responded and told me that they would lock me through, I proceeded forward under power.

However, the previous two times I went through the process, the light near the lock and dam was red, which meant that they were not yet ready for me to enter the lock. So, I slowed down, and then, if it still wasn't ready—green—I turned around and went back *up* the river.

Now, I suppose I should have developed a better plan—perhaps anchoring outside of the channel. But I was not yet confident enough to do that. I thought I should first attempt that at a location that seemed to be less intimidating.

I finally got the green light to enter Lock and Dam Number 5 and proceeded again under power.

Dylan, the young man at the lock and dam, threw over two ropes to grab onto, and I held onto them for dear life as he began the lower the water in the lock to match the water in the dam below. Sometimes only one line would be thrown, sometimes, as in this case, two would be thrown. The rope allowed me to pull the raft up close to the lock and dam wall and not drift into other boats in front of me, or into the massive gates that held back the river, preventing serious damage to the raft and injury to myself. While some boats were able to "float" in the center of the lock and dam channel while they waited, they also had the benefit of more powerful motors, newer controls and easier navigation systems

Dylan was a delight—kind, generous, and immensely helpful. I asked him on what side I would enter the next lock and dam—Number 5A, farther down the river—and he assured me it would be on the right. He then ran into the building and grabbed me a map that showed the correct side to approach and enter each lock and dam on the river.

Trust me, knowing if I was supposed to enter on the left or the right side of a lock before I got there was very reassuring!

The process of getting through Lock and Dam Number 5 and back underway was maybe fifteen minutes.

While at River Valley Power and Sport, I had been given a package of large sticks of chalk. I was told that "tradition" was that you would write something on the wall of the lock and dam as you were going through it. In what would become a ritual for me through as many of the locks and dams I could, I took my piece of chalk and wrote "Hope on the River" on the lock wall. I waved to Dylan. He assured me that there was little tow and barge traffic on the river ahead of me. Happily, I motored through the turbulence and began my drift again.

Throughout the day, I came upon remarkable scenery and gorgeous cities, like Minnesota City, Minnesota, and Fountain City in Wisconsin. From the river you can see the beauty of these historic river towns, their church steeples, the high bluffs, and the quaint and bustling shoreline. From the river it all looks bucolic and welcoming and warm and safe. Finally, I arrived at Lock and Dam Number 5A.

Some operators are more communicative on the radio than others, and the gentleman on this call was sparse with words. Plus, trying to hear him over the ear-shattering dull roar of my two-stroke Nissan was a challenge. Eventually, however, I got the signal to head into the lock and was met by Missy, another wonderfully patient, helpful, and professional lock attendant. Missy threw me the ropes and we chatted about the SS Hail Mary and my trip. Before long, I was waving goodbye to her as I proceeded once again under power through the turbulence.

Because I had to get to Winona before 7:00 p.m. to be assured of a slip at Dick's Marina, I powered through the rest of the way, which was good because the wind was high and would have kept me from making forward progress!

A while later, I saw the marina's entrance off my raft's port side and was met by a young man named McCoy Tekautz. He said, "You must be the boat they told me to watch for. I guess I couldn't miss you!" He pulled me in, gassed me up, and helped me into my slip. A bit later, I was met by Cynthya Porter, who handles marketing for Visit Winona. Not only did she bring me some gifts, including Bloedow's Bakery donuts, but she was also kind enough to drive me to Target to get some warmer clothes!

As I settled in for the evening, I repeated what became a near daily practice on my trip. First, I decided whether or not to put the acrylic signs up. When we designed the raft, we had spent a great deal of time figuring out how to allow the wind to circulate through the shed. After all, my living quarters non-streamlined design (a garden shed) had a profile that made it susceptible to catching the wind as I traveled down the river. I learned immediately that no matter how calm wind may seem on land, on the river it is something else. It whips around in circles. It changes direction. It gusts and calms and gusts again.

In my daily travels on the water, there was nothing but screen on the raft shed. I often had all three doors propped open to allow for free-flowing air throughout the raft as I made my way down the river. At night, however, a combination of cooler temperatures, bugs, and, yes, rain, created a different dynamic.

On warm evenings, without rain, I kept the acrylic windows off the raft shed. I liked the feeling of sleeping in a porch—with the screens to repel the bugs and the bats and all of the animal and insect life that creeped me out to no end.

On cooler evenings, and when it rained, I would spend the few minutes it took to slide the acrylic windows into the metal channels that ASI Signage had created and button up the raft pretty nicely.

Once "locked in" inside my raft shed, I had a few options before closing my eyes and drifting off to sleep. I could either spend time typing my blog at the desk that we built into the raft, which also served as the platform for my laptop and navigational maps and gear. Or I could try to catch up on some reading.

Sleeping on the raft, however, proved to be a challenge for me.

I need to note that I don't sleep a lot when I am not on a river raft.

For as long as I can remember, I go to bed late, I wake up early, and from time to time, if the opportunity presents itself, I will catch a nice nap to fill in for the lack of quality sleep.

Today, at age fifty-seven, I find that sleeping is even more difficult. I get tired enough and fall asleep fast enough, but I don't sleep for very long.

And, as I get older, so too do my parts! Especially the parts that wake up me at all hours of the night and morning and require me to use the bathroom.

One thing I tried to do as I trekked down the river was stay hydrated. During the daytime, hydration practice required a fair amount of peeking around before I relieved myself off the side of the raft. In the evening, when I was cold and tired, having to convince myself to get up and go to the bathroom became a nightly ritual that reminded me I have reached that "certain age" of life! The sight of me stumbling out of my inflatable cot and pushing aside plastic bins filled with food and equipment so I could unlatch one of the three doors of the raft to go to the bathroom would make most people laugh out loud.

I grumbled and I creaked and groaned until I finally get my business done, then would have to put it all back together in the same place before I could try to doze off to a fitful rest. When I really woke up for the day, which more often than not was around four o'clock in the morning, I checked my phone for messages and tried to delay getting out of the cot for as long as I could. Then I would finally flick on one of the solar lights attached to the raft ceiling, find my coffee pot, and try to get myself awake enough to start the day.

That Wednesday, I awoke and got ready to head to La Crosse, Wisconsin, but not before I took a moment to marvel at the generosity of the people I had met along the way. People who didn't have to help the way they did but did anyhow. I learned that McCoy was working at the lock while dreaming of being a professional fighter and wrestler. He had overcome injuries to work hard, train harder, and as he said, "grind it out." Others, like Dylan and Missy, are public servants who perform their duties and tasks with kindness, professionalism, and skill. They don't need to care about who is passing through their lock other than dropping them the rope and getting them in and out safely. But they do more than that—they want to know who you are, what you are doing, where you are going, and that you are prepared and ready. And they wish you luck and hope you have a safe journey.

And Cynthya, who had been introduced to me by my friend Patrick

Klinger, found me the place to dock in Winona, brought me tasty treats and gifts, and then had the generosity to drive me to get the clothes I forgot to bring with me.

Simple. Human. Kindness.

I began my journey with a commitment to bring hope to families living in each state along the river. But along the way I realized that I was going to need to rely on the kindness and humanity of others to help me succeed. So far, I was finding everything I had hoped to discover.

Chapter 7
Fred and Matilda to the Rescue

My departure from Winona could not have been more glorious. The day's weather was warm, with little wind, perfect conditions for the next stage of my journey. The previous evening's visit with Cynthya and McCoy made my stay in Winona even more special. And the day ahead of me looked ideal. Better yet, I didn't forget anything this time—and nothing blew off the raft—so I was feeling pretty darn good about myself.

The trip from Winona to La Crosse did not disappoint in terms of beauty and experience. The perspective from the water's surface provides a vantage point that everyone should find the time to see. The high hills, bluffs, and topography alone are enough to take your breath away. Add in the wildlife—the majesty of bald eagles, hawks, geese, ducks, swans, and other fowl—and you can understand that there is an entirely different world on this river than what you see from the road or walking paths along the shore.

Here, long before any of us were around, nature created a realm that is impossible to imagine unless you experience it in real time. The temptation is always to grab a camera and snap a picture—and, admittedly, I did that from time to time.

But there is also the unmistakable allure of merely sitting back, soaking it in, and marveling at it all.

Appreciating what you see simply because you can.

I readily admit that I am not much of an outdoorsman. Animals, if not within the context of their environment, scare me. Yet I am in awe of their power, purpose, and sheer tenacity. Each one, big and small, has unique characteristics so central to their place on the planet that it is impossible not to look in wonder at how they move, walk, fly, swim, or crawl.

Even while I wrote my blog, sitting in the SS Hail Mary in a harbor off the main channel of the river, fish were jumping around me. Ducks and geese were swimming back and forth, cranes soared aloft, and all sorts of animals were chirping, grunting, creeping, and crawling.

I imagined the bounty of this river before humans arrived on the planet. Imagine what it must have been like for Native Americans before non-native Americans arrived. Even then, for those who came from other continents the landscape and the animal kingdom which inhabited it must have been breathtaking.

Before long, however, my thoughts would turn from nature to commerce.

As I approached Lock and Dam Number 6, I began to see more and more river traffic composed of tows, tugs, and barges. These are not to be trifled with, and I did my best to remove myself from their lane as quickly and safely as possible.

My raft didn't move with astonishing speed, even though I had my two motors on the rear to make sure I could move. The key, of course, was to have my head on a swivel and make sure I didn't get so absorbed in my thoughts—focusing on my maps and charts, or talking on the phone to a reporter, donor, member of the Spare Key team, or family member—that I forget to look ahead of me. And behind me!

On that day, it was forgetting to look behind me that made me kick myself. Not because I was in immediate danger but because I was reminded of how quickly the situation changes on the river. One second I was musing about the bucolic scene of natural wonder and beauty and the next second I had a multi-ton tow boat catching up to me.

In this particular case, I picked up my radio, hailed the craft behind me, and asked its intentions and what side of the channel it wished me to be on. Right away, the skipper requested I stay on the channel's red buoy side, and I promptly complied.

By the time I reached Lock and Dam Number 6, I had encountered two other tows heading northbound and followed the same protocol. I radioed ahead about a mile before reaching the lock. The operator indicated that traffic proceeding upriver was already preparing to go through the lock and dam, and it included a large tow with barges and several pleasure craft. I was told to expect to wait for about an hour and a half. So I dutifully went off to find a quiet place to anchor and enjoy the wait.

Unfortunately, I went through another learning experience in this exercise.

About an hour and a half later, when I radioed the operator and asked for an update, he indicated that the tow and barge were leaving the lock and that I could begin preparing to enter it. I radioed back and told him that I would wait for the barge to get past me, and neither he nor I thought anything about it.

Which is where the learning experience occurred.

It took the barge about forty-five minutes to get by me before I left my safe perch. Once it had passed, I throttled up, and it took about twenty minutes for me to get back to my initial location near the lock and dam entrance.

In that time, other traffic had entered the lock and dam area wanting to head north, including additional commercial traffic, and I lost my place in line!

Lesson: Stay close, but not too close.

I needed to have a clear line of sight to the lock and dam to check when traffic was gone and then radio ahead to ask if it was okay to proceed forward and wait for the green light to enter the lock. Without that clear line of sight, I had no clue as to the traffic status in the area, and the operator had too many other things going on to worry about calling me back to say, "Hey, Erich, you're free to come forward."

That learning experience cost me three and a half hours at Lock and Dam Number 6.

Once in the lock, it took fifteen minutes, and boom, I was out and on my way to Lock and Dam Number 7.

Along the way, there was the nexus again of nature and commerce.

More tugs. More tows. More barges.

More wake and more waves!

So, another lesson learned.

While I had gotten fairly adept at getting out of the way of big ships and boats, and at learning to anticipate the wake and pointing the raft's bow into it to keep from being hit broadside, the waves created by bigger tows and boats were a different story. I discovered that I needed to wait another ten or fifteen minutes until the trailing wake caught up, because that can even be more challenging to the raft. These waves swell and grow in size and number and don't stop until they stop.

Several times, I found myself being pounded by waves that hit me minutes after the tow or tug went by me.

Another... ANOTHER... lesson learned.

In traveling farther, I got to see Mountain City and Fountain City and more tugs and tows and barges, and all of it reminded me again of the immeasurable impact the Mississippi has on our lives every single day.

The people who work on it. The people it feeds. The land it nourishes. The nation it built.

This river exemplifies so much of the human experience, it is hard to put into words.

Yet my day wouldn't be done until I got through Lock and Dam Number 7 and arrived in La Crosse.

By and large, Number 7 was uneventful. However, the operator did not respond to radio calls, so I called the lock and dam phone. I could tell the individual was annoyed, but I politely asked if I could proceed forward for locking.

At that point, he told me yes and that he would ready the lock and dam.

In between all of this, radio traffic began with northbound traffic saying they wanted to lock in as well.

Either I was confused, the lock and dam operator was confused, the northbound traffic was confused, or all of us were confused, but I know for a fact that nobody was completely clear about who was doing what, when, and where.

Finally, the light turned green to enter the lock, and so I did. Got my rope. Hung on. Doors opened. And off I went.

About this time, I decided to switch over to my kicker motor to drift the rest of the way to La Crosse, as the Nissan had done her job in getting us through the two locks and dams.

Before I got to the last turn to La Crosse I had to get past one more tow at a swing bridge right outside the bend to town, and I successfully did so.

Then it was onto the final stretch to La Crosse

When you enter this town via the river, you are struck by two beautiful blue bridges. The scenery is magnificent, and I can see why residents of this community love it.

I motored into the La Crosse Pettibone Boat Club Marina, where I was met by two television reporters and a radio reporter. After a couple hours of interviews, I waited for the arrival of Fred and Matilda.

Before they arrived, I carted my fuel tanks over to the gas dock to have them filled up. Later in my journey, I would learn to fuel up at the gas dock before I pulled in for the night, but at this moment there was a certain comfort in just getting the tanks filled and bringing them back to the raft.

And waiting for me at the fuel dock was a replacement acrylic sign for the one that blew off at Wabasha! As well as delivering on his promise to buy Matilda a burger in La Crosse, Fred would help me reinstall the sign and the metal channel that had flown off with it.

A couple of hours later, just before it got dark, my brother got the channel reinstalled and the windows back on for good measure. The three of us then went to the marina grill and ordered a pile of food. I was famished.

After quickly dispatching the food and warding off the giant mosquitos, Fred and Matilda packed up some of the excess equipment I wanted to offload and waved goodbye.

I come from a family of six boys and three girls. Of all the gifts I have been given in my life, the gift of family—the one my parents created, and the one my wife and I have made—has been the most meaningful of all to me.

My brother Fred is a wonderful human being. He is accomplished, smart, generous, hard-working, and conscientious. I am grateful to have him in my life and thankful he has been with me on this adventure.

So ended another night on my river journey.

Chapter 8
Losing My Keys and My Mind

My journey from La Crosse to Lansing was as pretty as a picture after a delayed start.

On Friday, September 4, I awoke to wind gusts of thirty to forty-five miles per hour at the La Crosse Pettibone Boat Club. It didn't take long for me to decide to spend another day in port. I spoke with Amanda at S&S Houseboat Rentals, my marina in Lansing, and she was gracious when I told her that my plans had changed and said I could arrive the next day instead.

The wisdom of my decision to stay in La Crosse became more evident as the day progressed, as little changed in terms of the wind. It was a good day to catch up on projects and to do some raft "chores."

The first task was to batten down all my storage bins, which I hadn't done despite reminding myself over and over to do so. Every time I encountered a wave of any significance, my storage bins were in danger of toppling. Storage bins toppling was both a matter of convenience and safety.

Oftentimes I found myself having to move around on the raft to prop open doors, rearrange fuel tanks and solar panels, or get a better view out of one of the windows. With storage bins falling over or sliding out from the sides of the shed into my path, it was an accident waiting to happen.

Some of the storage bins contained books, maps, charts, and other paper items, including some of my foodstuff. If the contents fell on the deck, which was sometimes soaked from the windswept river moisture, it meant I had to deal with soggy reading materials and wet food—neither of which was fun to have to dry out, repack, and rearrange, either at the end of my day or while underway.

Furthermore, I hadn't really done the type of weight distribution I had intended to do. This was a critical issue I needed to address early on in my trip, and one I needed to pay close attention to the further down the river I went. The top-heavy nature of the raft's construction (because of the shed cabin), where the weight was placed, and how it was placed had an impact on steering dynamics in good weather and most definitely in bad weather. Wind gusts, unexpected waves, and troublesome wakes already made the raft feel like it was unstable. Improper weight displacement transformed this perceived instability to real instability. As I learned more and more about how the raft operated under power, combined with the external forces of the river and weather, I became more mindful of how I needed to distribute weight inside the raft.

The SS Hail Mary's design also impacted how well the motors could operate while I was underway. An element of powering any watercraft is the concept of "lift" and "plane." The lift of the motor—that is, how it impacts the height and level of the aft and bow of a craft—typically will govern the "plane" of the craft—that is, whether the bow is up or down in the water when underway.

My raft barely planed because it was top heavy and didn't allow either of my motors to truly achieve any real lift while underway. Because I had such limited lift capacity, anything I could do to improve weight distribution would give me some additional control over the plane of the raft. This in turn would give me a few options for how I could attack the water in front of me as I traveled.

So, with a few eye hooks, some bungee cords, and some rearranging of items, I secured the storage bins satisfactorily. All this, of course, while the wind swirled around me!

I was also expecting a visit from Mike Wilson, the president of the Red Wing Marine Museum who had been an ardent supporter and advocate for my trip. He was bringing me a book called *Creeping Bear*, about a family's journey down the Mississippi River in 1916-1917. The author, Maurice Nelson, wrote the log journal when he was twenty-five years old as he piloted the Creeping Bear from Red Wing to New Orleans. The trip's purpose was to set up agents to sell Red Wing Motor Company engines, and the burgeoning entrepreneur was accompanied by his wife, son, and sister.

Mike gave me an unpublished copy of the book before I left Red Wing. I read passages of it throughout that day and mused about the similarities and differences between young Maurice's trip back then and this fifty-seven-year-old man's trip more than one hundred years later. I hope I did Maurice proud by the time I reached the end of my journey.

Before Mike arrived, however, disaster struck—again!

Upon returning to the raft from lunch, I decided to start both the

Mercury and the Nissan motors, just to make sure that both were firing and that fuel was moving through the lines correctly. I bent down to prime the key for the kicker motor and realized, to my horror, that there was no key.

I couldn't believe it.

I never removed the keys from either motor remote because I never wanted to lose them. Ask my wife and kids about me losing things. I can't find my glasses... my wallet... my keys! Truth be told, if my head weren't connected to my neck, I would lose that as well.

I called Joe at River Valley Power and Sport in Red Wing and asked if he had a backup key. He told me that there are so many different options of keys for the Mercury that it would be challenging to locate the right one and suggested I see if there was a local boat and marine company that might have some.

The previous day, I had met the harbor master of the La Crosse Pettibone Boat Club, Matt, who seemed like someone who must know something about boats. After all, everybody I know (except for me) knows something about boats!

Matt was a cool customer. He asked me a couple of questions about the motor and the remote, then had me try to find a number or letter on the ignition and tell him what it was. He told me he would call back after he reached out to the power sports company in La Crosse.

Once again, began to tear through everything on the raft to see if I had dropped the key or knocked it out of the remote somehow.

My heart sank when I still couldn't find it, and I was trying to think through how I was going to manage this latest crisis when, lo and behold, I spotted something silver on my camera bag.

It couldn't be, could it?

It was! There, stuck to the side of my camera bag, were two nondescript keys attached to one another by a thin circle of metal that was barely a key chain.

As I had walked by the steering console earlier in the day, the mesh fabric of the camera bag must have snagged the sharp metal tip of the key chain.

I quickly grabbed the keys and then calmly, but with a shaking hand, inserted one into the Mercury ignition switch. Suddenly the quiet roar of the 9.9 kicker motor came to life.

Hope had returned to my life.

So, too, did some choice curse words directed at myself for my absolute lack of organizational skills on this trip. I have few real skills in life, but I pride myself on the creative construction of cursing that can't be repeated here! It's all going in my Raft Book of Curses, soon to be assembled!

It's funny; I think I am pretty good at planning and logistics. I pay close attention to making sure I have prepared for the things I can imagine and sometimes even the things I can't. I build safeguards into systems, plan for worst-case scenarios, and rarely proceed into any venture without spending a significant amount of reviewing and re-reviewing plans.

But try to remember where I put a set of keys or my glasses or my wallet and my entire life comes to a dead stop.

I called Matt back and thanked him profusely for caring enough about the issue to help me figure out how to deal with it. He advised, wisely, that I write down the number that was on the key in the event I lost it (and its twin) again! I did just that and placed on one of the studs inside the raft the proper identifier for the kicker motor keys should I ever need to use it again.

After that disaster was behind me, Mike Wilson arrived. We chatted about my trip so far; he had brought me a funnel and a measuring cup as well as the newly printed copies of *Creeping Bear*. After a few minutes of discussing my various travel adventures, Mike bid me goodbye and returned to Red Wing for meetings. I settled in for the night. I planned to go to bed early so I could depart first thing in the morning to get to my next destination: Lansing, Iowa.

As dawn broke, I went through my usual routine: got my coffee made, readied the raft, and slowly departed the Pettibone Boat Club to present myself to the big river.

The view that morning was simply spectacular. The rising sun. The blue sky and calm water. The wind was considerably more sedate than it had been the day before. This was the perfect day to be on the Mississippi.

I traveled through many narrow channels as I made my way to Lansing. The benefit of narrow channels on windy days is that they provide a natural windbreak, keeping the water calmer, and this allowed me to relax a bit and enjoy a more sedate drift down the river, with the smaller kicker motor keeping me inside the navigation channel. The downside to narrow channels comes when traffic is heavy, leaving little room to maneuver inside the navigation channel. Whenever that happened, I needed to get outside of the channel—which, as mentioned previously, meant exposing the raft to submerged trees, rockpiles, and wing dams.

That day, I would find myself dealing with much of the latter and less of the former.

I made my way through miles of twists and turns and gorgeous scenery. Nature's bounty on the river is never-ending. Majestic trees, beautiful waterfowl, and little islands in the river made me want to constantly grab my camera and take pictures. But, along with nature's bounty would be the bounty of man, in the form of a massive number of towboats and barges.

It appeared that they would never end. The barges were ubiquitous, and it was on that day that my trip nearly came to an end.

Now, I want to pause a second here because the phrase "it was on that day that my trip nearly came to an end" is a recurring theme of this journey.

A leaky pontoon. Swamped motors. A white-knuckle adventure across the whitecaps of Lake Pepin. Signs blowing off the back end of the raft. These challenges were trivial compared to what was about to happen next.

I knew that ahead of me was a large group of barges being pushed by a towboat. I had become more adept at using a couple of different apps on my iPad to gauge the distance and speed at which these vessels were approaching me. So I wasn't shocked when I saw the upcoming conglomerate and thought I was reasonably prepared to address it. However, at the same time as this behemoth showed itself to me, I realized that I had gotten on the shallow side of the outer channel, the red buoy side, rather than the deeper green buoy side.

I decided to point my bow to the barges to absorb the wake and waves from this colossus and avoid doing any further motoring around in the shallow area. I threw in both of my anchors. They immediately caught hold and slowly began to turn my bow toward the intended target. When I looked up, my blood went cold.

Coming around the bend at high speed was a massive cruiser pleasure boat, cutting a wake and creating waves that I can only describe as tsunami-like.

Now, if my bow had been pointed to those waves, I would have simply gotten hit by a couple of uncomfortably large ones, taken some water on the bow deck, and bobbed a few times before settling down and going on my way. Unfortunately, my starboard side was fully exposed to the cruiser's wake, which only grew larger and faster and more ominous.

With my anchors in the water, and a barge coming from my other side, I quickly attempted to pull up the anchors and motor the raft into the cruiser's wake. But I couldn't get both anchors out fast enough and throttle up to direct my bow in that direction, and I knew it.

The first wave hit the starboard side and sent the SS Hail Mary bobbing up and down.

The second wave hit the starboard side at about the time the first wave was receding, knocking the raft to its port side. Everything on my table flew off. Flashlights, binoculars, and solar lights that were hanging on the walls and ceiling were launched off their hooks.

I kept trying to pull the anchors up, knowing that until I did, I couldn't hit my power and turn.

It was at this point that I could feel the raft begin to lose its battle with staying afloat.

I rushed back to the console and started the Nissan, determined to turn the raft even if I had to drag the anchors with me.

Then it hit.

A giant wave. The one I feared was coming.

The force of the wave blasted the starboard side of the raft out of the water. So much so that I could see the sky through the screen windows on the starboard side.

This wasn't the horizon.

This was straight-up gray cloudy sky that I was staring at. The SS Hail Mary was threatening to topple completely over.

Panic and fear and adrenaline and anger all kicked in. I pivoted my body to the starboard side of the raft, grabbed onto the header of the wall, and shoved my entire weight against it, all the while screaming, "No!"

The raft fell down onto the water.

I immediately shoved the Nissan into forward and then ran to furiously grab the anchors and pull them up.

Powered by my adrenaline, both anchors nearly leapt out of the water, and I ran back to the console and throttled the Nissan hard to starboard to get my nose into the next grouping of waves that were going to pound me.

The Nissan caught, moved, and spun the SS Hail Mary's nose perfectly into the next set of waves.

But I wasn't out of trouble yet.

I still had the enormous barge bearing down on me.

I wasn't going to take that beast on in the shallows, so I throttled the Nissan as hard as it would go, trimmed it to give me speed, and shot (okay, "shot" may be an overstatement!) across the channel into the broader and deeper off-channel side of the green buoys.

I sat there and idled for a while, then throttled to a low chug just to keep moving back and forth until the barge passed by me. I waited a few more moments for its turbulence to subside and headed back into the channel. I slowed the raft to a crawl, sat down, and let the fear and terror and anger and frustration mingle together.

I was shaking. My shirt was soaked with sweat. I could not believe what had just happened. I was so unprepared for it. As unprepared as I was for everything on the trip.

Losing my keys. My signs. But those were nothing, having no impact in real terms on my life or the trip.

My trip through Lake Pepin was frightening.

What had just happened—terrifying. To my core.

I have been afraid of many things at many times in my life. But usually that fear is directed at something that doesn't have to do with my life.

A brother hit by a car and nearly dying. Kids getting sick. Surgeries on a child, with an infection afterward that kept me up at night. Brothers and sisters, parents, spouses, and a host of other people I know, love, and care for who have faced threats to their life—I have had that fear and more in my life.

There have only been two times where I truly feared for my own life. The first was years ago at my cabin when, while eating a bag of pistachios, I had one lodge in my throat. No matter how hard I tried, I could not dislodge it. There was nobody but me at the cabin, and the odds that my neighbors were close by and could lend assistance were not good.

With my reflection in the side-view mirror of my car showing that my face was turning all the bad colors associated with not having much longer to live, I ran over to an aluminum rowboat sitting on a trailer and thrust my stomach down on the side of it.

Nothing.

Finally, with my consciousness leaving me, I tried one more time, and the pistachio nut dislodged.

I don't remember how long I was on the ground waiting for my breath, and my life, to come back to me.

I remember, though, knowing that I had barely escaped with my life. That was the first time.

The second time I feared for my life was the moment that had just passed me.

I had rehearsed in my head countless times how I would get out of the raft in the event it tipped over. Or sank. Or otherwise faced some type of devastation with me in it.

I traveled with all the doors open. The back screens removed. And, when I saw barges, I got rid of the chair, I stood, and I kept my head on a swivel.

Despite all this mental preparation, though, there would be nothing I could have done had the raft flipped over.

I wasn't ready. At all.

I drifted for a while, and I thought about the events that had unfolded. I went over them again and again in my head.

As the shaking subsided and my focus returned, I realized my mistakes.

I had seen the barges coming and should have anticipated that they would shift to the red buoys to prepare to travel the channel. In hindsight, the angle was apparent.

Once on the wrong end of the channel, I should have immediately reversed course to the green buoy side, paying attention to my depth finder and the app that was showing me plenty of space on that side, along with plenty of depth.

I screwed up.

My screw-up was exacerbated because of an unforeseen event, which was the arrival of the cruiser.

The one mistake was magnified with the addition of that boat.

I soon had to move on from this moment of contemplation and analysis and prepare for the raft's arrival at Lock and Dam Number 8. Coming up on Number 8 was, thankfully, uneventful.

Upon receiving the green light, I waited briefly to enter and accepted the operator's two lines thrown down. Usually when the operator throws the line, they throw them down to whichever door I am leaning out of when I approach them. This makes it easier for me to catch them and keeps me close to the steering console and the motor ignition. This allows me to quickly restart the motor when the locking process is completed and immediately proceed out of the lock and dam. The weight of the raft, because of how it was built, is also towards the rear so it makes it easier to control the raft while I wait to lock through if the ropes can be controlled from the back. Unfortunately, the lines were thrown onto the raft's front deck, not at the port door near the raft's bow as they usually were. This meant I had to run up front and pull myself forward to grab one of the lines from the port door and then radio up and ask the operator to throw the rope back down to me. It made for an awkward dance, with the raft's nose retreating from the lock wall while I pulled hard to bring it back up to the wall.

Finally, the lines did what they were supposed to do and brought me back. The gate opened and out I went.

The rest of the trip through the channel to Lansing was filled with more barges. More tugs. And more tows. Eventually, however, I called S&S Houseboat Rentals to ask which slip I should use and was told to pick any of the slips in which there wasn't a houseboat.

Now, trying to park the SS Hail Mary without a current was a delicate dance. Trying to park it with the river current, while slow and yet enormously powerful, is something else.

My first approach had me off-target and needing to put the Nissan in reverse. (Have I shared with you that there is *barely* a reverse on the Nissan?)

So I quickly reconsidered my approach, throttled the Nissan to spin me around, pointed the nose into the slip, and finally got the right angle and right direction and the right result!

After I got tied up, I went and introduced myself to Amanda, one half of the couple that owns the marina. Her husband, Blake, showed up a bit later, along with their two young kids.

They graciously allowed me to tie up for free, and I thanked them profusely. I got the raft squared away for the night and then walked into Lansing, which was about five blocks away. I picked up some items from the hardware store and then went to the grocery store and picked up four small steaks, a can of mushrooms, some dish soap, a scrub pad, and Milk Duds and Malted Milk Balls!

I walked back, pulled out my gas stove, and proceeded to pan-fry my steaks and mushrooms and unwind.

It had been an unforgettable day.

What could have been the end became the beginning of one more day of realizing my good fortune in being out on the river. And to meet remarkable people like Amanda and Blake, who owned this port that I would call home for the night.

It has been a privilege for me to lead Spare Key over the past eight years. I considered it my obligation to repay that privilege by doing my part as a member of the Spare Key team to keep our organization afloat, taking a journey that would catch fire—create a spark of hope with people—and raise money and awareness.

I was not trying to put my life at risk. The opposite was the case. I had every intention to finish the trip and return home to my family, having fulfilled the goal that my river expedition to find hope would keep alive Spare Key's mission of helping families "bounce and not break."

Chapter 9
Here's a Boat, There's a Boat, Everywhere's a Boat

I awoke the next morning to another lovely day. I began to pack up because I was going to get all my gas from the dock. However, before I did, I asked Blake if he could run me into town to grab a five-gallon gas can for the kicker motor and some additional straps and duct tape. As we drove, I asked him more about his business.

Born and raised in Lansing, Blake is a graduate of engineering school in Milwaukee, who, upon graduation, went to work for what he said was his dream job at Arctic Cat in northern Minnesota. Blake and Amanda later decided to make a living doing something that allowed them to dictate their work's terms and conditions—a job that wouldn't require them to travel somewhere other than where they wanted to be, live, work, and raise a family. So in 2017 they bought S&S Houseboat Rentals in Lansing.

They have worked hard to build their business, and 2020's Covid-19-inspired mania to do anything and everything outdoors created what Blake called "the year of business we've been waiting for." Their peers have recognized them for the business they have built, and Blake is proud, as he should be, of the work they put in together to make their company succeed and grow.

As Blake and I returned from the hardware store with my new purchases, I went to ready the raft for departure. As I did, Blake came down and helped me push off to approach their gas dock from the south. Gassing up took little time, but soon I was underway to Prairie du Chien, Wisconsin, to meet Mayor Dave Hemmer and receive a proclamation declaring it "Hope on the River Day" in the city. My plan was to dock for the night at the city's Riverwalk dock.

It was, again, a glorious day.

The scenery was gorgeous, and the boat traffic was pretty minimal. Most of it consisted of fishing boats hurrying and scurrying from one place to another.

However, after a few hours, when I was within a couple of miles of Lock and Dam Number 9, I could see the boat traffic heading north intensify. Nothing crazy—a lot of pontoons and cruiser boats and the like—but there were more of them, and they were more frequent.

I approached the lock and dam, radioed ahead, and the operator told me to proceed forward and he would lock me through quickly.

I arrived just as three other vessels were leaving, and the light turned green nearly immediately. As the only vessel in the lock and dam, I felt pretty darn good about my progress. I was looking forward to getting to Prairie du Chien in plenty of time to meet the mayor and unwinding from a long, but enjoyable, day on the raft.

Then the lock gates opened, and Hell was right in front of me!

Before I got one hundred yards from the lock and dam, I witnessed not only the most extensive barge system being pushed by a towboat that I had yet seen, but a line of fast-moving boats that were coming straight at me.

Well, not at *me*, but at the lock and dam I had just left.

My dilemma was obvious. I needed to get outside of the channel, but which way?

Outside of the channel to my right was open but narrow.

The outside to my left was occupied by these fast-moving boats.

I had to make a decision quickly and stick with it.

This time, I decided to go to the narrow side, where the barge entourage currently was, anticipating that it would turn its rear and point its nose towards the lock and dam.

Thankfully, I was right.

But the speed of the boats bearing down on me had begun to create their own wake, even before I got through the wake and churn from the barges I had to continually turn into the wake, turn out of it, turn into the wake, turn out of it, and repeat.

Yet this was just the beginning.

Finally, the barge got by me, and I thought I could proceed down the channel with abandon.

Not. On. Your. Life.

If you have ever played the game Frogger, you can appreciate what the next fourteen miles of my trip looked like.

There were boats *everywhere*. And by "everywhere," I want you to imagine any scene from *Star Wars* in which the Rebellion is in a battle with the Empire. TIE fighters disguised as boats were flying all around me.

On all sides... in front of me... behind me... and each of them creating their own wake, which was then exacerbated by someone else's wake.

I went flying from one side of the channel to the other and back again.

This went on for nearly two hours, and it was exhausting.

Finally, I saw the turn to the east channel for Prairie du Chien and breathed a sigh of relief! I could put in for the night. Hang out with the mayor. And recover from the nonstop onslaught of boats forcing me in and out of the navigation channel over and over and over again.

The plan was that I would leisurely pull up to the Riverwalk dock located on St. Feriole Island, tie up, meet the mayor, and call it a night.

That was not going to happen.

First, the channel leading up to the island and the Riverwalk, which was on my left, was supposed to be a no-wake zone. But people don't pay much attention to that in this particular stretch of the river. The channel itself was alive with waves and churn and foam. All of which pummeled me to and fro, and once again required that I play Frogger.

When I saw the dock ahead of me, I breathed a slight sigh of relief. Until I got closer.

This was a floating dock.

Which meant that it was not secured.

Which meant that every wave that hit the dock made it jump up and down like a kid on sugar in a bouncy house.

It was literally alive!

And I had to figure out how to angle between it and the Riverwalk.

This was proving not to be an incredibly good idea, as evidenced by all the people on the Riverwalk looking and pointing their fingers and a few shaking their heads.

I tied up. Within thirty seconds, I knew it was not going to work.

As I tied up, the dock moved. The raft moved. The dock moved up. The raft moved up. The dock flew down. So, too, did the raft.

And then the dock started to shake and shimmy up and down, sideways, and in every other angle. As it did, so too did the SS Hail Mary.

I immediately regretted my decision to tie up and immediately untied. I shoved the Nissan into reverse and persuaded the raft to back out as quickly as it could. Then I spun around and pushed it forward.

The raft moved right into the churning mess of waves in the no-wake zone and bounced around. I got on the phone to the mayor and told him it wasn't going to work. I asked if there was a spot to dock further downriver.

Determining that there wasn't, Dave Hemmer instructed me to head back north, hug the shoreline which would then be on my right, and come around the backside of the island of where I had tried to tie up. As I began to do so, there was one swarm of boats after another. They were not going to give me any rest! (Was this Labor Day weekend?)

Finally, and mercifully, I made it around the island's tip and found calm water and a channel that really was a no-wake zone. I motored slowly until I saw the mayor and then eased the raft's nose onto the shore.

The mayor was enormously gracious to meet with me at all. Even more so to have the patience to bear with me as I tried to get myself in a position to get off the raft and chat. It became evident to both of us that I couldn't stay overnight given the lack of adequate protection from what was being predicted to be a pretty severe thunderstorm. I shared my gratitude for Dave's support and for the proclamation, took some pictures, and then he helped me shove off.

The plan now was for me to head to Clayton, Iowa, to Bill's Boat Landing about twelve nautical miles down the river. First I had to retrace the channel to get back into the navigation channel, which was nearly one and a half miles away.

And, once again, I found myself in the chaos.

It was unrelenting.

This time, the boats that had raced past me as I entered the east channel were turning around to run back north up the river. But this time, it was even more daunting.

The channel was narrower. There was truly little room on the outside of the channel. And the boats were bigger. The biggest boat I had seen thus far on the trip came bearing down on me from behind. When I say bearing down, I mean that he literally came up fast behind me, and he apparently wasn't planning on moving.

In fact, it became clear that he wasn't going to move.

Finally, I swerved to starboard, and as I did, I could see the person driving the boat laughing at me and pointing to his friends at the wake he had created and then at the raft.

This was fun for him.

I knew it would not be for me.

There was no way for me to get away from this situation.

The onslaught of vessels everywhere was causing a deluge of angry waves that battered the raft. I didn't have much choice. I took the wheel and swung the nose into this boat's wake.

The waves hit and came flooding into the entire cabin. I figure probably a half-foot of water came in on the first wave—the second wave, about the same amount. The third wave, mercifully, was down to a stream. But hundreds of gallons of water had come flying into the raft, and I still had to contend with all the other boats flying around me.

Finally, I could see my break coming. Or at least what I thought was my break.

The river split was ahead of me. A quick turn to my left and I would be on my way to Clayton, where in two hours I could put the raft into a safe harbor.

But alas, the boat that nearly swamped me was turning around to make another pass. This time, though, I had made the decision that I was going to protect myself.

Running to the rear of the SS Hail Mary, I grabbed one of the two handguns I had brought with me, which was in a safe I kept secured in the shed.

This gun was the larger of two and cut an imposing figure.

As I cut in front of the cruiser, I leaned out my shed door and let him see the gun in my hand.

I waved it back and forth and then made sure he saw both my face and the gun.

He saw both, and I knew that I wouldn't have any more problems with him by the look on his face as he kept going. I was out of harm's way.

Finally, I made the cut to the left, got into the southbound channel, and began my journey to Clayton.

The boats didn't stop.

Ever.

At this point, I knew I had to get off the river. There would be no getting to Bill's Boat Landing in Clayton today. The question was, how was I going to do it?

I grabbed my Quimby's, found the closest marina, called Boatels which said it was in McGregor, Iowa the next town ahead of me, and made a call. Did they have a slip I could tie up?

They did! And it was less than a quarter of a mile in front of me.

I saddled up to the gas dock when I arrived. James, the attendant, filled me up with gas and directed me to my slip. I could not have been more thrilled.

I would tie up. I would put the pump in the pontoon and drain it. I would find some food. I would dry out the raft. I would be set for the storm coming that evening.

Except the pump didn't work. In fact, it literally started smoking when I put the tube into the spigot.

That wasn't good! Especially since I *knew* there was water in the pontoon. I put a stick down in it and saw that there were several inches of water.

I ran back to the gas dock to see if James had a pump.

He didn't, but called a friend he thought might have one.

The friend didn't answer the phone.

Finally, I called the closest hardware store, which was located miles away in Prairie du Chien. Did they have sump pumps?

Yes!

Could they deliver them to me if I paid extra?

Unfortunately, they had nobody available to do that.

I hung up, knowing that I needed to get that tube drained but I had no way of getting the sump pump to me from the hardware store.

Then, I said to myself, "Call the mayor!"

And I did. The Mayor of Prairie du Chien, that is!

Like every great mayor I have ever known, Dave Hemmer didn't even hesitate. As I explained the situation about the sump pump to him, he said, "I am putting on my shoes as we speak and will get them and bring them to you!"

Long live mayors! They get stuff done!

Within twenty minutes, he was at Boatels with two brand-new pumps.

I thanked him—again—profusely for his kindness and hurried back to the pontoon to drain the tubes.

But this wasn't going to be as easy as I'd hoped!

Despite knowing there was water in the tubes, the pump would not bring it out. I tried and tired and tired. Finally, I tried the other pump.

And, after two attempts, it finally began to turn out water.

After about ten minutes, and what I estimate to be about twenty-five gallons of water, the pump stopped. I threw a stick down into the tube, and it seemed pretty dry.

Whew!

I then spent the next few hours unloading my bins, drying things out, cleaning up, and secretly wanting to punch the guy who swamped me in the nose.

I was uneasy with having to pull the gun out. At the same time, I was glad that merely showing him the gun was enough to make him get out of my way. I hoped I wouldn't have to do that again on this trip.

I thanked God for getting me to this point safe and sound, then began to prepare for the night.

As evening approached, from the way the air felt, there was no doubt that there would be a severe thunderstorm. So I decided to get to sleep early, with the plan that when the storm hit, I would get off the raft until the storm passed.

Which is how things actually went.

About 2:00 a.m., I woke up. I could tell the raft was moving because of the wind. I grabbed the things I wanted—my wallet, my phones, raincoat, sleeping bag—and jumped off the raft. I found a couple of places to hide, including under the awning of an antique store and the overhang of a roof of a gas station waiting for the storm to roll on by.

Around 5:00 a.m. or so, I ran from the gas station and I ended up back at a picnic shelter about one hundred and fifty feet from the raft.

The lightning had passed, so I was comfortable sitting in the shelter with a metal roof and metal picnic tables less than one hundred feet from a fifty-foot aluminum flagpole.

As I sat there bundled up, I suddenly saw one of the acrylic signs on my raft fly off the raft's rear port side.

It went straight into the water and disappeared.

Then, the second one, a larger panel, detached from the raft, flew up in the air, and blew away out into the middle of the river somewhere!

Arrgh!

So I quickly ran down to the raft, grabbed my staple gun, put up plastic where the acrylic had been, and retreated to the safety of the picnic shelter.

With daybreak I went back to the raft and assessed the damage. Obviously, I had lost some more signs. There wasn't much I could do about that. I would need to let ASI Signage know at some point, but for now I wanted to make sure things weren't totally wet.

Given that I hadn't slept much, I decided I was going to spend another day in McGregor. It would give me a chance to catch my breath after what had been a pretty eventful forty-eight hours. I kept myself busy throughout the day, got caught up on some email, and also dried out those things that were wet inside the raft.

I made a few trips to the local convenience store, did some reading, took a nap, and pretty much enjoyed the day. I decided to get to sleep early and do my best to prepare for the next day.

Chapter 10
Damn Dam

I awoke early, as usual, and readied the SS Hail Mary. I had a plan to be off the dock by 7:30 a.m. and on my way to Clayton to dock at Bill's Boat Landing thanks to a generous invitation from owner Kim Kuehl.

McGregor had been a good stopping point to re-order supplies, re-evaluate my approach to entering locks and dams, and address how I would handle large cruisers in the future.

The trip to Clayton was roughly ten miles, and on this day the weather began to deteriorate with gusty winds and rain on the horizon. The route to Clayton was pretty cut and dry; it was merely a matter of hoping to avoid Labor Day boat traffic as much as I possibly could. Thankfully, the combination of wind, overcast skies, and threat of rain reduced the amount of boat traffic immensely. Here and there was a fishing boat cutting in and out of the navigation channel, but beyond that, I was pretty much alone.

I pulled up the Navionics marine navigation app that gave me a sense of the status of barges being pushed or pulled up or down the river and saw that the only one on the radar was a safe distance of six nautical miles behind me. A combination of drifting and motoring through the larger parts of the river would give me plenty of buffer all the way to Bill's Boat Landing in Clayton.

About two miles from my destination, a huge cruiser popped up behind me and was coming on fast. I decided to try to reach the ship captain on channel 16 to see if I could encourage him or her to give wide berth to my little raft and limit the size of its wake, as we were both coming into the narrowest area of the channel before Clayton.

I tapped the radio and spoke. "This is the skipper of the SS Hail Mary, a homemade raft, and I have just passed mile marker 626 and request that the vessel coming up on the same mile marker be gentle with me as you proceed my direction. Anything you can do to minimize your wake when you run up to me would be greatly appreciated."

I waited for a response but didn't receive one, so I assumed the captain was going to ignore it or didn't hear my request. Either way, I was preparing my deflection angle away from the cruiser, so I didn't have any time to make the request again.

About one hundred yards away, it was clear the boat was slowing dramatically as I tried to steer closer to the starboard side of the raft and prepared for an onslaught of waves created by the cruiser's wake.

Instead, a voice came on the radio and said, "Skipper, I got your message, and we have complied with your request. Have a safe journey. Over."

I returned the wish for a safe journey, ended the conversation with a smile, and continued along my way.

Coming around a bend was the river channel entrance to a section of the river channel that is as wide as any I have been on so far. Ahead of me was Bill's Boat Landing and as I approached it the view around me was breathtaking and eye-catching. This section of big and bold river that pushes out its banks on either side to form a body of water is not dissimilar to Lake Pepin. Like Lake Pepin, the wind is brisk, and the water can roil with whitecaps before you know it.

I could see Bill's Boat Landing, a bar and restaurant, at mile marker 624.7 to my starboard side. As I brought the raft up to the large dock that runs adjacent to the river, I had to step outside the starboard door at the aft and push my foot down to get the raft to slow down and heel. Finally, it slowed enough for me to fully jump out and grab the docking line and tie the raft up.

When I turned, there was Kim Kuehl, my host, and the owner of Bill's Boat Landing. We greeted one another and chatted a bit, and then I asked if it would be okay if I moved the raft to the inside of the dock to try to reduce some of the rolling action of the river waves. She readily agreed and said she would have her fiancée, Scott, come down and help me get the task done. She went back up to the bar and a couple of minutes later, Scott showed up; we shook hands and steered the raft off its previous mooring and into calmer waters.

Once the boat was tied up, I went up to Bill's Boat Landing and found Kim in the kitchen and ordered myself a Bloody Mary, which was exceptionally good! I then ordered a *big* breakfast—Bill's Omelet, which was packed with tasty things, and brisket as a side order. I attacked that food like I hadn't eaten in a week, and it was so, so good!

During breakfast, many people came up and asked me what I was doing, and some gave me cash donations that I stapled to the inside of the raft. Others just walked by shaking their heads. I don't blame them. I shake my head sometimes, too!

After breakfast, I settled down and had the opportunity to get some writing done, catch up on emails, return phone calls, and relax in a beautiful place.

I also had a chance to visit with Kim.

Her parents, Bill and Barb Kuehl, purchased Bill's Boat landing in November of 1976.

The place was originally a marina, bar, bait and tackle, and short-order shop. According to Kim in a post she shared on a website, "Throughout the years many physical changes have made many improvements. We have evolved into what some may consider a kinda dive bar, river bar family friendly bar n grill offering wide variety of menu options. We take pride in creating a welcoming environment for all that stop in and filling your bellies with flavorful food, your favorite cold beer or great cocktails. Cheers & we hope to see you soon! Be sure and check our Facebook page: Bill's Boat Landing."

Kim is as kind, genuine, and authentic as a person you will find. Like many kids of entrepreneurs, she wasn't sure if she wanted to follow in her parent's footsteps. Ultimately, with both of her parents passing, she decided in 2016 to fully engage in taking over the operations of the business her parents had bought and built over the past forty years.

She's done a remarkable job. And, in a community with a population of fewer than fifty people, she has struggled to find labor, dealt with floods, and faced not only the uncertainty of a global pandemic but the non-stop challenges that any small business owner has every single day. She handles it with good humor, pluck, and determination. Scott, her fiancée, is the bartender, but I suspect he is more than that in this relationship and operation. He is unflappable, courteous, kind, and friendly. I think they make a good team, and it shows in the business.

Later on, as the bar closed for the day, we were joined by Max and Bonnie Basemann. Max is the mayor of Clayton, and Bonnie is the city clerk. Kim is a member of the city council. Bonnie, it turns out, was the one who had heard about Hope on the River and shared the information with Kim, which is why she reached out to invite me to share their dock on my way down the river. What a delightful group of people!

Like every good mayor I know, Max Basemann is all about getting things done. He deals with issues ranging from the plowing of streets to assessments to people doing what they aren't supposed to do, and every other issue that big and little city mayors deal with every single day. One difference for this little city mayor is that everyone knows his name, knows where he lives, and can track him down in an instant.

Max and Bonnie lived in Colorado for years before they sold everything and came to Clayton. While both had roots in the Midwest, they had raised their family in Colorado before deciding that they wanted something smaller and less stressful in their lives. I am not sure how becoming elected officials of a city is less stressful, but they could not have been kinder. So kind that as I was preparing the raft for the evening, Max came down and invited me to stay in an extra apartment that he and Bonnie had available.

Who could turn that down, given that the temperature was going to be in the mid 40s! What a treat! A warm room. A hot shower. And I could see the raft from the windows of my apartment.

As I prepared for sleep, I gave thanks for my good luck that day and prayed for the people I'd met along the way. I prayed for those in my life that I missed and cared for and worried about. And I called it a very, very good day!

As I woke, I could hear wind chimes, letting me know that it would be breezy. However, the wind was coming from the north, which was a good thing as it would help push my raft a bit faster on the current.

The day before, Scott had indicated he would be up by 5:00 a.m. and that when I was ready to shove off, I should come and find him. So at six o'clock I lugged my equipment down to the raft, started the motors and let them run a bit before I turned them off, made sure the anchor lines were free and clear, removed the remaining acrylic window signs, and made sure that everything that needed to be tied down was tied down.

When I went back up, Scott, greeted me with a hot cup of coffee!

After a few minutes of conversation and warmth, I told him I would go down and get the raft motors started before coming back up for his help. When Scott came down with me, we turned the rear of the raft to the opposite side of the dock, the bow to the front, and then I powered up. As I prepared to leave, I thanked Scott and headed toward the navigation channel.

There was something comforting about getting out on the river at 7:00 a.m. and slowly making my way south without having any other boats in the water.

I enjoy solitude. Not all the time. But I admit that there is a comfort for me in moments of isolation and solitude that goes back to when I was a young man in Fairmount, North Dakota. I would leave my home and go for long, extended walks on the gravel backroads around the small rural community I lived in for seven years. With nothing but myself, a pack or two of cigarettes (yes, I know, a filthy habit for a fourteen-year-old!), and my thoughts, I would walk for hours. Often I would whistle, happy to be alone, and think about nothing and everything simultaneously.

I want to say that I figured out the solution for World Peace or the cure for diseases on these walks, but I lack the necessary intellect to accomplish such worthy tasks. But when I returned, tired and blissful, my soul was calm, my heart was full, and whatever thoughts I had in my head had been dealt with along the way. The journey down the river had many of the same elements. However, I was not often left alone with my thoughts for long.

On this day, as I made my way, I came across several confusing markers in the river that made me question where I was in the navigation channel. Furthermore, the wind was increasing, the sky was getting darker, and I would soon be upon Lock and Dam Number 10. Soon enough, I was within a mile of it. I switched to channel 14, tapped the radio, and said, "This is the pleasure vessel Hail Mary coming southward on the river and checking the status of Lock and Dam Number 10, please."

The response was quick. The operator indicated a towboat was coming upriver, and it would be nearly forty minutes before I could approach and be locked through.

Dang it!

Don't get me wrong; a forty-minute wait on any other day wouldn't have been a big deal. I would have slowed down to a crawl, and it would take me about thirty minutes to approach the lock and dam. Then I would turn idle in place or turn the raft back upriver for a half-mile or so just to turn around and repeat my slow return down.

That day, though, the wind, coming from the north and the northeast, was blowing ten to fifteen miles per hour, with gusts up to twenty-five miles per hour. Furthermore, the area approaching the lock and dam had virtually no wind barriers, and the areas outside of the buoys on both sides were shallow and filled with hazards.

I got to the lock and dam in about twenty minutes and didn't see any evidence that the towboat had been brought into the lock. That wasn't a good sign. That meant it might take more than forty minutes, and it was going to be a white-knuckle forty minutes at that.

I powered the Nissan and turned the raft around hard and fast so that the wind wouldn't catch my starboard side for any longer than it needed to and then pointed the raft directly into the wind.

The SS Hail Mary's front door was held open by a bungee cord, and I removed the screens from all five windows on the back of the raft so that the wind could fly through unabated. That, along with the screens that remained on the sides and the front of the raft, helped to reduce some of the lift that worried me about my vessel.

After about twenty minutes of barely crawling forward but doing enough to keep myself from going backward, I turned my head and saw, with relief, that the towboat and its barges had gotten fully inside of the lock.

But that meant another twenty minutes before it would be high enough to proceed up the river.

I was being buffeted hard by the wind, and it was cold and blustery. I thought about going upriver again but was concerned that if I got too far out of sight of the lock and dam, I would find myself in a situation where northbound traffic might take precedence over my turn.

To my port side was a marina, but I wasn't confident I could get in there and hang out and still get back in time.

On top of that, the wind was blowing harder. It would have required me to expose the entire starboard side of the raft to this wind, and I wasn't ready to take that chance.

So I continued up the river at a snail's pace and then saw the lock's gates start to open. At that point, I toggled the radio and asked the operator where he thought I should be when the towboat came out of the lock.

He instructed me to continue to stay to the channel's red buoy side, which I dutifully did, both motors churning to keep me pushing against the northeast wind without going backward.

Finally, he called me back and instructed me to proceed directly back to the lock and dam.

With a sigh of relief, I swung the raft back around and pointed it directly toward the lock's opening. About five minutes later, the green light instructing me to enter came on. I had to power across the channel under power of both the kicker motor and the Nissan, and at the same time, get through the churning backwash of the towboat that had just left.

This, along with the wind, was giving me all I could handle for the day!

As I entered the lock, the turbulence was intense. I yelled up to the operator that I would likely need two ropes and perhaps even some help from him to keep the raft against the lock wall.

He threw down two ropes and assured me that the water and wind would soon calm down. But until it did, I was holding onto those ropes for dear life!

I was being pushed away from the wall constantly, and I dug my feet into the base of the inside of the raft and pulled hard on that rope to pull myself back into the wall.

I have to be honest; this was exhausting. Spending more than an hour out in the wind trying to keep from being blown around was already more than I had bargained for. Now I held on for dear life, waiting for the gates to close behind me and the water to begin dropping.

Eventually the gates closed. The water calmed. And the water level began to drop. I still had to hold hard and tight onto the line because the raft was still being hit by wind, and I strained to keep from being taken out into the middle of the lock.

I am not sure how long all this lasted when, out of the corner of my eye, I caught sight of the gate doors downriver starting to open. I sighed and gave a little thank you to God for this joyful reality.

The doors fully opened, the horn sounded (permitting me to exit), and on my way I went.

About a quarter mile beyond the lock and dam is a place called Landing 615. This was to be where I would tie up for the day, as I had decided to break up the next fifty miles into a few days because of the weather.

Unfortunately, the location I had been given to tie up put me directly in the wind and river channel line. But I dutifully tied up. Got the raft secured. And then tried to figure out how this was all going to work throughout the day and night.

After a few hours of being bounced around, I noticed a marina right behind where I was docked. I walked down and realized the city of Guttenberg owned it. Duh!!! How could I have not seen it! After all, it was in my *Quimby's* marina guide. Not sure why I hadn't called them to begin with. So I did now.

The individual who answered the phone assured me that not only could I have a slip for the night but I could have one that would keep me out of the direct line of wind and rain! So I got the raft ready to go and began to untie her.

The challenge now, though, was that I had to contend with a raging, nonstop north to northeast wind, and rain, and the current of the river.

I had both boat motors running and tied together. As I untied, the raft began to fly out of the slip. I held on as long as I could and then finally had to jump into the front of the raft, run back to the console, shove both motors into a fast reverse, and turn.

Now here was the tricky part.

The Nissan's reverse required me to slide the lever straight down for reverse. The Mercury kicker motor required me to slide the lever straight up for reverse. Remember, this is me we're talking about! Trying to remember which lever went which way at the right time, much less keep track of everything else I was supposed to be doing, was its own particular challenge.

However, I got lucky and remembered to shove them in their appropriate opposite directions, so I was able to back the raft quickly into the channel, then turn it around just as quickly and motor into the marina.

What a relief!!!

No wind. There was rain, and there was nothing I could do about that.

But I could tie up, plug in, and button up the raft and be out of the wind and the current and protected from the rain for the evening. On top of that, a friend covered the cost of me to stay at the local inn a half-block from the marina. I could not have had a better outcome to the day.

Chapter 11
A Pirate Pit Stop with No Pirates

Once tied up in the Guttenberg Marina, I had time to kill, even though the weather continued to be wet, windy, and rainy. I also had to get equipped.

First and foremost, I had lost a piece to my percolator coffee pot, which is, to me, just as fear-inducing as coming unexpectedly upon a barge on the river! I was cleaning the dang thing out and kept saying to myself, *Whatever you do, don't drop anything into the river*, which of course ensured that I would drop a piece into the river. So I had to find a replacement and dutifully walked myself down to the local Guttenberg Hardware.

I also had to pick up a new storage bin to replace the cardboard box which contained the Hope on the River t-shirts that had gotten wet near Prairie du Chien.

In rooting around the hardware store, I located coffee pots. Still, the only thing they had in the form of a percolator coffee pot was electric, and I didn't want to deal with any additional electrical needs on the raft.

So I stumbled upon a French press!

I have never used one, and frankly, everybody I know who uses one always seems so pretentious. But I figured I was on a raft on a river, so how pretentious could I possibly be? Plus, it was pretty cheap, and I needed something to make coffee with before I left Guttenberg the next day.

I brought it up to the counter, where two women stood behind a massive plexiglass window with masks, and tried to communicate effectively with them. Easier said than done, especially since I, too, was wearing a face mask. Eventually I was able to articulate that I didn't know how to use a French press, and did I need filters or anything other than what was in the box?

They were, I have to say, as confused as I was about the question.

We opened the box, looked at the parts, and all shrugged at one another.

Since I was determined to figure out how to make coffee, I bought it and put it in my storage bin along with some other items and thanked them for their assistance.

My next stop was the grocery store, which was about five blocks away.

I needed something to eat, and I didn't want to eat in a restaurant or bar or grill. I was determined to get a loaf of bread, some luncheon meat, cheese, and chips and bring this tasty feast back to the hotel room I was fortunate to be able to stay in that evening.

Walking into a grocery store in a small town in the age of Covid-19 was its own unique challenge.

First, there were varying degrees of people wearing masks.

Second, in this particular store, an exceedingly small one, trying to politely navigate around one another was a challenge.

Eventually, I got myself a loaf of bread, some American cheese, a package of luncheon meat, chips, and a can of jumbo black olives. I was going to enjoy this feast!

Unfortunately, as was to be the case for the ensuing days, the skies opened up and the rain poured down on me.

By the time I got back to my room I was soaked to the skin.

Yet I was able to dry off, sit down at my table, and enjoy a meal that brought memories flying back to me.

I recall as a young boy going on road trips with my dad and siblings. Eventually we would pull over to a small store along the way, and my dad would grab a loaf or two of bread, whatever kind was the biggest and cheapest, and get cheese and some sort of sliced sandwich meat from the store. Sometimes there was a meat market in the store, sometimes merely a cooler section with pre-packaged luncheon meat. If it was pre-packaged, it was baloney or summer sausage. If there was a butcher, it was more elaborate! It might be salami, baloney, ham, or roast beef, and cheeses of all kinds. And blood sausage and head cheese!

If those last two sound bad, trust me—they tasted equally nasty.

My dad had an uncanny knack for getting things he liked but that nobody else would eat.

Yet we never went hungry on those road trips. In between whatever slices of bread we had were some kind of meat and cheese, washed down with chocolate milk in Styrofoam glasses.

I remember those days as clearly as if they happened yesterday. As I sat in Guttenberg eating my sandwiches with baloney and American cheese and washing them down with a Diet Coke, I smiled.

Finally full, I spent some time catching up on emails and phone calls, brought my new storage bin down to the raft, filled it with T-shirts, started my motors for good measure, and made sure that everything was tied up tightly on the dock.

With that done, and my belly full, I took a nap in the bed that felt like Heaven.

A couple of hours later, I got up and decided to walk down to the lock and dam I had come through earlier to take some pictures. It was wet, very windy, and cold, and as luck would have it, a large tow with barges was getting ready to enter the lock!

What a treat to watch this remarkable process and to be able to show it on Facebook Live.

These massive vessels inside a lock and dam with barge workers bracketing the ship's front and back is a sight to see! It is also a reminder of the difficult conditions that these workers labor under to get these barges successfully up and down the river.

On this particular evening, the wind whipped cold rain in their faces, yet they looked up and me and waved and said hi.

One worker, holding onto the lines that kept the barges and the tow in check, walked by as the vessel began to lock through. I shouted out and asked what they were carrying; he responded, "Grain!"

The process was complete within the hour as the towboat and barges continued their procession downriver. I returned to my room, grateful for the opportunity to share this experience with people via the Hope on the River Facebook page. I took a shower, got my belongings ready for the day ahead, and hit the hay.

The next morning I got up early. At 6:00 a.m., I began to transfer all the things I had in my room back into the raft. My goal was to be underway by seven thirty and make the short trip to Pirate's Pit Stop in North Buena Vista, Iowa.

The Guttenberg Marina had worked out perfectly. It had kept me off the river's main channel and allowed me to get things put together for my short trip that morning.

Of course, it's always an adventure as I am leaving!

As I was backing out of the slip, trying my best to keep myself straight, I realized that the bow of the raft was heading starboard before I could get the rear of the raft out of the slip. This meant that the large cruiser to my starboard ran the risk of my pointed pontoon tubes gashing a hole along its port side.

I held my breath as I leaned harder on the remote lever for the kicker motor, trying to get it to engage faster in reverse. As I did, a piece of the frame on the aft port side of the raft caught on the dock and began to pivot the front end around to starboard, but thankfully not any closer to the cruiser.

Once the entire bow made it past the cruiser, I heard a crunch and looked back to see that the frame of the SS Hail Mary had buckled slightly. However, that buckled frame section saved me from tearing a hole in the cruiser, so I was grateful!

So, on to North Buena Vista and Pirate's Pit Stop Marina less than fifteen miles away. To be honest, I was skeptical about this next stop. I had called and messaged earlier and was assured that I would have a place to tie up but that it would be on a barge on the channel. What I heard was, "You can tie up in the middle of the river on a floating dock."

So I continued onward with some trepidation and began to casually look for an alternative place to dock in the event the Pirate's Pit Stop wasn't the best one for the raft.

About three quarters of a mile away from the designated location, I spotted the marina—which was literally nothing more than a small barge with a structure on top of it, barely out of the river's navigation channel.

It was a floating raft marina! Kindred spirits, I figured.

I called the owner, Linda, and asked her to confirm that what I saw was, in fact, the place I was going to tie up for the night.

She assured me it was and then directed me to go past the marina, come back upriver, and dock my raft between the marina and the shoreline. She said she would be down to meet me.

Within thirty minutes, I was safely nestled between the Pirate Pit Stop barge and the shoreline and could not have been happier! Not only was I off the main channel, but the location kept me out of the wind and rain elements quite nicely.

Linda came down, introduced herself, made sure I had what I needed, and said she would return in a bit to talk. Later her husband, James, came down to assess me and the raft and seemed satisfied that while I might have been nuts to do what I was doing, I appeared to be generally pretty harmless.

The Pirate's Pit Stop Marina is a remarkable place. I have since learned that this is one of the most popular stops along this river stretch, in large part because Linda and James are such gracious hosts. Plus, it's simply fun. Tie up to a barge, get gas and supplies, and venture up to one of the courtesy docks to enjoy food from their outdoor grille, cold beverages, and good conversation with smiling people with warm hearts.

I was content and safe and out of the weather.

I also had an opportunity to do a little fishing and caught a few small fish. Later that night, Linda and James came down to check on me and confirm my departure time the next morning so I could gas up. They also brought me a container of chili—how nice!

I ate the chili, did some more work, got the cabin of the raft squared away for my evening's sleep, and went to bed feeling grateful for the generosity of my hosts.

The next morning I was up early again. I got my stuff packed up, battened down, started the motors, made some coffee with my new French press, and at about eight o'clock texted Linda to let her know that if we could fuel up at eight thirty, I would love to be on my way at nine. At about the same time, I decided to call ahead to Lock and Dam Number 11, which is right above Dubuque, Iowa.

The man who answered at the lock identified himself as Willi. I let him know that I was coming down on a homemade raft and wondered what traffic at the facility would look like around noon.

He said that he anticipated heavy traffic and that I should be prepared for a long wait if I got there and they were locking commercial traffic through. He also assured me that if a more extended stay was required, they had a "pool" off to the starboard side of the lock area that I could anchor in, out of the wide river and away from the wind that would buffet me if I had to stay exposed out there. While I had some consternation about a several-hour wait for the lock and dam, I was comforted by Willi's kindness and assurance that "we will take good care of you."

Not long after, Linda and James came down and she handed me a plate of hot food—sausage, scrambled eggs, and fried potatoes! Simply amazing.

We then gassed up the raft and Linda gave me a T-shirt and a koozie. I paid for gas and thanked them both profusely for their generosity.

After a few more waves and thank you's, I was on my way to Dubuque and the Dubuque Marina and Yardarm. Not long after my trip was announced, I had received an email from Craig Phillips, who offered to pay for my slip and gas. At about the same time, I received an email from Jeremy McDowell at Mid-Town Marina in East Dubuque, offering me a place to stay as I came through.

I would travel about twenty-one miles that day and go through some reasonably vast swaths of the river. As I proceeded, I frequently checked my apps for any large vessels approaching from my aft or bow. I also watched with increasing concern as the weather deteriorated.

I was resigned to the fact that the day would be wet and somewhat windy. However, I had not seen forecasts of the kind of wind guests I had been dealing with for the past several days. And as I got closer to the lock and dam, the weather began to get wetter, the wind faster, the gusts more intense. Fog and low clouds started to drop further into my line of sight. I began nervously checking the shoreline to see where I might tie up if the clouds and fog began to envelop me. The idea of being socked in and not being able to see where I was gnawed on me with each additional mile. I was making mental notes of how I would prepare to tie up outside of the navigation channel if necessary while at the same time hoping I could make it to the lock and dam—and, more importantly, through it before the weather fell apart completely.

As luck would have it, about two miles from the lock and dam, the clouds and fog lifted a bit and the wind gusts died down. I called the lock and asked for a status update. As I feared, the operator shared that there would be at least a two-hour wait as two vessels would lock through ahead of me. However, the same operator suggested I head to the pool I had been told earlier in the morning.

My relief was palpable, as the voice on the other end of the phone was kind and reassuring.

As I got to the pool, I slid in as far as I thought wise given the depth, threw in my anchors, and toggled my marine radio to ask the operator if I was far enough out of their channel.

He assured me I was and told me that they would update me as things went on to let me know the lock and dam status.

After about an hour or so, and after I saw one towboat get through the lock, I radioed and asked if I should still expect to wait an hour or so before I could get through. To my genuine surprise and delight, the operator said I could begin moving forward and that they would be able to lock me through shortly.

Yahoo!

I motored into the lock and dam with my small kicker motor, and a young man threw me down the line. I happily accepted it, pulled myself up along the wall, and took my chalk and wrote HOTR #11. I took a picture to mark the moment.

As the water began to go down (at this lock, it would go down eight feet), the lock employee leaned over and we chatted a bit. He told me that it would be a fast drop and wanted to know about my trip. I shared briefly and encouraged him to go to Spare Key's website to learn more.

Soon the front gates swung up and the horn sounded, and I was on my way. Suddenly, on the radio, the familiar voice of the young worker I had chatted with in the lock came on and said, "This is Lock and Dam 11 to the small passenger ship. I just checked out your website. Your organization is amazing and thank you for what you are doing to keep it going. Safe travels along your way."

I radioed backed my gratitude for their kindness and ended by saying, "Your kindness today is evidence that there is hope on the river."

The men and women operating these locks and dams are public servants. Every single one I met along the way reminded me of the importance of public service and the even more important people who are willing to do these jobs to serve all of us. Truly remarkable.

I saw the mile marker for Dubuque Marina and Yardarm about a half-mile out from the lock and dam. As I approached it slowly, I could see two no-wake buoys, and then to my starboard a horseshoe of what I can only describe as orange buoy balls with a mannequin in the center standing up with her hands in the air.

Confused, I called the marina to ask how I should proceed. Eventually, after a fair amount of confusion on my part and the marina's, I made it safely into a slip.

I tied up and was looking forward to doing laundry and having a hot shower. But first I had a chance to meet Craig, my host, and thank him for his kindness. He and his family spend most of their time living on their fifty-foot cruiser docked at the marina. He's from Cedar Rapids, Iowa, which had experienced devastating storms a few weeks earlier. He was planning to drive up there the next day to deal with insurance issues related to property damage from the recent derecho. I had to look it up, but derechos are fast-moving bands of thunderstorms with destructive winds. The winds can be as strong as those found in hurricanes or even tornados. Unlike hurricanes and tornados, these winds follow straight lines. Like many residents in the area, Craig had significant damage inflicted on his property.

He told me he would not just cover the cost of my slip but pay for any gas I needed the next day. As has become a common theme, I thanked him profusely.

Also as usual, I needed to pick up a few things. For one, realized I didn't have any laundry detergent. In addition, at my previous night's stay at the Pirate's Pit Stop, Linda had loaned me a space heater that I used to keep warm and to dry the floor of the cabin. I was determined I would get myself my own space heater for the raft, given that the rain showed no evidence of letting up. I called a taxi, and not long after I was at the store picking up detergent, extra socks, a space heater and some extra duct tape.

A couple of hours later I had clean laundry and a clean Erich and settled into my raft to do some work and enjoy a couple of MREs for supper. That night the weather was cold, and the space heater was a welcome addition.

Morning came quickly, and I knew I didn't have to get up early because my trip to East Dubuque was only about three miles downriver.

Craig called me while I was having coffee, and we chatted for about a half hour as he gave me additional advice on marinas, navigation, radio chatter, and locks and dams. I told him how much I appreciated his kindness and that I looked forward to talking to him in the future. At about 10:00 a.m. I slowly made my way past the orange buoys towards the river's main channel. As I did so, I saw three magnificent bridges ahead of me; one of them was a railroad swing bridge.

I also saw a colossal towboat coming upriver.

Or at least it looked like it was coming upriver.

My app showed it making no headway. My binoculars didn't pick up any movement. Frankly, as I looked at it, the vessel seemed like it was stationary in the water.

About that time, Joe Soucheray and Garage Logic, the official podcast of the Hope on the River trip, called to chat about the journey so far. At nearly the same moment, I realized that the previously inert tow and the barge were underway and coming right at me as I was coming down the river.

I am sure that there must have been some kind of optical illusion that made me think that the ship wasn't moving. But right now, it was moving and FAST!

I was waiting for a scolding horn from the ship, but I quickly motored to my starboard as it slid by on my port side. As Joe and I talked, I was also navigating the churn that the ship's turbulent wake had dug up. Finally, I was able to focus on my conversation with Joe and proceeded forward to my next destination—Mid-Town Marina in East Dubuque.

Joe and I chatted for the next few minutes about the trip, the people I had met, and the trials and tribulations of being on the river in a homemade raft. We had a few laughs. The guys on his podcast, Chris and Rookie, are great guys just like Joe. They care deeply about their community, their country, their families, and this guy on a raft on the river!

We said goodbye and I began to look for my entrance to Mid-Town Marina. I called the marina several times to confirm that the entrance to the slough I saw on my portside, which looked like it couldn't have been deeper than a couple of feet, was indeed, the marina I was going to.

I was assured multiple times that it was, and with gritted teeth I made my way slowly through the entrance and then finally to the location of the marina itself. This would be where I would stay for the next couple of days until I left for Bellevue, Iowa.

My arrival at Mid-Town Marina was happening at the perfect time, since I needed to rest the raft, dry it out, and get things back in shape after what had been days of nonstop rain, wind, and storms. Nestled away from the main channel, the marina is a quiet place that would be perfectly situated to keep the raft out of the elements and give me time to assess the situation with the warping of doors, leaking of pontoons, and a host of other little raft ailments.

When Jeremy McDowell first reached out to offer me a place to stay if I were to end up in East Dubuque, I'd taken him up on the offer. I'm sure he regretted the decision after I'd called him about a half dozen times to make sure I knew exactly where I needed to enter his marina.

The challenge of hip-hopping from a marina upriver to one less than three miles downriver is that things quickly sneak up on you. Not only that, but the Mississippi is vast in that area, and there are a series of three bridges. The navigation maps I had, both paper and digital, didn't always do the best job of articulating specifically where one would need to turn. Or at least I didn't do a good job of understanding where they said to turn!

I finally figured out that I needed to turn to my port side once I made it through the last of the three bridges. However, as I approached the last bridge, I was confused by the channel navigation markers. Suddenly I realized I was heading right into a wing dam. I reversed course quickly while also trimming my motors at nearly the last minute.

Whew!

Finally, I saw the slough I needed to enter and noticed red and green colored sticks bracketing the entrance. Once again, I called Jeremy to confirm that (a) I was going the correct way, and (b) I was supposed to stay inside those sticks. Calmly, but I am sure with his patience tested, he assured me I was going the right direction, that I should stay within the sticks, and he would see me shortly.

A quick side note: I tend to ask a lot of questions in life about most everything. It is how I learn. It is also how I avoid getting myself into trouble and screwing things up. Sometimes, admittedly, I ask a *lot* of questions and it may seem, to the person who is being asked them, to be the same question over and over. To me, however, they are not. They are simply a slight modification of the question intended to get me closer to an answer that I think I can better and more fundamentally understand. I appreciate that it must get annoying, but at fifty-seven years old, I am not sure I can come up with a better way to get the answers I think I need to stay out of harm's way!

In this situation, I figured that when I got through the sticks, the way to the marina would be obvious.

Alas, it was not. In fact, in front of me was a pile of rocks and one channel that went to the left and one that went to the right.

Arrrggh!

Yup, you guessed it! I called Jeremy again and apologized profusely but said, "I really can't tell which side of these rocks you are on!"

Thankfully, one last time, he calmly assured me that I should go left and not right.

I did, and there, in front of me, was the glorious Mid-Town Marina!

I quickly tied up and introduced myself to Jeremy, thanked him for his patience and generosity, and assured him I wouldn't cause him any additional problems. He laughed and we chatted for a bit, and then he directed me to a package that had been delivered to me. As you may recall, two of my acrylic signs had blown off during the thunderstorm in McGregor. Inside the box were two replacement signs and a replacement channel for one of the signs, and longer screws for all the channels into which the signs slid.

Wendy Pajor and the lead on the sign project, Paul Benick, must have thought I was an idiot for losing signs. But the signs were amazing. They really made the raft stand out, and I finally had figured out how to keep them secured! "Trial and Error" seemed to be my nickname on the trip, and "trial and error" was the phrase of the day when it came to those signs.

I took my package of signs, asked Jeremy for a drill, and walked back down to the raft. It was starting to rain like crazy, but I wanted to get these and all the other signs up, button up the raft, and then figure out how to dry it out. After about thirty minutes I was able to call the job complete, with the signs in their appropriate place, and begin to assess the soaking wet condition of the raft itself.

I called a taxi service and took a quick trip to the store to get some towels, and plastic and a fan to help dry the floor. I made it back and mopped up a bit and turned on the fan. After a few hours, it was apparent the fan wasn't going to do the trick, and I could now see why. As the rain poured down, it was clear that the raft itself wasn't leaking from the roof or the walls—water was leaking into the floor from the front of the raft. We had missed an area of caulking between the frame of the front of the cabin and the outside vinyl flooring, and it was pooling up and leaking through the door.

Unfortunately, nothing I could do now would stop the leak until after the rain stopped, so I spent a generally miserable night sopping up the water, staying off the floor, and sleeping on my inflatable mattress atop plastic storage boxes.

The next day I took another trip into town, grabbed a powerful floor fan, and brought it back to the raft. I also attempted to patch the area in front of the leaking door, which seemed to do the trick. After a few hours, the fan began to do its job, and by the evening the floor was bone dry!

The Mid-Town Marina had an onsite bar and restaurant. While this wasn't the case at every marina I visited, there were a handful of them that did have such a luxury and it was my luck that Mid-Town not only had both, but they were pretty good! I was able to have lunch there a couple of times and also dinner. The food was excellent, reasonably priced, and stuffed me! If you are ever at Mid-Town Marina, I would highly recommend their homemade pizza and burgers.

On September 13, I woke up to blue skies and a warm morning. It was going to be a beautiful day to raft down the Mississippi. I started my motors, battened everything down, and proceeded to the gas dock, but not before I forgot something...again!

One of the things that the folks at River Valley Power and Sport provided me with when they installed the kicker motor and tuned up the Nissan was a metal bar that connected the two. This allowed me to steer the kicker motor from the same wheel as I steered the Nissan. When it was connected, of course!

That morning, I had decided to use the kicker motor to move out of the harbor and onto the river, so I started it, untied the raft, and throttled it into reverse. But without it being connected to the steering arm!

Duh!

So the raft kind of squirted out into the water, and I had to quickly put the kicker motor into neutral, reach back and attach the bar, and slowly creep to the gas dock to fill up. Once done, I headed slowly back through the channel I'd entered and backed out onto the big river.

It was a spectacular morning, and I knew that I would be traveling to Bellevue, Iowa, to tie up a few miles from Lock and Dam Number 12 at Spruce Creek Marina and Campground.

As I was leaving, the Coast Guard came on and warned mariners that a vessel had gotten hung up on the ground near mile marker 560.

Spruce Creek is at 559.5, so this was going to be interesting.

Mile marker 559.5 was also twenty miles away from me at the moment, so it was the least of my concerns for the time being.

The river valley in this area is too stunning to describe with words. Suffice to say that anything I could write would be insufficient to convey its glory. The shoreline, the foliage, the wildlife, and the water combine to create a landscape that is a feast for one's eyes. And on sunny, warm September day, I could not have been more grateful for my time on this river.

I drifted a great deal of the day, but then found myself on several stretches of really wide river with high winds, so I had to motor through that. Additionally, I encountered a series of fishing boats that required me to power through their wake. But by and large, this was as relaxing a day as I could imagine. I did a couple of videos to share for an upcoming event and prepared myself as well as I could for the next couple of days' stays.

One of the things I had initially planned to do as I approached Spruce Creek was to enter the area via the Bellevue Slough. When I'd spoken to someone the day before, they had assured me that not only would my raft be able to get through the slough, but if I chose to, I could easily tie up anywhere along the shoreline.

In looking at my navigation maps, though, it was clear that there were multiple obstructions along the way. I think the person thought by "raft" I meant something a bit nimbler, that created less of a draft.

Or I misread the maps.

Or both.

At this, I am literally laughing out loud!

In any case, I chose to bypass the slough and proceed down the main channel to mile marker 559.5 and the Spruce Creek Marina.

This stretch of river was one of the narrowest I had been on. In fact, someone at Pirate's Pit Stop had warned me about it and said to keep my eyes open if I found myself approaching a tow.

Sure enough, as I came around a dog leg in the river, there in front of me was a colossal towboat pushing barges upstream. Neither side of the river was wide enough for me to get out of the channel safely, so I turned around and went back upriver about half a mile and found a deep spot out of the way. I idled until the vessel went by me about twenty minutes later.

I turned back into the channel and proceeded down the river, where I came upon a boat that created massive and deep wakes in the water. It was an odd-looking boat and it seemed to run very deep in the water and it was the second time I had encountered one like this. I didn't yet know that these were Army Corps of Engineer boats, but each time I had and would encounter one, they came fast and deep and required me to nose the raft's bow toward them to ride out the waves.

Once past that ship, I knew I was about a mile from my destination.

I also had radio traffic from the Coast Guard saying that the ship that had beached earlier at marker 560 was now clear. And as I got around the bend, I figured out later why!

Approaching me was another huge towboat with barges on either side. The entourage wasn't moving fast, but fast enough for me to move to its starboard as I began to angle my way towards the marina where I would spend the night.

In approaching the Spruce Creek Marina, one has to go through a small opening into a closed harbor. I found my space, paid for it, and tucked in for the night. It had been a good day on the river, and I was pleased to be in a safe space for the night.

Chapter 12
The Angel of Clinton Marina

I awoke early in Spruce Creek and realized that I wasn't likely going anywhere. A deep and heavy fog had set in overnight, and as I emerged from the cabin of the raft, I could see nothing.

All around the raft in the small harbor area, the fog was thick and unwavering. Out on the river, it was as if a white sheet had been pulled down along the riverbank and nothing was going to be seen in it, on it, or around it.

Knowing that the sun wasn't going to burn this away anytime quickly, I retreated to the cabin, made myself some coffee, put away my bed, made some breakfast, and began preparing for the moment when the fog would finally dissipate.

I also decided to call ahead to Lock and Dam Number 12 to get a sense from them of what they thought traffic through the facility would be like that day. Assuming the fog was disrupting everything, I wanted to be sure that I had a good sense of how long I might need to wait should I need to factor in commercial traffic that morning.

The lock staff were enormously helpful in sharing with me that they anticipated a busy morning; with the fog, it was likely to be even more active. However, they indicated that I would be okay one way or the other.

I thanked them, hung up, and at about 10:00 a.m., almost like magic, the fog faded away and I was able to get myself underway.

When I arrived at the lock and dam, they indicated that they had a towboat going through with barges but that I should be able to lock through as soon as that were done. The weather was glorious—bright sun, truly little wind, and the water like glass. I asked for advice as to what side of the towboat they wanted me on when I exited the lock. They directed me to my starboard side, near a green buoy, and said I would be fine if I stayed in that vicinity until after the towboat made it through. As I waited, two other pleasure craft arrived to wait with me. About an hour later, we were summoned forward into the lock and dam.

In this lock, the other craft were not tied up, although I did request and received a rope. I asked Austin, the lock operator, why the other vessels weren't using ropes. He responded that because of Covid-19, they weren't providing ropes and assistance unless specifically requested. That made sense, and I appreciated the answer.

After about twenty minutes, we got the signal to proceed forward. I thanked Austin and headed out from Lock and Dam Number 12 to my next destination: the Savanna Marina.

As I approached Savanna, Illinois, I traveled under a lovely bridge. I saw that a large paddleboat was making its way behind me. Fortunately, my entrance to the marina was directly ahead and I proceeded to my port side at a leisurely pace to enter the marina. It was a wonderfully clean little location owned by the city of Savanna and had two transient docks for overnight stays, set up as "first come, first served." I was a bit concerned that I would find both taken but was relieved to see that they weren't. It didn't take long to tie up, and then I went up to talk to whoever was operating the marina.

However, as I had learned over the previous several days, when nobody answered the phone there was nobody available to meet with. So I knocked on the little cafe's door and the woman who answered gave me some direction on how to pay for my slip. Then I called another number I found and a voice on the other end of the line assured me that someone would be available to provide fuel the next morning at seven o'clock.

I spent several hours running errands—picking up some supplies, getting food for dinner, and purchasing a new inflatable mattress. My first two had expired after hitting nails that were pounded in through the outside wall, their pointed tips sticking into the cabin. I realized that at night I must be brushing up against the sharp tips and poking multiple holes in the mattresses. The fact that I had now gone through two air mattresses proves once and for all that I should have gone with a hammock or a folding cot from the start!

Next time.

My evening in Savanna was, as has been the case at other marinas, frequently punctuated by the evening sounds of freight trains and their whistles and horns sounding on the hour. As if to announce the trains' arrival, several fish jumped seconds before the trains passed through. It was a unique early warning system that repeated itself every single time the train came thundering through the area.

I made myself some dinner and got caught up on emails and writing and decided to treat myself with an earlier than normal bedtime. The next morning, the man I had spoken to on the phone the previous day arrived as promised at seven o'clock and I fueled up, at a cost of $31.70. Just as I was getting ready to cast off, however, he came running up to me, horrified, and told me he had accidentally charged me $317.10 instead of $31.70. I chuckled and said, "Well, at least this morning I didn't screw something up!"

Try as he might, he could not figure out the credit card machine or how to reverse the charge and repeatedly apologized for the mishap. I assured him I wasn't worrying about it and somehow, we would get it figured out.

On to Clinton, Iowa!

As I left Savanna Marina, I knew I was in for a lovely day of traveling. As I made my way south, a few miles ahead of me were Sabula and a gorgeous swing bridge. I proceeded with caution toward eighteen-foot clearance, nervously re-estimating, again, the height of my raft. I knew I was well under that height, but, as with all things on this trip, I had to reassess whether my calculations and assumptions were correct.

Thankfully they were, and I made it under the bridge with room to spare!

Just after I made it through, I got a call from the Savanna Marina manager, who was also apologizing profusely for the mix-up of the wrong charge. As we chatted back and forth on the phone she asked if I could give her my credit card number so she could try reversing the charge. Soon enough she said she thought it was taken care of but I should call my bank and confirm that it had been resolved.

But when she tried to run the correct amount, her machine said my card had been declined!

This was getting to be a lot of work for $31.70 worth of gas.

I told her I would call my bank and get things figured out and make sure she could run the card through again and get the marina paid and the overcharge taken care. I called my bank, explained the problem, gave them my credit card number, address, social security number, and all my private information. Then, after a few minutes of back and forth, it was determined that because of the wrong charges, plus other charges, etc., the card had been declined because I had reached my daily limit. They nicely suggested I could increase the credit limit if I gave them my account information, address, passwords, etc.

At about that time I happened to see a message flash on my computer screen where I was casually watching the Facebook Livestream I was broadcasting. Someone said, "Hey Erich, I'm not sure you want to be sharing your bank account information online!"

Yikes!!! I had completely forgotten that the trip that morning was livestreaming, so everything I was saying—including my bank account information—was being broadcast to thousands of people on Facebook!

This $31.70 was becoming more expensive by the minute.

I called my wife and asked her to call the bank and make sure that our account was safe, changing passwords, etc., so that passwords or codes that might have gotten broadcast would no longer be working. After more frustration and anxiety, we finally got it all figured out and put my credit card drama behind me!

I continued on my way as the river began to twist and turn, more and more, and then it started to open up. And when I say open up, I mean *open up*!

This section of the river was beginning to look an awful lot like Lake Pepin, and in a few miles, I was deep into a massive area of the Mississippi that was not only wide but had extraordinarily little protection from the wind.

The wave chop began to increase in intensity, as did the winds from the south and the southeast. Pretty soon, my casual drift was no longer adequate and I had to turn off the kicker motor and fire up the Nissan to power through the wind and the waves.

About five miles from Lock and Dam Number 13, I found myself coming upon a very narrow channel in which I would eventually turn to my starboard side. I quickly checked my iPad app to gauge the depth on either side of the buoys and found that I was surrounded by a stump field on my right and downed trees and obstructions on my left. In front of me, a towboat with barges suddenly appeared and was bearing down on me.

I decided to radio for instructions about where the tow wanted me to be when we passed by one another.

A mumble from the captain came in reply: "One whistle. One whistle. One whistle."

What the hell did *that* mean?

Before I left Red Wing, Matt Stokes had walked me through some of the language from towboat captains that he thought would be important for me to know.

Somewhere in the back of my mind, and inside the cabin, was the definition of what "One whistle" meant, but I simply could not remember or find it! And the towboat and I were getting closer and closer to one another.

I meekly got on the radio and said, "Captain, this is the small little pleasure craft in front of you approaching your towboat. I apologize but I cannot recall what 'One whistle' means and would be grateful for additional guidance."

He promptly radioed back and said, "Your port to my port. Your port to my port."

Aha! That I understood! He wanted me to get out of the channel and keep my port side to his port side. In other words, pass him on the green buoy side of the channel.

I promptly did as he said.

Now, because the channel where he and I were to pass by one another was so narrow, I decided to sneak outside of the navigation channel on my starboard side. I figured I wouldn't need to be out there very long but didn't want to be particularly close to this towboat.

This is the point where having a depth finder is an absolute lifesaver.

Because I was, in fact, in the stump field.

And while my iPad app was great for telling me about stump fields ahead of time, it wasn't particularly good at telling me where the stumps actually were.

I was, in reality, in a stump minefield and it was getting more and more crowded by the minute.

Stumps and boat motors do not go together well.

I quickly got my face down into the monitor of the depth finder to see what was beneath me. The depth finder kept giving me soundings of three feet, four feet, three feet, two feet, four feet, and so on.

I figured that the raft was drafting high enough to keep me safe if I stayed around two feet above the top of the stumps, but any lower and it was likely to tear off my prop and potentially grab my transom and motor, grinding the raft to a dead halt.

The barges and I were taking longer than I had planned to get by one another, in large part because the towboat was pushing upstream against the current. Finally, after about twenty minutes, they went by.

Not long after, the captain jumped back on the radio and said, "Captain of the little pleasure craft, I would suggest you get back into the channel sooner rather than later, before you get hung up on a stump."

I thanked him and did exactly that!

Once past the channel, the river got even bigger... windier... and the waves turned to whitecaps. I knew that this was starting to get more serious, and dangerous to the same degree that I had experienced on Lake Pepin.

I got both motors going and got my speed up to about eight knots to power through as water began to crash over the front of the raft. I moved my sandbags back off the bow to get some more lift, and shifting the weight accomplished that. About a mile and a half out from Lock and Dam Number 13, I called the lock operator to confirm their status. Tony, the lock operator, indicated that if I got there within the next hour, I should be able to lock right on through.

Music to my ears! I thanked him and hung up and floored my motors. Saying they roared to life sounds a bit dramatic given that I topped out at about ten knots, but it got me to the lock and dam in plenty of time to radio Tony and let him know I was ready to enter when he was ready to have me.

After a ten-minute wait, I got the green light and entered.

Tony, like most operators, was conversational and helpful and supportive. He provided me with a little booklet on lock and dam etiquette, we chatted a bit, and about twenty minutes later he gave me the all clear to exit. As I came out of the lock and dam, I was met with more choppy water.

Before I left, Tony indicated that the pool of water above the lock and dam, referred to as Pool 13, was the second-largest pool on the river. Only Lake Pepin was larger.

That made sense.

I was relieved to hear that the next-largest pool was near Lock and Dam Number 14, right down the river. That being said, every large area of water in the river after the final lock and dam in Illinois—which is where I would enter the Lower Mississippi—was going to be a big pool of water. I had better be ready!

As I faced the waves, I reminded myself that I would soon be meeting a woman named Jean Lashelle, the manager of the Clinton Marina. Jean had reached out to me with an offer to stay at their marina, and for the past several days we had been communicating about my location and when I anticipated getting to Clinton.

She also notified the press, and I was delighted to hear that not only would the *Clinton Herald* be there to cover the trip but that a TV station would be, as well. As I came around a bend of trees, I could see the Clinton Marina, and there, standing on the dock, was Jean taking pictures and waving her arms. I was thrilled!

She directed me around a dock and into an inside slip. I followed her instructions and quickly tied up. Then I got a wonderful hug and we greeted one another, both saying how glad we were to finally meet!

Jean had been with the marina for seven years. I could tell she loves her job, and she loves people. She has a quick smile, a big laugh, and a warm heart.

As we were tying up and I was getting things battened down, Winona Kay Lawson Whitaker, a reporter from the *Clinton Herald*, arrived to interview me. Winona had actually been at Lock and Dam Number 13 to get pictures of me coming through, and I jokingly said that I hoped she had gotten the raft's good side in her photos. I told Winona and Jean that I was going to need to get water out of the pontoon before I could settle down for the day and grabbed my pump and hose. As Winona and I chatted, and Jean helped me out, I took about ten gallons of water out of the port side tube—roughly eight pounds of water I did not need back there!

After about thirty minutes, the interview wrapped up. Jean went over the gas dock to serve another boat and I continued to tidy up the raft.

A few minutes later, a television camera and cameraman showed up and we did another thirty-minute interview. Once that was done, I made my way up to the Clinton Marina office. There I chatted more with Jean and met her daughter, Rebecca. Rebecca had been kind enough to get me some Dunkin' Donuts coffee and donuts and we spent a few minutes chatting, as well. Rebecca had served in the military for five years and discharged out and had, like many veterans, been struggling to get access to services in the era of Covid-19. I listened and then shared with Rebecca and her mom that I knew a few folks in Iowa who might be able to connect with some congressional offices that could support her in getting her VA services.

After about an hour or so, Jean was kind enough to lend me her car and I drove into town to the Farm & Fleet and picked up a new transfer pump. *Yahoo!* I figured since I was near a Walgreens, I might as well stop in and get a flu shot as well.

I returned to the marina, gave Jean her car keys back, and walked up the stairs above the marina to grab lunch at a restaurant. After about an hour or so, I went back to the raft. Soon a couple traveling the river from Otsego, Minnesota, pulled up.

Their names were Bob and Amy and they were going to take what is called the Great Loop—a trip from the Great Lakes to the Gulf of Mexico, and from the Mississippi River to the Atlantic Ocean. It's quite a feat. They were excited, anxious, and ready to go!

We had a nice chat about our mutual adventures. They had a much bigger boat than I did—a nice fifty-foot cruiser with a double deck and massive motors. I jokingly asked if they wanted to trade and was not surprised when they declined!

As I prepared for bed, I was struck once again by the kindness of strangers. Jean and her daughter could not have been nicer or more generous. Jean, in fact, gave me the tips she received for the day as a donation to Spare Key. I wished them and my Great Loop neighbors good night and got ready for bed. My morning in Clinton was going to be busy!

I had a call to make to the Realtor Convention of the Dakotas in the morning, and I knew I had a call from a radio station in the afternoon. My plans that day, as often happened, were going to change—in some good ways and some not-so-good ways.

The Realtor Convention of the Dakotas is one of the absolute highlights of my year, and a tremendously beneficial relationship for Spare Key. We first were invited many years ago to participate in their convention in Bismarck, and the event has become one of our most successful fundraising—and friend-raising—annual events. Every year since we have been invited to attend, make a presentation, and, during the luncheon when the Realtor of the Year Award is given, pass around little cardboard houses shaped like our Spare Key logo. The amount of money we have raised in those ten-to-fifteen minutes is jaw dropping!

When the Spare Key team takes the cardboard houses into an adjacent room so the convention can continue its business, we are always humbled and grateful to find them stuffed with wads of cash, checks, and all sorts of notes and greetings. It never ceases to amaze me! The Realtor Convention of the Dakotas has allowed us to raise well over $150,000 over the years. Their generosity is heartfelt and genuine. Each year as Spare Key sets up our booth, there are REALTORS who come by to confirm that we are doing the passing of the houses at the next day's luncheon—they already have their check written out, or money prepared, or credit card ready to be scanned.

In 2020, however, like nearly every other organization, hosting a traditional convention was simply not possible for them. The event had to be virtual, but, true to form, not only did they invite us to participate, but they asked me to speak to them from the raft. I was thrilled to do so!

So, at around 9:30 a.m., I went *live* from the raft and shared the journey of Hope on the River with however many REALTORS were watching. I don't know how much money we raised from this event, but that was less important to me right then than it is was for me to remind the REALTORS how much they mean to us and how grateful we are for them keeping us in their thoughts.

It was a great way to start my day.

I had originally planned to stay two nights in Clinton, especially because of the kind generosity extended to me by Jean and her family. But, given the glorious weather of the day, I made the decision that if I got underway to LeClaire, Iowa—and, equally important, through Lock and Dam Number 14—it would be well worth my time to start out again sooner rather than later.

I thanked Jean profusely, got all my tanks and motors filled with gas, and set off down the river. The Mississippi started out lovely and "small" and easy to travel. By the time I reached mile marker 516, barely three miles from my departure point, the weather began to change.

And when the weather changes, so too does the wind.

Not to fear, however. I didn't have too far to go that day, roughly 24 miles, so I decided I would run mostly with the kicker motor and take my time.

As I went past home after home built up on stilts and big concrete walls, the water became bigger and choppier. The river turned from a lazy channel to a big booming lake, and by the time I was moving into marker 512, I was fighting waves and wind.

This was becoming a recurring theme. Nice, laconic morning starts followed by daunting bodies of water and equally daunting wind, followed by even more daunting waves. Today would be no different, just more intense.

By the time I reached mile marker 504, I was in the midst of what felt on the raft like gale-force winds. The wind was rushing at me from the south and then the south-east, and it hit hard.

The nose of the raft kept pushing down and water coming up on board—so much so that I pulled my ballast off the front end and shoved it in the middle of the cabin, then turned up the throttle on both motors to get the front up to plane. That helped a little until I got to an area around mile marker 499 and Port Byron. At this point, I was bombarded by both water and wind. Not only does the choppy water bounce the raft around, but it also pours into the transom and pushes up through the bottom of the steering console, so my feet get soaked as river water rushed in and drained back out the rear of the cabin. I was six miles away from my day's planned final destination, but it may as well have been sixty miles away given the rough weather.

This time I was not going to make the same mistake I made in Lake Pepin and go to the wrong side where I would be at the mercy of the treacherous wind and waves. Unfortunately, even going to the correct side offered me little respite. The waves were already roiling, and then, worse, a recreational boat loaded with people who should have known better came flying by me, creating a wake that only added to my misery. I not only had to contend with nature but now the inconsiderate boaters who simply waved and gawked at me as they rushed by.

At this point I was caught in a crossfire of waves and wakes. The SS Hail Mary shuddered and I turned her quickly into the wind, then shot her short end around and headed back upstream to recover.

I did this three times, and each time I did it I had to choreograph my turn as the wind died down so that I did not end up showing the largest surface of the raft to the wind any longer than necessary. The last thing I needed was a huge gust of wind to grab the raft with my side fully exposed, possibly tipping me over into the river.

These maneuvers kept pushing me further back up the river, but I was trying to buy time to figure out how to get out of the worst of this blustery weather. Finally, I got the courage to turn the raft back into the wind and try to make a beeline for the area of the channel that was beckoning me, to (I hoped) get out of the wind.

With a wet floor, due to having navigated the wake of another boater coming by at high speed without any concern for me, I found myself coming around the bend to LeClaire, Iowa, and now respite from the wind. Ahead of me, I could see the faint outline of Lock and Dam Number 14. I knew that not far from there was the marina where I would spend the next two nights.

I was relieved but also nervous. As I powered down the kicker motor and the Nissan and looked back at my tubes, I could see they were heavy with the water they had taken on in their most recent beating from the waves. I didn't want to dillydally much longer without getting to a secure place to pump the water from the pontoon. I went forward with the knowledge that I was going to be docking for the night.

Unfortunately, that wasn't going to happen quite yet.

The marina I planned to stay at was unfortunately not off the main river. This meant that while I would be off the navigation channel, I would still feel the impact of towboats, pleasure boats, their accompanying wakes, and waves, even as I was tied up.

But first I needed to figure out how to get to the marina! The directions were complicated, and my exhaustion from the beating I had just taken didn't help my state of mind. The directions seemed to indicate that I needed to go a couple miles past the marina and then turn to my right and come back upstream to avoid submerged rocks.

Unfortunately, I had read the maps, and the directions, completely backward. I was actually supposed to come to a landmark in the river *above* the marina and then turn to my right, proceed close to shore, and travel along the shoreline and between the submerged rocks to get to my location.

About two miles past the marina, I looked more closely at the Navionics app on my iPad and compared it to my navigation charts from the Army Corps of Engineers and realized I had made a mistake. I then powered back upriver, which added more water weight to my tubes, and finally circled around and made my way to the location along the "No Wake" shoreline.

Upon reaching the dock, my heart sank.

The marina itself was closed for the day. The instructions I had were to tie up to its gas dock and then settle up with the owners in the morning. The gas dock was a disaster. Not only was it nearly falling apart, but because of its proximity to the navigation channel, it jumped up and down as each passing wave and wake hit it full blast.

I reluctantly tied up because I knew that I had to do my radio interview, scheduled with Minnesota radio station KTOE. I talked about my trip with radio host Al Travis. Al and I had a great conversation but my mind was elsewhere, namely on the water in the pontoons. I was wondering how I was going to drain it before the raft sank too low in the water to be pumped out.

We finished the interview and, as I hung up, the raft and the gas dock were bouncing all over the place. I knew there was no way I could stay at this location overnight, plus I wasn't even sure I could drain the water from the pontoon.

Glancing around the marina, I noticed an empty slip and decided I would park there and take care of the raft and the water in the tubes. Because there was no staff present, I figured if the owner of the slip showed up, I would simply exit and go back to the gas dock. If not, I would pay for the slip in the morning when the staff showed up and be on my way.

I was surrounded by boats much larger than mine, so I figured it would be easy to get in and get settled.

Boy, was I wrong!

As I got about halfway into the slip, the raft came to a hard stop.

I had been using the kicker motor to slowly make my way into the slip and it was hung up on the bottom of the river. I quickly pulled it up, but then realized the Nissan had gotten stuck too and knew I had to get it up out of the water. Once both motors were up I figured I would just push the raft out with my push-pole, restart the motors, and get the heck out of there.

Alas, the raft itself had gotten stuck in the slip.

There was a reason the slip wasn't occupied. The silt and the mud from the river had collected in this area and had not been dredged away for some time.

At this point I was stuck halfway in and halfway out of the slip and this wasn't going to help me deal with the very real problem of water in the pontoon, nor allow me to be safely harbored for the night.

I took off my shoes and hoped, as I jumped out of the raft into the water, that I would not sink or get stuck in the mush. My plan was to put my feet up against the dock and my back on the raft and push until it broke loose.

It took all the muscle I had, but finally the raft moved and broke free.

I quickly got back up, shoved the push-pole down into the water, and slid the motors back into the water and started them. I quickly hit reverse, turned the raft back to the river, and floored it!

Despite all the effort it took to get to that marina through the nasty weather, I decided it was *not* going to be where I spent the night. So, while I slowly moved the raft back along the shoreline, retracing the path I had taken to get to the marina, I looked at my *Quimby's* guide and found three marinas downriver, beyond Lock and Dam Number 14. I called to see who was open and might have slips available.

After a fretful few minutes, I finally reached one that said they did and as long as I got there in the daylight, I shouldn't have any issues tying up for the evening. Now it was time to get back into the navigation channel and get to that lock and dam.

Of course, nothing is that easy!

As I turned into the channel, there in front of me, coming upriver, was a towboat pushing twelve barges and essentially blocking my path to get to the lock and dam.

My salty sailor language got a blast of new words around this time!

I had to get out of the channel and wait for the behemoth to get by me. As I did that, I called the lock and dam on the phone. They told me they currently had no one approaching, either upstream or downstream, so if I could get there quickly they could get me through.

"Quickly" and the SS Hail Mary are not synonymous with one another!

Finally, I was able to run south, parallel to the northbound towboat and barges, and get clear enough to shoot my way back into the channel and continue south.

Of course, my run-ins with massive high-speed cruisers were not done for the day.

This time, one came up behind me, fast and big and relentless, and then finally went off to starboard and slowed down to enter her home port. The massive wake left behind, coupled with the wake of the twelve barges, sent me bouncing over and into the waves, with more water pouring into the front of the raft but thankfully not into the cabin.

At that point I didn't even care anymore. I just needed to get to that lock and dam, get through it, and get tied up before dark.

As I sped closer, I called again, and the operator told me that he should be able to get me through quickly. I was nearly at the head of the lock and dam when, out of the blue, a pontoon inexplicably saddled up on my starboard side, at high speed and less than twenty-five yards from me.

I figured they were trying to beat me into the entrance of the lock, which seemed kind of dumb as it wasn't going to get them through any faster than me. They all waved at me as I grabbed my horn and blew it at them, putting my hands and shoulders up into a "What the heck are you doing?" shrug.

Or maybe I said some other words that are not appropriate for this book.

Whatever I said, it got their attention.

They simply stopped, turned around, and went back the other way!

But their wake didn't, and I had to bounce through that as well.

This particular lock and dam did not have a light tower on it for me to be able to know when to enter. So I had to radio the operator yet again and ask for instructions. He indicated that when the horn blew, I could enter. When that happened, I moved forward. In this lock and dam it was relatively easy to grab my rope and put my chalk on the wall and wait to be lowered.

Soon I got the all clear (although the gates were not completely open) and sped forward.

The seven miles I had to go to get to my final location for the night—the Isle of Capri Marina in Bettendorf, Iowa—could not go by fast enough for me. I was running both motors and going about nine knots, which meant I should, assuming no big waves, no big wind, and no big boats, get there in plenty of time to tie up and get the water out of the tubes.

After a few confusing conversations with the staff at the marina about which way I needed to enter, and clarification from a friendly pontoon driver a mile before I got there, I saw the entrance and relaxed.

I was thrilled to see that my Minnesota friends Bob and Amy, the couple doing the Great Loop, had also pulled into the marina. They had run into engine problems and decided to spend the night there after getting them ironed out. Bob came over and helped me pull up and tie up, and I told him he was a sight for sore eyes. I quickly pulled out my pumps, plugged them in, and ultimately drew about twenty-five gallons total out of both tubes—far less than I feared but more than I cared for.

But I'd made it! I was there! I had ended up traveling nearly forty miles instead of twenty-four, but I made it and I could not have been more grateful for that.

I got dinner at the nearby hotel, came back and did some work, then called it a night, knowing that the next morning I would do a call to the North Dakota REALTORS contingent which was having their meeting as part of the REALTORS Convention of the Dakotas. In the evening I would do a Zoom call into the Lend Smart Mortgage Mike Lust Golf Tournament that was being held to raise money for Spare Key.

As I woke in the morning, I made coffee, a breakfast of spam, ham, eggs, and processed cheese, and did a couple of Facebook Live broadcasts promoting the golf tournament.

Bob and Amy were in the process of leaving the Isle of Capri Marina, and I wished them a safe journey and went about finishing my breakfast, chatting with a few folks who ended up donating some money to Spare Key, cleaning my dishes, and beginning to get caught up on my blogs, maps, etc.

I got a call from a young guy named Joshua Lamberty with the Quad Cities area TV station WQAD. He wanted to do a story and asked if he and a camera person could come over.

Of course!!!

A bit after 10:30 a.m., I saw them pulling up and let them know that I wanted to finish my day segment of Hope on the River News by discussing what my daily life looked like on the raft. I also knew that I needed to be done by 11:30, in time to be on the air with my friends from the North Dakota Association of REALTORS.

Joshua was accompanied by a young womaned named Stephanie who would film the segment. We exchanged greetings, I clipped on a microphone, and we began to do an interview. I introduced the SS Hail Mary, how it was built, how it worked, and everything in between. We then boarded the raft and took her out into the navigation channel.

As with all things, we ran into a couple of issues.

First, for some reason the kicker motor wouldn't go into forward—or reverse.

Second, as I turned my attention to the kicker motor, I saw a large towboat pushing forward down the channel from my port side.

I fired up the Nissan and with a loud, clanky roar, she started! I smiled and told Joshua and Stephanie that it might be a bit louder but at least we would make it back to the marina in one piece.

I shared the story of Spare Key, Hope on the River, and why I felt this trip had a bigger purpose than just raising money and awareness. We all enjoyed the brief time on the water, and then I began to pull up to a different slip than the one I had been tied to the night before. My previous spot was next to a fish that had expired and was making us increasingly aware of its plight as the weather heated up. I didn't feel like spending the night next to it, hence this to move to the other side of the marina.

It should have been easy.

But it wasn't.

As Stephanie stepped onto the dock to pull the nose of the raft in, the wind pushed the SS Hail Mary around and the rear part swung hard to port. Soon the raft threatened to get stuck with its rear on one side of the slip and her nose on the other.

That would not be a good thing!

I quickly ran over to the opposite side dock, where Stephanie was standing, intending to get the back of the craft pushed over far enough that I could throw her a rope to grab and pull the raft over to her.

Then it happened.

I lost my balance and I fell into the water of the slip.

My first thought was, *How deep is this?*

My second thought was, *Okay, not too deep, but it's a lot colder than I thought it would be!*

At this point I grabbed onto the front of the raft and then hopped back up to the dock.

I instructed Josh to give me my push-pole and told him to exit the cabin, go to the end of the same dock that Stephanie was on, and be prepared to grab the rear of the raft as I pushed it toward him with the push-pole.

Finally, the SS Hail Mary swung around. Josh grabbed it and we tied up, then spent the rest of our time together laughing about my latest misadventure!

I had a great time with Joshua and Stephanie, and I think they enjoyed the experience. I hope they enjoyed getting their story ready for the evening's broadcast! As the day was ending, I made my call into the Lend Smart Mortgage Mike Lust Golf Tournament from the Isle of Capri

Marina, and I was grateful once again for this journey, the people I had met, and the places I had been.

Chapter 13
The Kindness of Family and Friends

I took off from Bettendorf early in the morning and was met by a gloriously sunny, if breezy and chilly, morning. The Isle of Capri Marina had served me well, and now it was time for a quick jaunt to Andalusia for the night, followed by an equally quick trip to Muscatine, as we prepared for a long slog between Muscatine and St. Louis.

The trip from Bettendorf to Andalusia was beautiful, quiet, and serene.

On this day, I was going to have to journey through Lock and Dam Number 15, which was barely two miles from where I got back in the channel to continue my journey south. I made a point of calling before I left to check on the status of the lock and emphasized to the operator that I was making way at about six knots per hour in a homemade raft!

He quickly shared with me that he did not anticipate any up or down river traffic taking priority and that it was likely they would lock me through in their auxiliary lock, 15A. I was pleased to hear this as it would make quick work of the day if I could make it through the lock and dam in short order.

When I got to within a mile or so, I toggled my radio to ask the operator if things were clear for me to proceed forward into the auxiliary lock. He indicated that given that there was no traffic at that time, he would simply bring me through the main lock channel.

That was fine by me! Shortly after that, I got the green light to proceed forward. The lock was uneventful until near the end.

For some reason, the undertow and current at the end of this lock was much stronger than in previous locks I had gone through. Because of that, I scrapped my original plan to simply proceed under power with the kicker motor and powered up the Nissan, as well. After a couple of uncomfortable minutes, I was able to make some decent progress, then settled in to enjoy the wind pushing me along from the aft port side of the raft down the river at a decent, if chilly, pace.

As I proceeded, I saw more and more single towboats moving back and forth along the water, most of them outside of the navigation channel and none of them requiring me to take any kind of action to get out of their way.

I was hoping that would be the case for the rest of the day, and it sure seemed like it until I got to an area around mile marker 476, where it was obvious there was a *ton* of towboat and barge action going on.

I was a bit concerned since as luck would have it, I had a 10:30 a.m. radio interview with Jeff Angelo of WHO Radio in Des Moines, and then right after that, Joe Soucheray and the gang from Garage Logic. I needed to focus on these interviews and keep well out of the way of the busy traffic that was happening all along the route.

I was able to finish the interview with Jeff with no problems. It was a fun interview, and he was a good chat and obviously quick to understand Spare Key, the purpose of the trip, and how to share information with his audience in a way that didn't feel cramped or rushed.

After the interview was over, I received the expected call from Chris Reuvers with Garage Logic. I had shared with Chris the antics of the past few days: getting stuck in mud, nearly being blown over, and falling in the river the previous day. Joe, as only Joe can do, moaned and asked again when I would end the trip and go home and be safe.

I have a lot of fun on these calls with Joe and his Garage band. The guys are smart, casual, funny, and quick. I have known most of them for decades, so it often feels like I am talking to an old friend, which makes the interview fun for me.

On this particular day, the fun got combined with a couple minutes of anxiety as I saw not one, not two, but four towboats either coming either directly at me or cutting directly in front of me as I was working to finish up the interview with Garage Logic. To my surprise, each of them suddenly pulled over and out of my way and stopped.

The crews from each towboat waved at me, and some were taking pictures, but all were smiling and friendly. They had obviously seen me coming or heard I was coming and were kind enough to allow me to proceed without having to avoid them.

It was a good thing that I hung up the Garage Logic interview when I did. I teared up a bit out of simple gratitude for the good will of those on board the tugs. Maybe I was tired, maybe a bit worn out and river-weary, but the fact is that they reminded me again of the hope of this trip, and of the people who have extended so many kindnesses and courtesies my way.

They of course did not need to get out of my way. Although we all share the river, my use of the river was something temporary, and in due time my journey would come to an end. But for them, it is their livelihood. It's how they put food on their table, pay their bills, and build their own part of the American Dream. In the navigation channel it was me, not them, that should have moved out of the way. That fact that each one of those towboats took the time and effort to allow me to pass through without having to deal with their wake was a wonderful gift for my heart that day.

I took a minute to collect my thoughts and then proceeded to my location for the day, Kelly's Landing. As I approached my exit from the channel, I had to make a sharp left to get through an opening in between two little islands. As I did and shot through them, I could see the fuel dock where I would pull in for the day and ultimately, would spend the evening.

Once I got in and tied up, I began to put things in place. I looked around the location to get my bearings and then walked about a half mile into the town of Andalusia, which has a population of about 1,400 people. I grabbed a bite for lunch at Luebbe's Restaurant and then stopped over across the street to the gas station and grabbed some drinking water and nightcrawlers. I figured since I would be hanging out for the night in this area abutting the Andalusia Slough, I should try my luck at fishing.

My luck was, as usual, lousy. A few nibbles but not much more than that.

I had a nice, hour-long phone conversation with Owen about the day, about history, about how to melt cheese for his sandwich, and the current political situation in America. Owen is always a blast to talk to. He is funny, quick, and wicked smart. I missed him and his wit and it was well worth staying up later than usual to hear his voice.

After we hung up, I got myself put together for the night; I wanted to leave early in the day to test out the fuel consumption of the Nissan. Not too far ahead, as I came off the upper river and began to journey into the lower river, the lack of readily available fuel was going to be a challenge. I needed to have a better sense of how much fuel both motors consumed to try to measure just how much fuel I would need to carry on the raft. So, after making sure everything was tied up, the signs were slid into their channels, and the bed was inflated, I tucked in for the night.

About 4:00 a.m., I woke up shivering like crazy. It was *cold!* I checked my phone and it said it was hovering at around forty degrees and I believed it! Not only that, but the back windows leave a crack open of about four inches and I forgot to put anything in to block the breeze. I got up, threw on another coat, and crawled back into my sleeping bag. It must have worked because I woke up about an hour later. It was still cold, so I tried to plug in the space heater I had purchased several stops earlier.

The damn thing kept stopping.

It was at this point, of course, that I learned something else new.

The power draw of the space heater was too much for the power pack, which was why it would not stay running. I only figured this out after I started up the generator and plugged in the heater, only to hear it laboring to run.

Oh well!

I made my coffee and readied the rest of the raft. At about eight o'clock, I ambled out of the slough under the noisy power of the Nissan at about two knots.

Once through the slough I powered up to four knots and kept it there.

The weather and the water were simply perfect! Barely a breeze, the water was glass, and nobody was in sight behind me or ahead of me.

This was the perfect day to begin to test the fuel consumption of the Nissan. About an hour into the trip, I looked behind me and saw a kayak piloted by a guy with a hat on. I stopped the motor and he slid up beside me.

His name was Kevin, and he was traveling from Itasca to St. Louis in his kayak. Just because.

I told him I thought he was pretty brave considering how low in the water the kayak sits. We both agreed that the weather had been bad for us and that it was pleasure boats, not towboats and barges, that caused us the most grief. After a few more minutes of banter, we wished one another well and went off into our own paths in the channel.

About two hours into the trip, I saw my stop in Muscatine, Iowa: the Fairport Landing Marina. My brother Hans and my sister-in-law Julie were going to meet me there while traveling south and bring me supplies, as well as take some of my excess equipment back home with them.

As I pulled in for the day, the owner of the marina came up to help me tie up and get fuel. Along the way I had lost one of the plugs to my gas can and unless I could get the right type to keep the fuel port of the tank plugged, the gas would leak out. Thankfully, the marina owner had an extra one and we were able to fill the tanks.

Not long after that, Hans and Julie showed up. I was glad to see them both!

They brought me the additional gas tanks I would need for the lower river, and I handed them a bunch of things I simply no longer had room to carry. We hurried into town and stopped at Walmart, where I picked up a cot to replace the third air mattress that had failed me and some snacks for along the way.

We visited for a while, and then Hans and Julie had to get underway to continue to Nashville where they were meeting one of their daughters. We said our goodbyes and I went about tidying up the raft, securing my new purchases, and doing some writing.

The evening was quiet and calm, and I spent time at the Torchlight Restaurant, which is onsite at the Fairport Landing Marina. Onboard the raft, all four fuel tanks were full: nearly fifty gallons of mixed fuel and eight gallons of regular fuel. Tomorrow would be a long and productive day, I hoped, of moving farther down the river. I planned to travel nearly fifty miles to reach Oquawka, Illinois, and a place called Sum-R-Daze Marina. As I did every evening, I hoped for "fair winds and following seas" in the morning as I drifted off to sleep.

Chapter 14
An Elephant of a Story

The glory of the morning in Muscatine was simply wondrous. I awoke early to prepare to be on the river at first intense light. I began my morning ritual:

Make sure both motors start.

Make sure that all my navigational tools, communications equipment, and digital maps are fully charged and in working condition.

Retrace my planned route for the day. I typically did that about a dozen times, as I was sure the first eleven times I calculated something incorrectly.

If I knew I would be traveling through a lock and dam, I removed all the acrylic windows and detachable screens on the back five windows.

I took a bungee cord and made sure that the port and starboard screen doors were open, and that the front screen door was open as well.

I said a prayer to God to give me wisdom, courage, and bravery, and that I would avoid moments of sheer panic and terror. And, if sheer panic and terror must be had, that I would have the wisdom, courage, and bravery to confront it.

Last, I heated water for my coffee and sat back for fifteen minutes to simply be calm.

As I sat back, I decided to do a time-lapse video of the rising sun and take my other phone and start a Facebook Live to allow others to see the great beginning of the day. Just moments earlier, a large towboat with about twelve barges began moving upriver next to the marina where I was docked. It was such a confluence of Mother Nature and human-made wonder that it was hard to comprehend this early this morning. Especially before I had a full cup of coffee!

My goal that day was to reach the Sum-R-Daze Marina. To travel the fifty miles, I would need to navigate through Locks Number 16 and 17, but the weather forecast was promising, the wind was light, and I was confident that if I could lock through quickly, I could get ahead of much of the stronger wind that was expected that day farther down the river.

Once the tow and barge passed by, I collected both of my phones, secured them, and prepared for my departure. The day before, when I pulled into the slip, I'd had to come in from above it—in other words, I had to go back upriver and approach from the north. While the current hadn't been fast, it was strong. I'd had to throttle up to get the nose of the SS Hail Mary into the slip while Tim, the marina owner, grabbed the front. He then pulled it forward and I had to throttle up again and shove the motor in the other direction to bring the rear of the raft to the same side as the bow.

It had taken a bit of effort, but we had finally been able to secure her.

This morning, without Tim's assistance, I would need to motor quickly, and straight out, to prevent the port side of the raft from slamming into the ship tied up next to me. I untied the front of the raft and held on to the rope as tightly as I could, then quickly did the same with the starboard rear side. Then I jumped through the starboard door, where the kicker motor was already in idle. I slid the kicker into reverse, powered up, and was able to back out without incident.

As I pivoted the raft to the starboard and upriver, I shared with those watching my livestream on Facebook another couple minutes of the beautiful rising sun. Then I throttled up the Nissan, turned off the kicker motor, and turned the raft into the channel to head south.

I would encounter Lock and Dam Number 16 a few miles from Muscatine, and as I moved further in its direction, I enjoyed the calm breeze and water that looked like glass. I had the Nissan moving at a six mile-per-hour clip.

I was still trying to figure out, roughly three weeks from the day I left St. Paul, the balance between drifting, floating, and motoring. To be candid, the difficulty in simply drifting or floating in the waters north of St. Louis had been a challenge for three reasons. First, as described earlier, was the presence of significantly large pools of water above and below the locks and dams, which I needed to actively traverse. Second was the tremendous number of pleasure craft, with wake, that required evasive action. Third was the need to navigate through and around the locks and dams, along with towboats and barges I encountered.

Unfortunately, even with the use of the motors, my progress was slow. I had averaged only about twenty miles a day, which caused me to re-evaluate the amount of time I would be on the river before I got to Baton Rouge. It was my hope that once I was past the lock and dam system, and into the faster waters south of St. Louis, I could make more time and spend more time drifting.

Today would be a perfect example of that *not* happening.

As I prepared to enter the pool above Lock and Dam Number 16, I called the lock and dam on the phone rather than the radio. I had found this method to be more successful than attempting to reach the operators by radio. It might well have been a function of the distance of my radio signal, but it could also have been that until you are close enough to be in view of the lock, or within proximity of entering it, the operators are dealing with other issues.

I don't really know, because it has been six of one and a half dozen of the other at different times. In any case, on that particular day I was told that a tow and barge were locking through so it would take about an hour. I asked for advice on where to wait and was told to stay on the starboard side, near or behind the green buoys. That made sense, and it was what I did for over an hour until I saw the tow make it through and begin to make its way upriver.

I sped forward and let the operator know I was on my way. He indicated that he would get me into the lock as soon as I arrived. At this point it was clear that the wind was picking up and the weather was starting to deteriorate.

It took me a bit longer than I anticipated but I finally made it into the lock. They told me that I wouldn't be using a rope; rather, I would "float" in the middle of the lock.

Floating means just that. You sit in the middle of the lock in the water and wait until you are lowered, then you start your motor back up and motor through.

Here's the problem with that concept and the SS Hail Mary: she didn't float in place!

The design of the raft was such that it was top-heavy and could quickly catch wind. Often in these kinds of spaces, what might be a relatively uneventful wind gust for a large cruiser ended up spinning me around.

And that is what started to happen. The raft started to spin to starboard.

I decided I'd had enough before it got to be too much. I toggled channel 14 on the radio and asked for a rope to be thrown down. The operator complied immediately, and I grabbed the rope and held on tightly. I pulled the raft into the wall and waited. After a couple of minutes, the gates in front of me began to open.

And then trouble started.

I could tell that the turbulence at the exit was much rougher than usual.

But to make matters more challenging, directly in front of me was a tow pushing barges straight into the lock I was getting ready to leave! I figured I would need extra power, so I throttled up the kicker motor as I started the Nissan.

Except the Nissan didn't start.

And it wouldn't start.

The turbulence grew worse, and what made it even more difficult was that the tow was clearly advancing without regard to the challenges I was dealing with. Significant turbulence. High wind. Big waves.

The raft began to bounce from port to starboard and wasn't picking up speed quickly enough to get through the waves. I tried the Nissan again and again and again and nothing.

I could tell it was flooded but I couldn't understand why. After having run just fine for the hour or so previously, the motor was now refusing to catch.

The tow then blew its horn to warn me to get away from it. Believe me, I wanted to be nowhere near it!

The problem was that the wind was pushing me toward it while the waves were keeping me from making progress. I was also seeing out the corner of my eye that I was still way too close to the base of the dam for comfort.

In this chaos I knocked over my chair near the steering wheel, groaned a bit, and finally got into calm enough water to be able to get the raft's nose into the wind. This reduced the sail effect of it, and I made some forward progress.

After a few hundred yards of being definitely clear of the dam and the churn of the tow and barge, I quickly stepped to the back of the raft, unscrewed the gas cap to the Nissan's tank, and repumped the fuel bulb. After two attempts, it caught, and I then threw the idle switch up to increase the idle and let it run like that for about a minute. As soon as I idled down, I threw her into gear and went forward, picking up my pace from six to seven miles per hour.

I wanted to get plenty of fuel running through the motor, making it hot enough to keep firing without worrying if it was going to stall out on me. I then proceeded down the river for several miles at that pace, inside channels that wound around but were also relatively calm. After a few miles, the mouth of the river got bigger.

The wind, too, began to pick up in earnest, pushing at me from the east and the south and then together. In this kind of situation, the wind basically forced me backward while at the same time pushing up against the water and creating a churn of waves that eventually became white-caps and started to roll right at me.

A regular boat doesn't have many issues with this kind of situation.

I am not on, as you know, a regular boat.

The SS Hail Mary doesn't plane, and she doesn't knife cleanly into waves. She kind of grunts and groans and plows into them. Intermittently the raft will shudder, and the steering column itself will shake as water pushes up beneath the steering console and ends up atop the floor, soaking my feet.

As I continued to plow forward, I thought of how much further I had to go. First I needed to get through Lock and Dam Number 17, then I had to proceed another twenty-two miles to get to the Sum-R-Daze Marina in Oquawka.

Another twenty-two miles of the blustery south wind and waves seemed pretty daunting. However, I had decided to make that stretch today. I had plenty of fuel and figured that if I just proceeded carefully and with purpose, I would get to my location with much of the day still intact.

I got to Lock and Dam Number 17 after about an hour, called on the phone, and got clearance to proceed. Once into the lock, I was again instructed to float in the pool. I commented that I didn't know if that would be such a good idea given my raft, but by then the operator had gone back to monitor the closing of the gates.

At this point, I did call him on the radio and request a dropped line.

He provided me one but at this particular lock and dam, the wind simply would not quit. As tightly as I held onto the line, my front end would not cooperate and began to spin out into the lock pool. My plan to chalk the wall seemed awfully quaint and unnecessary at this point and given that I did not want to have the front of my raft suddenly facing the back of the lock, I let go of the rope, turned on the kicker, and throttled my nose back to port to get straightened out.

Luck was on my side with this lock and as I straightened out the raft, the front gates began to open. Before proceeding forward, I turned on the Nissan and used both motors to get me through the lock quickly and out without any further incident.

Two down! No more to go—for today!

Now I just had the remaining miles to Oquawka and the wind and the waves to contend with. It was a struggle to move forward, as the wind was pushing me to the side while I tried to cut through the ever-increasing height and intensity of the waves.

Pulling the 1970 Kayot aka the SS Hail Mary to St. Paul

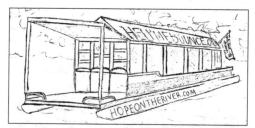

Original rendition of the SS Hail Mary by Maisie Mische

Owen Mische pondering his work on the SS Hail Mary

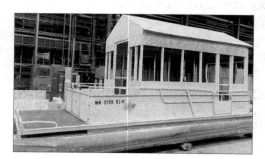

The SS Hail Mary from the Port

The SS Hail Mary from Starboard

Dry dock where the SS Hail Mary was built

Members of the Build Team inspecting the floorboards

Looking dapper at the South St. Paul launch site

Television stations onsite to see if the raft will float!

The Build Team celebrating a successful test launch!

Our signs are complete thanks to ASI Signage Innovations, Minnesota

The SS Hail Mary at port at the Padelford River-boat Company

The SS Hail Mary towed by the Padelford Riverboat on Launch Day

Crew of Red Wing River Valley Power & Sport

My food bins - ramen, MRE's, and SPAM!

Being towed after a near disaster on Lake Pepin

Pirate's Pit Stop, North Buena Vista, Iowa

One of my chalk drawings celebrating my arrival at a Lock and Dam

Captain Erich at the controls of the SS Hail Mary

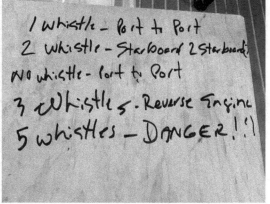

My table with the whistle commands and meanings

Captain Gus Gaspardo as we leave
Grafton Marina

Failed "Rubber in a Can" effort to stop the leaks

My successful parking of the raft for the first time!

Each house represents someone who
helped me along the way

My favorite picture of my trip taken by Captain
Michael Coyle

Gus Gaspardo, Bob Deck and I in St. Louis

Karl and I parked at the Kaskaskia
River Lock and Dam

Riverboat Captain Michael Coyle

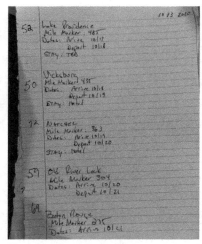

The schedule of our final stops to Baton Rouge

My brother, Karl, watching for towboats

On the rocks at Caruthersville, Missouri

I look like a Riverboat Captain!

Locking through a lock and dam

Final photo of the SS Hail Mary on the Mississippi River

The SS Hail Mary leaves Baton Rouge Harbor

My brother Karl and I in Baton Rouge

Louisiana Secretary of State R. Kyle Ardoin and me

Spare Key now registered to serve in all 50 states and D.C.

Me!

Sailor making sure it's me after two months away

I started to think about my backup stop, a place called Keithsburg. I had seen and read about it and it appeared to have some potential for me to at least tie up for a while and switch out my ever-diminishing fuel tank that was powering the Nissan. Soon enough, I saw the Keithsburg railroad bridge and began to shift my raft to the port side to line up with anything I thought I might see in the city.

What I saw was not promising. First, the wind was still shoving me rudely all over the place. Second, I saw a massive sandbar that looked like it was nearly vertical at ninety degrees. Third, the little dock I did see was near a boat ramp and I couldn't make out whether or not it was deep enough or protected enough for me to circle in and dock.

A crowd began to gather on the shoreline where the campground above the sandbar stood. This, of course, only served to make me more nervous and anxious about the situation. After a couple of minutes of indecision, I finally decided to turn the raft back into the channel and stick to my plan—on to Sum-R-Daze, which was a good ten miles ahead of me.

I plowed ahead in search of calmer water. I knew that the Nissan tank was getting low and I didn't want to be going through this water and have it come up empty! I must admit the process of switching out gas tanks, one of which weighed seventy-two pounds, in a raft on the water had its own moments of peril. I readily admit that it wasn't the smartest or safest thing to do, but at the moment I simply wanted the comfort of a full tank of fuel to finish this trip to the marina.

I took my time and unhooked the existing tank. I then removed the nozzle and replaced it with a screw to keep the extra gas from coming out. Then I took the nozzle, put it on the full can, and heaved it over the frame of the back between the windows. I got it tied down, hooked it up to the motor, primed the fuel bulb, and quickly attempted to start it.

Once. Twice. Three times.

Finally, it fired! I threw the idle switch up hard to keep it chugging and then moved all the empty tanks and detritus out from underfoot and proceeded south with the Nissan running hard. Every wave hit hard and as it did, I winced—thinking that another ten gallons of water was getting into the tubes. But I had committed to this course of action, and I was going to get to the marina today before dark and be done with the day!

Finally, I was within three miles of the marina and slowed down the motor to a five mile-per-hour crawl. I backed off the throttle because I wanted to give the tubes a break, too. Within a half mile of the marina, I called Rhonda, who with her husband Paul owns Sum-R-Daze Marina. She answered and was delighted to hear that I was close by.

She gave me great instructions on how to proceed downriver and then come upriver and at an angle into the marina. I slowly powered in and slid into the slip; she grabbed the raft and I was locked in! I jumped out, gave her a fist bump, and told her how thrilled I was to be there and that I needed to hurry up and pump out the tubes!

She laughed and told me that she had other errands to run that day and simply to make myself at home.

I got my pump and carefully removed the spigot cap, placing it safely inside the raft. I primed the pump, slid the hose down the tube, and the water began to flow. Surprisingly, as was the case for the past few weeks, the amount of water drawn stayed fairly consistent. I got twelve to fifteen gallons out of the starboard tube, and five to seven gallons out of the port tube. It varied a few gallons here and there but overall stayed remarkably the same.

I didn't want to jinx myself, but I felt that if this was the extent of the leak after a hard run of fifty miles, I could probably manage the process of water removal as long as I had access to the tubes and to power.

The challenge, however, would be that further down the river, as marinas became scarce and I had to slide the raft to the shoreline for the night, I likely would not have unimpeded access to the tube tops even if I had access to generator power. That could be a problem, and one I was hoping to fix.

Eventually I got the raft squared away. I had asked Rhonda if I could stay for two nights, and she readily agreed and told me it was free. Plus, they had a clubhouse with a shower! *Glory!*

I cleaned up and walked into town, about a mile away, and picked up some water and snacks. But before my night was done, I would be doing a Zoom call with some of the folks who have been with me on this journey from the beginning.

The topic: How to fuel the raft past St. Louis!

It was a topic I knew had to be discussed but one that, given everything else I had been dealing with, I just hadn't had time to focus on.

Now, with St. Louis about a week away, I had no choice.

I reached out to Fred, Owen, John Apitz, Dave Ritter (my wife's cousin's husband), and Gus Gaspardo. Each of them was intimately aware of the details of the trip from the beginning and I trusted their judgement and advice. They did not disappoint.

Dave estimated that I would need about ninety gallons to make it from the last fuel stop, Hoppies Marina in Missouri, to Memphis. Fortunately, my Hans and Julie had brought me the additional tanks that allowed me to get to ninety-gallon capacity. Gus thought the solution would ultimately take care of itself and I would figure it out along the way. I trusted Gus and he had been right about what it was I had to learn, when I learned it, and how I learned it. He told me that nobody learns without the mistakes.

I should be a genius soon enough!

Once we resolved the fuel situation, we talked about where I would dock downriver and how to handle the incessant nosediving up and down of the raft—known as "porpoise-ing"—along with a variety of other issues. Gus planned to meet me in St. Louis and help me through the city. I could not have been more grateful. It was truly a relief to know I would have his wisdom and guidance through what I could only imagine was going to be an absolute minefield of tows and barges.

By the time we finished the call, we had figured out a few things, including some of the specific cities I would need to stop at past St. Louis. The dates and specific locations remained to be determined. This much, however, was true: without those folks, and others, I would not have succeeded. Their friendship, encouragement, kindness, and wisdom were critical to the Hope on the River effort having any chance of coming to a successful conclusion. In the end, it wouldn't be any lack of effort or support on their part that decided the outcome. The Good Lord and how he guided me along the way determined when the trip, and how the trip, came to its conclusion.

With the Zoom call done, I was beat! It was time to call it a night, and I did.

The upside of that busy and eventful day was that I didn't have anywhere to go the next day! So whether I slept in or didn't, I had a lazy morning to look forward to and a full day to prepare for the next phase of the journey.

The next morning, I got a text from Rhonda apologizing for not being able to spend more time with me. Goodness gracious! Clearly no apology was necessary. She was so kind to allow me to stay at this beautiful marina, I could not thank her enough. I did text her back and ask if she had a wagon or wheelbarrow I could use. I had an empty fuel tank I wanted to fill and if I could haul it into town, I could take care of it on my own.

Ten minutes later a guy named Larry Carlson showed up. Larry was and is a gem! He gave me a ride into town so I could get gas and groceries, then we headed back to the marina. This grandfather of thirteen was clearly proud of his family. He is a retired engineer with the Burlington Northern Railroad and has a deep connection to this community and the river. As we sat and chatted for a while about my trip and what I had seen so far, he shared with me an amazing story of a circus elephant, Norma Jean, that had been tied up to a tree in an Oquawka community park, hit by lightning, and died instantly. I cannot do justice to the story, but it was crazy!

After the elephant was killed, the city showed up and dug a big hole and pushed the poor beast into it and buried it. Obviously, the story doesn't end here!

An actual memorial was erected, and Larry told me to get in his car and we drove to see it. Sure enough, there it was in all its glory – a large and impressive memorial to the Elephant Norma Jean! Norma Jean's memorial was something any human would have been proud to have had erected in their honor. After that adventure, Larry took his leave and told me he would back around 4:30 p.m. to bring me a tenderloin sandwich. I couldn't argue with that.

So I continued to do some work, get some writing done, and make phone calls. Larry showed up with a breaded pork tenderloin sandwich as big as a catcher's mitt and smothered with pickles and onions! It was made by a couple of guys down at the local gas station and it was *amazing*. I devoured it, and then we sat around and I had a scotch, he had a rum-and-something, and we chatted about life and the world.

At about six o'clock, Rhonda arrived with her husband Paul. For the next several hours we had a delightful time! A conversation about the world, about politics (but not too much), the river and accidents and adventures that we had all been on throughout the years. I really enjoyed my time with the three of them. They are all accomplished people, proud of their community, their neighbors, their family, and the jobs and businesses they have worked and built. After a few hours Paul suggested I spend the night in the clubhouse and I quickly agreed. Spending the night in a warm place instead of the cold raft sounded perfect given my early morning departure.

We said our goodbyes and I thanked them profusely for their kindness, their generosity, and the amazing story I would carry with me for the rest of my life.

I awoke at 5:00 a.m., made some coffee, and gathered my belongings. As soon as the light began to poke through, I hurried down to the raft and got ready to go. I started both motors... got the windows and screens and doors ready... made sure that my newly filled fuel tank was secured... and prepared to make way.

The weather was perfect. There was barely any wind, the water was nearly glass, and it seemed like I had nothing in front of me except Keokuk, Iowa, which was an "easy" fifty miles ahead. I left the dock around

7:30 a.m. and around an hour later came upon Lock and Dam 18. I radioed ahead and they told me to proceed forward.

Once there, they threw down a line, and I turned off both motors and waited as the raft lowered down to match the water in the pool outside the lock and dam. Cody and Jim were the operators, and they could not have been kinder or more helpful. Within fifteen minutes, I was ready to go but again I had an issue with the Nissan similar to the previous day's issue in Locks 16 and 17.

She would not start.

I couldn't believe it, but I wasn't going to wait around, either. I floored the kicker and away we went. Once I was past the dam and in calmer water, I played around with the Nissan and finally got it to fire and stay running. I then shoved the throttle up to seven miles per hour and decided to keep it there for as long as I could go or the tank ran out, whichever came first.

Along the way I encountered several tows and barges, including two that were passing under Burlington's railroad swing bridge. Both ship's captains were kind enough to provide polite guidance as to where they wanted me to wait, and once they went past, I thanked them and motored on.

My next big moment was going to be the Fort Madison Swing bridge. According to my charts, it showed an elevation of thirteen feet. I had taken great pains to measure the height of the raft multiple times and decided to add an inch or two. I felt confident in my mind that the SS Hail Mary was ten-and-a-half feet high, which would give me more than enough room to get under the Fort Madison bridge.

But people had warned me that water levels change—that wakes and waves can move you up and down—and pretty soon I was convinced I was going to slam into the bridge!

A few days earlier, a bridge operator up the river had shared some pictures of me coming through the lock and dam near his bridge. He and I chatted on Facebook and he encouraged me to call ahead to the Fort Madison bridge operator on my radio to ask for guidance.

As I began to approach the bridge, I have to admit it did not look like I was going to make it under. In fact, I was starting to doubt my own measurements. Add to that a tow and barge coming through. At about that same time, the Nissan started sputtering and choking and threatening to stop.

I turned on the kicker and got her up to equal speed as the Nissan just to make sure I was definitely under power. As soon as the tow got past me, I called the bridge operator and requested guidance and assistance.

Unfortunately, for the first time on the trip, someone I reached out to for help would not give it.

The bridge operator was short, curt, and essentially told me I would find out soon enough if I was short enough to pass. Furthermore, she indicated that there was nothing she could do to assist me because a train was passing over the bridge and there was an unlimited amount of other traffic that would need to pass through before she could swing the bridge if it needed to be swung.

I was in a pickle, frustrated, and mostly just concerned about the raft's height and the Nissan's condition and how long it might take before the bridge operator actually would be willing to swing the bridge for me.

I finally got a call on the radio from someone who said, "Pleasure craft raft with a height of ten-and-a-half feet, you should be just fine given that the height of the bridge is thirteen feet. Proceed slowly and you will be fine. Next time, I would advise you to get a navigation chart so you know the height of the bridge."

I had no intention of telling him I did have those charts and I knew the height. I simply thanked him profusely and proceeded forward. He then indicated he had heard about my trip and wished me the best going the rest of the way.

I slowly proceeded forward and at the moment in which impact would occur if I was too high, I closed my eyes, gritted my teeth, and prepared to shove the kicker into reverse.

Slowly, but surely, I got through it and breathed a sigh of relief!

That being said, the Nissan was still sputtering.

I had been texting people I knew all day asking for suggestions. In the end, the suggestions all came back to things related to fuel. Either the mixture was too rich, the tank wasn't working right, the tank valve to release vacuum pressure needed to be adjusted... I ran the motor hard to burn out any potential carbon but each time I brought it back to between six and seven-and-a-half miles per hour, the motor would sputter.

Finally, I got the motor to stick at six miles per hour and I did not appear to have any problems. This was good news, as the next ten miles or so would be vast areas of very wide sections of the river exposed to wind and rough water, so the Nissan was going to be important. That being said, the weather was fantastic. There was virtually no wind, and the water was mostly calm. I was making good time. Yet the Nissan acting up was a problem that I needed to resolve, especially since the next day I would be tackling another lock and dam and a big one at that!

Finally, around 3:00 p.m., I spotted Keokuk Yacht Club and called ahead to get guidance on how to approach the marina. Once in the marina, I paid my bill for the slip and immediately pulled water from the tubes. Again, it was around twelve gallons in the starboard and about half that much in the port. This despite having had the tubes underwater a great deal because of needing to keep the Nissan up to full throttle to deal with the sputtering.

An hour or so later, Brad Mader from River Valley Power and Sport and I connected by Facebook and then by phone. He thought that the problem might be the fuel filter and called me to guide me to the source of the issue and how to resolve it. To be honest, replacing the fuel filter might as well be doing heart surgery for me. I didn't know the first thing about it. Brad assured me that the fix was simple, and that any hardware store should have the filter I needed.

I went into the marina and asked the young man operating the bar if he could help me get a ride to the local auto parts store. He arranged for a guy named Roger to bring me, and Roger was a delight. Born and raised in Keokuk, he had worked for the past ten years for a family-owned business driving a truck for their products.

He got me to the store, and after I purchased what I needed and came out, he handed me twenty dollars for Spare Key. He told me he appreciated the organization and the trip I was on.

Hope. On. The. River.

Roger dropped me off and I thanked him again.

I got to the boat motor and gave some thought to the project ahead of me. As I began to replace the filter, I made sure to pay close attention to how the old one was installed so I could replicate it with the new one.

Unfortunately, the new ones I got were too big.

Arrrgggh!

I called the parts store and they assured me they had the smaller size I needed, so I approached the bartender again, who told me to ask Josh, one of the patrons at the bar, to drive me up.

I meekly approached Josh, explained the situation, and in no time he and I were on our way back to the auto parts store.

The young man at the auto parts store made quick work of the exchange, instructed me on how to replace the part, and away Josh and I went back to the marina. In ten minutes, I got the fuel filter replaced and then, at Brad's suggestion, I also replaced the spark plugs.

I turned the key and waited, and it started! It started!!!

The filter clearly had been dirty. The question was, when I was back on the water the next day, would this be the solution to the problem?

Who knew? Tomorrow is always a new day and a new adventure.

Chapter 15
DIY on the Big Muddy

This day would be like no other so far on my journey. First, of course, I awoke to a glorious morning in Keokuk. The sunrise was punctuated by the deep, hazy smoke of wildfires half a country away. It reminded me again that nature—resilient, brilliant, and ultimately untamed—pushes back against that which man has made, time and time again.

This would be a different day for another reason, too.

Lock and Dam Number 19!

Since my journey began, I had locked through seventeen dams. The only lock I did not go through was in St. Paul, Minnesota, near the Ford Bridge, because my journey started downriver of that lock, on Harriet Island at Padelford Landing. Each of the seventeen dams has had its own unique character, people, and of course challenges for me.

But all of them were generally the same size and required the same type of process to approach, enter, lock, and exit. I would call ahead to let them know I was coming. They would give the go-ahead for proceeding forward as they prepared the lock or else said to wait for other traffic to work its way through. Once given clearance to proceed into the lock, I would head in, grab onto a rope or float in the lock chamber, and wait to be lowered to about ten feet. Once lowered, I would power up and exit the lock.

The difference with Lock 19 was threefold: its chamber was twice as long as the other locks at 1,200 feet; it had a drop of more than thirty feet; and, instead of floating or holding onto a line thrown over the side, I would have to hang onto, or tie onto, a floating bollard.

A floating bollard???

Everyone I had spoken to who has gone down the river, or who knows someone who has gone or imagined themselves going down the river, has an opinion on this kind of lock and dam. Nearly all of them suggested I was in for quite a ride—and the definition of what this meant was up to your own interpretation.

In my mind, it sounded terrifying.

So much so that I didn't sleep well the night before, and I couldn't wait for 7:00 a.m. to come around so I could call the lock and dam and plead for their assistance.

I got up early and put everything in its proper place. I got my coffee, took some photos and videos of the morning sky made brilliant by distant wildfires, and waited impatiently for the clock to turn.

You might remember that I had been having issues with the Nissan the day before and had to change the fuel filter and spark plugs.

That, too, was making me queasy. While I got the motor to start easily enough in the morning—in fact, on the first turn of the key—I wasn't confident that my mechanical skills were what had done the trick. The Nissan seemed to be idling fine and, perhaps, even a bit smoother than previously. But until I got out on the water and throttled up, I would not know.

I am, by nature, pretty superstitious. Not in the kind of way that has me wearing the same pair of underwear for months at a time or scream-ing in terror when a black cat walks across my path. More in the way of assuming that something I'm not sure will work works until it does, indeed, actually work. It's a way of life that has served me well for fifty-seven years. It's why I don't plan to die until I am one hundred. And, until I get there, I don't plan to think it's going to happen until it does, indeed, actually happen!

The clock turned to 7:00 a.m. and I jumped on the phone. Anxious-ly, I waited for the someone to pick up. A guy named Mike answered and I explained my situation.

"Mike, I'm a guy on the river in a homemade raft built on top of a pontoon boat and I have two motors, a 60 HP two-stroke Nissan and a 9.9 HP Mercury kicker and I am at Keokuk Yacht Club getting ready to proceed to your location and I have been through seventeen locks and dams but never any like yours and I have to be honest I am a bit worried about how all of this is going to work and a bit nervous that I am going to screw it up and I wanted to see if there is any traffic coming through right now and if so how long will it be and would you be able to help me figure out how to use the floating bollard system so I don't mess up when I get there?"

(Please note that I did, indeed, say all of this in one breath for the editors out there. Therefore, no commas are required!)

Mike chuckled a bit and explained to me that there was a tow working through, that I should proceed on down, and he would make sure I was taken care of when I got there. He also said that another ship had called earlier from my same location and was headed towards the lock and dam, and I should follow them down.

As he shared this information, I saw the sixty-four-foot cruiser from Stillwater that had tied up about an hour after I arrived at Keokuk the day before. She was beautiful, and she was big, and I would need ten motors to follow her anywhere! I figured if I got going now, I could at least see what they were doing to get a sense of how to approach the lock and dam.

I thanked Mike, got the motors back on, and began my slow journey through the Keokuk Yacht Club's harbor channel.

So far so good with the Nissan. I got it up to about seven miles per hour, and it seemed to be firing fine. But I had decided the night before that I would keep it idling while in the lock and dam and ask forgiveness later. (Typically you are asked to turn off the motors, but I didn't want to be sitting in that massive structure with only the kicker motor to get me out. I had done that before on smaller locks, and it wasn't fun.)

As I got closer to the lock and dam, I suddenly appreciated just how massive this structure really was. To the left of the actual lock and dam is the huge Soviet-style Keokuk Plant, a hydroelectric facility. It is an imposing facility by itself. When coupled with the equally imposing concrete and steel giant that is Lock and Dam Number 19, it renders my little raft to a speck of dust on the water.

I radioed to say I was just on the facility's outskirts and given that a tow and barge was coming out, asked which side they wanted me on.

They instructed me to stay to the green buoys and near what are called the "cells," which I now know are numbered areas that indicate where you are in relation to reaching the entrance. I putted around out there for a good twenty minutes, keeping the Nissan running at low speed and waiting for the towboat to come through and the light to turn green to permit me to enter the chamber.

I had one radio on channel 14, the lock and dam channel, and heard the tow's captain indicate he was prepared to move through.

The operators gave him clearance and then added, "Hey Captain, there's a small homemade pleasure craft outside on your port side, and I know he sure would appreciate it if you steered clear of him at the lowest speed you can manage."

I heard the captain laugh and say, "Will do, and thanks for the head's up!" I would have chimed in to thank them both, but the light turned green at the point, and I needed to move and slide past the port side of the tow and into the channel.

As I approached, the anxiety increased in my chest. The fact is, the angle of the entrance to the chamber was hidden from the angle I was approaching. I was staying as close to the green buoys as I could without going into shallow water. I had been instructed to avoid, at all costs, getting too close to the Keokuk Plant. The reason given was that the turbulence and suction was so strong that it might grab me and pull me in and under.

Um, NO! With that kind of warning, I sure as heck was going to be careful!

As I approached, I saw two men, a younger guy and an older one. The younger one I assumed was Mike. Both of them were watching me intently come in, and as I did, I turned the Nissan to idle and kept the kicker motor pushing me forward. The older guy asked if I had called earlier that morning and I nodded, and the younger guy told me to follow him down on the three-wheeled bicycle he was on, which allowed him to move quickly up and down the platform of the lock.

As we went forward, I told him I had never done this kind of lock before. He told me not to worry and that he would show me how to do it. We arrived about one hundred feet behind the sixty-four-foot cruiser that had gone before me in the morning.

(A side note: A reminder here that the race isn't always won by the fastest. While the sixty-four-foot cruiser was faster and bigger than the SS Hail Mary and had a half hour head start on me to the lock and dam, the fact is, if there was traffic in the lock, nobody got through until it was their turn. I felt slightly smug that that big boat wasn't getting through that lock and dam any faster than me despite its large size and superior speed.)

As the raft came to a crawl, Mike indicated that I should take the piece of rope I had in my hand and simply throw it around the top of the floating bollard.

It was time. I would meet the floating bollard.

And there it was!

It was a massive round cylinder with a head on it that you tossed your rope around and then held on to. The way the process worked, according to Mike, was that I could either tie it onto the raft or simply hold onto it. (I didn't want to tie onto the bollard. Too many warnings from folks telling me that people forgot to remove a rope as the water receded and left their boat hanging in the air!)

As the water level decreased, the bollard and you and the rope and the raft would go down with it, but in a slow and controlled way. Mike also told me that the chamber wouldn't have any kind of turbulence or wind in it, so it should be a smooth ride all the way down.

I thanked him, and he assured me I would be okay. He told me that he was glad he could help and that everyone had to go through this kind of lock and dam if they traveled on the river. Finally, the back gates closed and the water began to lower. The descent was completely smooth, and I thought it was a lot easier to deal with than the other seventeen locks and dams I had gone through.

Ultimately we dropped, I believe, over thirty feet. The front gates opened, and I saw the cruiser begin to move. As it did, I also noticed that to my starboard side was a massive barge. Similar to one of the last locks and dams, there was a tow with barges waiting to enter the lock. However, this time I had the Nissan and the Mercury running hard and pushed through the lock's exit turbulence and the turbulence being kicked up by not just the tow but the cruiser, as well. I was enormously grateful for the motors!

After a few minutes, the water smoothed out and the wind died down. I put the Nissan at a nice seven miles per hour, sat down, and relaxed and enjoyed the rest of my coffee. The motor was running nice and quiet, and for that, I was grateful. I had decided to simply let it be and run it at this speed all day to make sure it was functioning correctly. And for several hours, it did beautifully.

A few hours in, a large tow pushing barges approached me from the south. I got on channel 13. Up to this point I had been using channel 16, which was an emergency frequency but also for more routine communication with and between vessels. I don't know why I hadn't known earlier, or paid attention when somebody told me, but nearly all commercial towboat traffic on the upper river used channel 13. It would make my ability to talk to towboats so much easier now, armed with this knowledge! I called the ship's captain and asked what side he wanted me on. He asked me to inform him of my actual location, which I had not when I told him I was a pleasure craft coming his way, and so I checked my maps quickly, told him approximately where I was, and he said, "Two whistle."

Now here's the thing. When the captain several days earlier told me "one whistle" and I didn't know what that was and had to ask him to explain it, I should have learned my lesson. I should have made a mental note to check what other similar commands were supposed to mean and, if necessary, write them down somewhere to check if I didn't remember.

I should have. But I didn't. And now the price I had to pay for my continued lapse of nautical judgement was to ask this towboat captain what he meant by "two whistle."

He patiently said, "Starboard to starboard," and I quickly moved in that direction. He then asked me to go to channel 67 to talk, and I thought I was about to get scolded for being one of those idiots who doesn't know what "two whistle" or, for that matter, any whistle meant.

Instead, he asked me where I was going and how long it would take, and then shared with me some helpful tips on how to remember some of the whistle commands. He could not have been nicer and more helpful. As we prepared to pass one another, he also suggested I get back inside the channel and stay starboard of him because the water where I was would get shallower. I followed his advice, and as we passed one another, he exited his cabin and whistled and waved at me. On the radio, I thanked him, and I was back on my way.

Not long after this, I heard a loud boom on the port side of my raft. I thought something, perhaps a motor, had blown up. Whatever it was had me looking frantically around the raft.

I looked out my port side door and just then I saw a shiny white object flop into the water. Followed by another white object flying out of the water and smashing into the side of the shed.

It was a flying carp!

Holy smokes! I had seen a couple of them jump past the ship's bow, but this one had actually hit it. These are not small fish, and I can see why people are worried about them. Now *I* was worried about them! If they hit the side of the raft, that was fine; it would just knock them back into the water. But if they flew into any of the windows or screen doors, they would come right into the cabin. And given that when I traveled I keep all my doors open, including on the port and starboard sides, a flying carp could fly in and hit me!

Crazy! In all my life I had never thought I would be on a raft on a river being attacked by flying carp.

As I continued that day's journey to Quincy, I was hit by multiple flying carp. I also had one more lock and dam to go through, Number 20. Thankfully it was wide open, and I was instructed to proceed forward and directly into the chamber.

A young man named Aaron threw me a rope and told me he had been working there only a month. I asked him how he liked it, and he said it was a blast. We chatted a bit more, and then the water lowered, the horn blew, and I was back on my way.

I continued along my way, being hit by flying carp, and came upon La Grange. As I did, I saw a tow sliding in behind a parked barge on my starboard side and stayed vigilant in the event they might turn to their starboard back into the channel. The towboat didn't, and so I proceeded forward. As I did and got past them, I began to encounter some rough, rolling waves.

These waves weren't huge, but the rolling effect they made sent the raft's nose down and up and I porpoised like crazy. All I could do was try to ride the waves out, find calmer water, and wait for things to even out. But this water wasn't doing that. It was getting more intense.

To add to the misery, a guy in a small fishing boat was drawing a ton of water and creating additional wakes on top of the rolling waves. Pretty soon I was bouncing all over the place and looking for calmer water somewhere. I don't run into these kind of locations a lot, but they made me nervous as heck when I did. And in this particular area it seemed like I was in a channel of waves that wasn't going to end anytime soon.

I finally decided to throttle up both motors and accelerate my way out of the location, and soon enough I found myself in calmer waters. As I turned to look back, I also saw that the tow that I had passed in La Grange was now entering the water behind me. The next few miles were going to be tricky, navigating a narrow channel with shallow water on the outskirts of both the red and green buoys.

I knew I had about five miles or so left before I got to Quincy, so I quickly looked at my fuel and decided to keep the raft's motors running at top speed to stay ahead of the ship behind me. I also knew that at 1:00 p.m., I would be talking with Joe Soucheray and the gang at Garage Logic, so I wanted to be far ahead of the guy behind me.

Soon I saw a series of bridges in front of me, which I knew was Quincy. And at about that time, Garage Logic called. Also at that time a tow with barges appeared ahead of me, pushing upriver.

Yikes!

As we began our conversation and laughed about my previous day and my current day's predicament, I decided to contact the towboat and ask where they wanted me. Joe and I had just been discussing the different whistle commands, shared with him by a listener and he'd told me to write them down.

As if on cue, the captain of the tow said, live on Garage Logic, "Two whistles."

Starboard to starboard!

So that's where I went.

My phone connection that day with Garage Logic was challenging, and at some point, I was muted. I think Joe was concerned that I was too busy talking to focus on the ships behind and ahead of me, and we ended the call with a promise to talk next week. To be honest, if the encounters with those tows had happened weeks earlier, I would have been terrified to have a phone conversation while dealing with them. Now, I was becoming more comfortable—not cocky—with the situation and thought it was going just fine. I appreciated Joe's concern about my safety out on the river—if I'd thought I was in any jeopardy, I would have excused myself and taken care of the matter at hand.

That being said, I proceeded past this tow and barge only to see another one right behind him! I called him on the radio and he instructed me to "stay in the tube," and to be honest, I had no idea what that meant. He came back on and said I was fine where I was and to continue. Two whistle.

About the same time, the tow behind me asked what my speed was. I indicated about ten miles per hour, and he responded, "Perfect, thank you!" My guess is that as long as I was running at that speed, he and I would be far enough apart that he wouldn't need to ask me to give way so he could pass.

After passing the second towboat I called the marina I was going to, Art Keller Marina, and spoke with a young guy named Dalton to get instructions on how to enter the marina safely. He was kind and patient and spent fifteen minutes helping me figure out which bridge to get under, where to turn, what side of the channel to be on, and where to meet him at the gas dock. I finally arrived at the gas dock and filled up all my tanks, including the three new ones that my brother Hans had brought me.

By the time we were done, I had nearly ninety-two gallons of fuel onboard the raft, or about 550 pounds. Lots of fuel and lots of weight.

Since as I traveled further down the river it would be tough to get fuel, and I couldn't be in a situation where I was short on fuel, I was getting stocked up. Since this made my load heavier, I released some of my sandbags. I paid for the fuel and then motored to a slip.

It had been a long day but a good day. Tucked into a quiet marina slip, I was grateful for the chance to unwind. There also happened to be a shower facility for the marina that was a couple blocks away, so I took full advantage of that and came back to the raft refreshed, clean, and relaxed. I planned to spend two nights in Quincy, anticipating my trek to the end of the upper river and preparing for what would come next on the lower river.

I took a mile walk to stretch my legs, made myself some of the last of the remaining MREs, and called it a night.

Chapter 16
A Sinking Feeling

My trip from Quincy to Rockport was one of adventure, discovery, and sheer terror. (I want to warn you in case you want to skip to the end of this chapter!)

The day before, in Quincy, I had spent a great deal of time catching up on emails, blog writing, and the like. I also rearranged the containers inside the raft to accommodate the addition of the extra fuel at the front of the raft. This would help keep the raft from porpoise-ing, which is annoying, frightening, and ultimately dangerous if the raft porpoises too deeply, as the entire vessel can slide into the river, sinking. Obviously not a good thing!

To that end, I decided to move much of the weight from the front of the raft closer to the middle and the back. I anticipated that doing so would balance out the addition of the fuel up front and help mitigate the porpoising. Unfortunately, I miscalculated many things in approaching this effort.

After my morning ritual of preparing for a day of the journey, I contacted Lock and Dam Number 21 via cell phone and spoke to a man named Dallas, who shared with me that I should be able to lock through quickly that morning if I got there within the next thirty minutes. I made a quick mental calculation and assured him that I could, and I began my exit out of the harbor that had been my home for the past two days.

As I made my way to the lock, it was a lovely morning. The wind was light, the waves were small, and I made quick work of the trip, thereby confirming that I had both the Nissan and the kicker motor under power.

At this point, I should have paid more attention and realized that both motors were not picking the rear of the raft up enough to keep the water from rushing over the surface of the top of the pontoons. This is important because it was commonly accepted by myself and my team that any leakage I was getting in the raft was likely coming from surface cracks on the top of the tubes. I should have paid more attention, sooner, to see how the raft was running and whether or not I was running sufficiently with the tubes above the waterline.

This would come back to haunt me later in the day.

I approached the lock, and as promised, Dallas and Paul got me in quickly and got me out quickly to allow me to proceed toward Rockport.

I thought it was a good omen that this hadn't taken long, and I felt pretty confident about the rest of the journey even though I knew I had a second lock and dam downriver that I had to journey through before reaching my destination. It was twenty-three miles away, so I wasn't going to spend much time thinking about that now.

The next encounter I had nearly ended my trip.

A few miles past Lock and Dam Number 21, I came upon a large towboat pushing barges up the river. Nothing unusual, and not a large enough entourage to cause me much concern.

I looked at my navigation app on my iPad and quickly determined that I had plenty of room on the port side of my raft, the SS Hail Mary, to exit the navigation channel and just let the towboat go by. For some reason, though, I got on the radio and asked the tow's captain for his opinion. I was quite sure his first set of instructions aligned with my thought: that I should go to my left and stay out of his way until he got by me.

However, his response was not clear, and I repeated my request for guidance from him.

He then said, "One whistle"—meaning that we should pass port to port—and instructed me to go by him on the green buoy side, my right.

I was skeptical, but he assured me that the water on my side was deep and we would get past one another uneventfully.

I should have stuck with my original plan.

The space from the shoreline to his rolling wake—with me in the middle—was not very wide at all. As I approached his port side, I regretted the decision immediately.

I could tell that I had extraordinarily little room to wiggle between him and the shoreline, so I picked up speed in the hope that I could ride past his wake quickly.

Unfortunately, that tactic didn't work this time.

The wake he created was not a simple chop; it was a rolling tsunami. I quickly assessed my options.

I couldn't go right, because I would go directly into the shoreline.

I couldn't go left, because he had not yet gotten far enough past me to allow me to get back into the navigation channel.

So instead I rode head-on into the first of several massive, rolling waves.

The raft pitched straight down into the river and stopped. I gasped as I felt myself being flung forward and down.

The water poured in and the motors labored under the brick wall of water I had hit.

It happened a second time, and this time the raft went down deeper and I nearly flew over the steering console.

I knew I wouldn't survive a third time.

I stopped the motors and let the third wave wash over the deck as I pushed myself to the front of the raft and desperately threw three sandbags off the front, into the river.

I then throttled up the motors, turned the nose sharply to port, and made my way back into the navigation channel. I decided that I would fight the roiling backwash and turbulence of the towboat in the channel rather than battle any more of the wake outside it. It took me a good fifteen minutes to ride out this roller-coaster. As the waves got smaller, they came faster, until finally I made it to calm water.

I was exhausted. Sweating. The raft was soaked. And I found myself shaking. Not from the cold but from the realization that the SS Hail Mary had nearly ended up seventeen feet down on the bottom of the river, with me in it.

I quickly rearranged some boxes inside the raft to shift the weight.

I took gas cans off the front of the raft, sat down, put the Nissan throttle at seven miles an hour, and tried to catch my breath and gather my wits.

My mistake in how I had rearranged the weight that morning was multiplied by the error of not trusting my judgment and going to the left side of the channel. Had I done so, the encounter would never have happened. The near sinking would have been avoided. And I would have been in a better position a couple of hours later when the next catastrophe struck.

I continued on and soon felt that the raft was sluggish and not responding well to the wheel. I was confused about the situation and continued to mess with the Nissan's speed and trim, all to no avail. I then stuck my head out the port and starboard screen doors and looked down at my tubes.

Instead of rising above the water as they typically did, the back halves of the tubes, from the raft's mid-section to the back end, was riding underwater. This wasn't good. Mainly since the tubes collected water from the top, or so we believed.

I tried trimming, changing speed, moving weight, and nothing changed.

I was beginning to fear that I had already been underway in this condition too long, and that so much water had collected in the tubes that any chance of changing the raft's plane was gone.

I continued to make, nervously glancing behind me at the level of the rear of the raft and down at the back end of the tubes. I pondered whether I should pull over, tie up to the shore, and attempt to pump the water out. I considered, reconsidered, thought again, and delayed the decision.

It shouldn't even have been an argument. I should have pulled over and done precisely that. A quick slide of the pump into the tubes and I could have remedied the water situation quickly and then proceeded with the goal of resolving it entirely upon my arrival at my next stop—Two Rivers Marina.

But I hesitated.

The fact that I didn't take advantage of that situation was an important reminder that being tentative on the river could cause problems later.

As I came through Hannibal, Missouri, I had to deal with multiple towboats and barges, including railroad bridges and the like, and I knew that eight miles ahead of me was a lock I had to get through without any knowledge of its status. Unfortunately, when I got within range and contacted them, they told me it would be two to two and a half hours before I could enter the lock.

Ugghh! More water collecting in the tubes!

I motored to a calm area of the pool above the lock, threw in my anchor, and waited until the raft swung into the current.

As I sat on the bow, looking down at the dam, I could see that the raft's rear had settled.

I also knew that the water coming from the north was spilling over the tops of the tubes, only adding more volume to these quickly saturating pontoons.

I was going to have to wait until two tows, one with and one without barges, worked their way through the lock. When I saw the second tow enter the chamber about an hour after the first one locked through, I called the operator and asked if he still thought it would be another hour to an hour and a half. To my surprise, he said it would only be another thirty minutes. I was thrilled!

I waited until I saw the tow lock through and then pulled up anchor and waited for the light to turn green, inviting me into the chamber.

As soon as it did, I proceeded forward.

I radioed and asked for a line to be thrown over and was informed that it would be done.

However, whether it was bad communication on my end or merely a lack of decent execution, after the young lock operator dropped the rope down and I began to pull on it to bring myself up against the lock wall, the rope went slack. He had either not yet tied it to the railing, or his knot didn't hold, but it came splashing down into the water.

I grabbed it and threw it back up to him, but it dropped through his hands.

He then raced off for another rope while I grabbed my hook pole, retrieved the rope, shouted up that I had it, and two more throws later, he grabbed it and tied it on.

I asked him to tie it tighter, and he did.

Unfortunately, during this entire transaction, the raft got caught in the wind, and I had to yank the rope hard to get the rear end up against the wall so I could then use it to wedge the raft's front end to the right, to push it up against the wall.

It was a mess.

Finally, after a lot of pulling, grunting, and cursing, I got it all back under control and the raft safely up against the lock wall.

When the dam water reached level, I exited and sped off as quickly as I could.

Of course, the day wouldn't be complete without another tow with barges coming upriver to a lock as I was exiting. Thankfully, we both went by one another and that was that.

However, I still had eighteen miles to get to Two Rivers Marina, and the raft was clearly listing to starboard.

I concocted a plan that I would find a slough and go off-river, pull the raft to starboard, throw a rope in the air over a tree branch, and pull the raft up high enough out of the river to be able to shove the hose from my pump into the pontoons and pump out the water. This was not the soundest strategy. After all, the raft was heavy, and now with hundreds of pounds of additional weight due to water in the pontoons, it would have required an extreme amount of effort to pull the raft up. Then I would have needed to figure out a way to tie it while it was up in the air. And then, assuming I was successful, I was going to need to pump the water out. (As I realized then, and as I write this now, it clearly was a ludicrous, impossible, and desperate idea!)

Anyway, each time I found myself approaching the shoreline in an attempt to try this strategy I got cold feet. Water was already well over the top of the access I needed to pump out the water. More importantly, I wasn't confident I had enough muscle to make this plan work.

I had one choice left, and that was to get to Two Rivers Marina without any further delay, tie up to the gas dock, and be ready to pump!

With each passing mile, I could feel the raft sinking deeper into the river.

And I could feel the Nissan laboring against the additional weight as I tried to throttle it to move it faster to my final destination.

As luck would have it, I came upon another tow pushing barges. This one had me pressed against the right side of the river. There was nothing I could do about the situation other than hope the tow's waves and wake were sufficiently weak to allow me to avoid another porpoise episode.

Thankfully, after many quiet prayers and some loud and creative cursing, I moved through its wake quickly, which meant I only had about four miles left before I got to my location.

I kept talking to the SS Hail Mary, urging her on, telling her not much further, and doing my best to avoid looking back.

Unfortunately, what I didn't see behind me I could see in front of me on my starboard side. The list had become so pronounced that even the bow was listing to starboard.

Three miles.

More listing.

Two miles. I was looking for an exit, a dock, something that would give me relief.

One mile.

I called the marina to confirm its location and where I needed to turn.

Finally, I saw the buoys that marked its entrance and pushed on.

The Nissan worked hard to keep the raft moving forward with all the extra water weight in its tubes. As I came into view of the gas dock, I knew what my plan was going to be:

Grab the gas generator.

Plug in the extension cord.

Prime the pump.

Stick it into the tube.

Remove the water.

As I approached the dock, a young woman waved at me. As I got closer, she grabbed hold of the starboard line I threw to her, and I leapt off the raft and pulled it tight against the dock. I grabbed hold of the aft starboard rope, put it around my shoulders, and stood straight up, pulling the raft as high up off the water as I could. In doing so, I realized I could create just enough space between the lapping waves and the top of the spigot to get a clear shot of getting the hose into the tube without more lake water invading it.

However, three jet skiers suddenly and slowly pulled in to fuel up, and their wake washed over the spigot I was getting ready. If I opened it now, the water would pour in and send the raft even deeper into the river.

I turned to the young woman and asked if anybody at the marina might come down and help me lift the back end. Two big guys showed up within two minutes, asked me what I needed, and then took the rope I had been using and heaved the back tube up, which allowed me clear access to the spigot.

Unfortunately, the spigot top wouldn't turn with my bare hand. I quickly took off my shirt and grasped the top with it in my hand, and it turned and came off.

I carefully placed the spigot top inside the raft lest it bounce into the river.

I primed the pump and then shoved it into the tube.

Immediately water began to pour out.

After a couple of minutes, I had extracted enough water that I could thank the two guys and let them know I could take it from there. Exhausted, I put my face on the dock with my bare back to the sun and laughed.

After a minute, I thanked God once again for getting me there safely.

A few minutes later, the harbor master, Laurell Hamilton, came down and confirmed how many nights I would be staying and which slip I would take. She then asked, "This isn't going to sink in my harbor, is it?" with a twinkle in her eye.

I assured her it would not, thanked her for the place to stay, and then continued to remove water from the tube.

Finally, I buttoned it back up and shoved off from the gas dock to the slip.

Once there, I again pulled water from both tubes, and by the time I was done, I had removed nearly sixty-two gallons from the starboard tube and almost twenty from the port tube.

In total, there were nearly 650 extra pounds of water weight on the rear of the raft!

Too much water. Too much weight.

And I cannot believe the good fortune that, along with prayers, got me to the marina without a worse outcome.

After cleaning up the raft and catching my breath, I walked up to the office, and Laurell and her friend Missy were there to greet me with a cocktail.

I needed it!

And, to add to their generosity, they not only gave me the slip for free but gave me a key to a sweet cabin for two nights, access to laundry and showers, and finally took me out for dinner.

Amazing!

At dinner, one of the guys who had come and given me a hand on the dock, Randy, proposed that the next morning we either take the raft out of the water or use some floatation devices at one of the slips to get it far enough out of the water to treat the tubes with some sealant.

I agreed to the latter approach, as I remained concerned that taking the raft out of the water would add more wear and tear to the infrastructure.

After dinner was done, I bid my new friends good night and retired to the lovely little cabin they had provided for my stay. It was glorious! Comfortable bed. Warm shower. And a quiet place to sleep for the night.

The next morning I got up, made myself a pot of coffee, and thoroughly relaxed and reflected on my good fortune. The plan was for Randy to come by around nine o'clock and we would figure out the exact strategy for taking the raft out of the water.

Randy arrived and we spent some time talking. He suggested that I back out of the slip I was currently in and travel to the other side of the marina harbor, then pull into a slip where a lift system would bring me far enough out of the water to take a look at the tubes.

Randy went to prepare the lift system. I went to get the raft and began my short trek to the rear of the harbor.

Once I turned into the lane where Randy was waiting at the slip, it became apparent immediately that we had a problem.

Unfortunately, we hadn't considered the fact that the slip had a roof and that the clearance between that roof and the top of the raft would only permit us to bring the tubes up six inches out of water.

Not far enough to gain access to them.

I capitulated and told Randy that if he was willing to use their crane device to take the raft out of the water, I would accept whatever the outcome was, even if it didn't end well.

The reality was, I could not let the scenario from the day before play itself out again.

Randy took a closer look at the raft and the crane and felt that we might be taking too much of a chance that the pontoons would crease if we pulled them out. Finally, we agreed that he would back a trailer down the boat ramp and we would pull it out of the water that way.

Frankly, we needed to get the pontoon out of the water so I could get underneath it and look about for any obvious cracks and try to formulate a plan to seal them. The only real way to do that was either to use the crane or take the raft out of the water on a trailer, as we were about to do.

Thirty minutes later, we had the raft on his trailer and out of the river.

Inspecting the tubes showed no apparent signs of problems or where the water might be accessing the tubes.

I didn't think it would.

I had decided to get a product that is widely advertised on television. This spray sealant has the consistency of rubber, and my plan was to coat every weld on the tubes I could find and hope that somehow that would solve the problem or mitigate it substantially.

Missy, who I had met the day before, was kind enough to get me six cans of the product, and I spent the next hour coating the tubes. The can instructions indicated it would take at least twenty-four hours for the product to cure, but with the raft in the blazing sun I hoped that it would expedite the process.

The goal was to put me back in the water the next morning and have me underway—hopefully with a pontoon that no longer leaked!

Chapter 17
Danger Comes Calling

I was up early in Rockport and began to collect my belongings. I waited outside the cabin that the folks at Two Rivers Marina were kind enough to provide to me during my stay. Randy would soon be calling me so we could return the raft to the water, and I would continue my journey to St. Charles.

It would be one of my longer trips so far, nearly fifty-two miles, and I would need to get through two locks and dams: Numbers 24 and 25. I was anxious about whether or not the fix we applied to the tubes was going to work. There was only one way to find out, and that was to get on the water and get going.

I got a text from Randy at about 6:30 a.m. that he was ready to go, and at about 7:15 he rolled up, hooked the trailer, and slid the SS Hail Mary into the river. Within fifteen minutes, I waved goodbye to Randy and was underway.

I had paid close attention to the weather reports over the previous twenty-four hours. Each report showed rain and wind along the way, but all the reports shifted the worst of it to later in the day. With luck and good timing at the locks and dams, I might make St. Charles ahead of any severe rain, wind, or potential storms. I decided to run hot with the Nissan all day to get there with as much time to spare before nightfall as possible. I did so with the knowledge that the fix we had applied might or might not work, and I wanted to do what I could to keep the tube tops running as high above the waterline as I could.

I removed the three Attwood gas tanks from the very front of the raft and put them inside a little area inside the original frame of the raft in an area I called the "porch." I also redistributed the weight to do my best to equalize the port and starboard bow. I had already shifted the weight inside the raft back to where it was before I'd moved it in Quincy.

As the boat ran, she seemed to be in just the right balance, so I felt particularly good about it all.

The weather was mild, and so was the wind, and I made quick time to Lock and Dam Number 24. I called ahead, as had become my practice, and was told that if I could make good time in the next thirty minutes, they should be able to lock me right through.

I got both motors turning and sped up, mindful that in doing so, I was pushing the tube tops under the water despite my best efforts to trim up the raft. Given that I needed to cover fifty-two miles that day, waiting for any amount of time to enter the lock and dam was going to be a challenge.

When I arrived, I saw that both the green and yellow lights were flashing. I had not seen that before and got on the radio to indicate I was confused. The lock guy informed me that it meant I should proceed forward with caution into the chamber. I did precisely that, and they got me in and out and back on my way. I eased back on the throttle, and the SS Hail Mary returned to her normal run placement as she had before I sped up to the lock.

Along the way, I was once again pelted by flying carp. I have to admit I was shocked at the prevalence of these fish. More so at the frequency with which I saw them flying out of the water ahead, behind, and on the sides of the raft. That they hit the raft is both amusing and a bit scary, and I kept waiting for them to leap onto the bow of the raft or, worse, into the cabin!

I soon approached the city of Hamburg. I had decided that if the weather was going to be an issue that day, or if the tubes appeared to be taking on water, Hamburg would be my midway stop even if I had to change the rest of my itinerary for the week.

Several people told me that Hamburg had a boat dock that I could tie onto if necessary. So with that information in the back of my head, I felt pretty comfortable about the journey. The weather continued to cooperate, and I frequently checked several weather apps that showed the weather continuing to hold until I reached St. Charles.

About five miles out of Hamburg, a guy on a fast-moving flatboat pulled up alongside me and started having a conversation. We both had our boats running, and it was hard to hear very well, and his dog was anxiously running from the bow to the stern of his boat, concerned, I am sure, about why his owner was rocking the boat.

I made out something about him having done this trip before, and that his ex-girlfriend had a place for me to stay if I needed to (if I could find it), and how far was I going? I tried to answer as best I could. He was having difficulty keeping his boat stable. I didn't want to reduce my speed any further given the need for me to get to St. Charles—plus, to be honest, I could barely hear what he was saying—so I waved, and he waved, and we went off on our separate ways.

As I approached Lock and Dam Number 25, my heart sank slightly as I saw several large tows and barges near the facility. I took that to mean I would likely need to wait a long while. If I could just get through that lock quickly, I only had about another ten miles to go before I reached St. Charles and the marina where I was going to stay for the evening.

I got on the phone, and to my delight, the lock operator said if I could arrive within twenty to thirty minutes, they could get me right in before they turned the lock around to let others come up. I asked him about the huge tow and barge sitting in front of me, and he told me they were waiting to come down but that they were parked.

So, once again, I throttled up both motors and began going as quickly as I could. Again, I was mindful that doing so was pushing my tube tops deeper into the water. If the seal wasn't working, or we hadn't caught everything due to limited access to some spaces, I would once again be in a bit of trouble.

As I approached the lock, I could see that they already had the green light on to enter the chamber, and I did so promptly. Within fifteen minutes, they had me locked through, and while there was an approaching tow and barge, I was able to quickly get to their port side on my port side and get past them.

At this point, I down throttled the motors again and got the raft back up into the position I had been in all day. I did notice a slight dip in the starboard tube on the back but nowhere near what I had seen in the two previous incidents. I felt reasonably confident that while there was probably water in the tube, it might not be very much.

I continued on my way and approached an area of the river that was as remote as any I had encountered on the Mississippi's upper part. Long stretches of water with dense brush and uninhabited shoreline on either side, punctuated from time to time with pockets of structure in and out of the channel. My two motors, the 60 HP Nissan and the 9.9 HP Mercury, running at full speed in water that wasn't particularly fast, meant that I had plenty of noise keeping me company along this stretch. So the fact that I didn't hear the approaching boat until it was nearly upon me shouldn't have been a surprise.

What was a surprise was that the four men in the boat didn't seem particularly friendly as they came up alongside me about seventy-five feet from my raft. Their boat was something that I now know is called a "jon" boat, and the occupants were outfitted in various forms of camouflage and there was a big pile of what looked like brush near the middle of the boat. As they got closer, I leaned out my starboard side door and waved at them as I was accustomed to doing during my travels. And most of the time when people saw me, they waved back or offered some kind of gesture to acknowledge my greeting.

But not these guys. They just stared at me. The guy steering the boat gave me a menacing look that bordered on outright hostility.

To my knowledge, I hadn't gotten in their way on this stretch of the river. I hadn't seen them before, and I assumed that they had been inside one of the many little cutouts on the river, channels I didn't dare bring my raft into for fear of getting hung up on submerged trees. They passed by, all of them staring at me. I went back inside the cabin and mentally shrugged it off. I thought it was rude of them not to wave, but it wasn't going to wreck my day.

About two hundred yards down the river, though, the jon boat turned to port and come back up the river.

I took note of the change of direction and moved my raft onto the other side of the river.

They responded by heading straight toward me.

Again, I adjusted the raft to get out of their way. But they also changed direction, keeping their boat heading right at me.

Now I was concerned.

This wasn't normal, and it was escalating from rude to threatening. At this point, I wasn't in a position to steer any further out of their way and simply shouted to them, "What are you doing?"

About one hundred feet away, they suddenly veered out of my way to my port side. In doing so, they created a wake that I then needed to traverse to avoid having the raft careen from side to side.

I mentally swore at them and thought, *Jerks!*

A few seconds later, they were back. They came up behind on my starboard side, then veered in front of me, yelling and shouting as they created more wakes. They raced in front of me, around me, and behind me, creating a circular motion of wake that was getting rougher and deeper. It was becoming more and more difficult to keep the raft from tipping over.

Now I was scared.

My initial reaction after the first assault was that they might be trying to get on the raft. But now it was clear what they were trying to do: they were trying to get me off the raft. What their ultimate motive was—

to sink the raft, steal the raft, or dump me in the river—I didn't know and at that point, I didn't care.

What I did know was that whether they tipped me over or forced me out of the raft, I would be in trouble. Once in the water, I would be at their mercy—whatever their motive—and I knew that no matter what, I couldn't let that happen.

I had my Sig-Sauer P238 loaded and sitting in the gun safe that was right behind my steering console. I popped the latch and reached in. I grabbed the small handgun and turned off the safety.

The gun was not particularly big in my hands. Yet, at the moment, it felt like a cannon. It was also equipped with a laser sight. Never in my life have I pointed anything more than my finger at another human being. Now, I had a gun in my hand and had to decide whether I would use it to protect myself. (In retrospect, the irony is not lost on me that my journey to find Hope on the River was beginning to look more and more like Horror on the River!) As their boat came back behind me on my port side and crossed over in front of me again, I made my decision. I believed I had no other choice.

The jon boat crossed in front of me, moved to my starboard side, and ran about one hundred yards in front of me before turning back around.

I switched both motors to idle and double-checked to make sure the gun's chamber was loaded and the safety was off. I had loaded it with hollow-point shells and knew that whatever they hit, they were going to cause some damage.

As the raft bobbed precariously from side to side, the front end dug into the wake, pushing water up on the bow. I walked carefully across the wet deck over to the pontoon railing outside of the cabin.

I looked down at the gun and clicked on the laser sight, bringing the Sig up with my right hand while holding tight to the railing with my left hand.

I put the red dot on the face of the guy steering the boat.

He didn't see the dot, but the rest of the guys on the boat did. I could see them yelling and screaming at him to turn away. He finally made the connection between their yelling, my extended arm, and the gun clenched in my hand.

I hadn't decided *when* I would pull the trigger, but I had decided I *would* pull the trigger if they didn't turn away. At that moment, I knew that if I had to, I'd pull the trigger and shoot him to protect myself.

The jon boat turned hard to my port side, and I followed them with the gun, not knowing at that point exactly where the red dot was because

I was trying to keep from falling off the raft while still maintaining eye contact with them.

I also wanted to make sure that they kept going because if they didn't, I would have fired off some rounds even not knowing where, or if, they would land.

They didn't stop. They kept on going.

I went back into the cabin, throttled up both motors, and got underway. I kept looking back, expecting to see them coming back up on me, this time with their guns drawn. I didn't know exactly what I would do if they returned. I grabbed another magazine from the safe and put it in my pocket, and grabbed the loaded Beretta I had in the safe and stuck it in the back of my pants. I was in no way prepared for a gun battle with anyone, but I knew that if they came back at me, that was precisely what was going to happen.

With a heightened sense of caution, I continued along my way. I was tense, my heart was pounding, I was sweating and the adrenaline was pumping. If it was physically possible for every hair on my body to be standing straight up, I felt like it was.

Here's the thing—I would have shot the driver of the boat. There is no doubt in my mind that I would have done so. That thought alone, to this day, continues to cause my heart to race. Truth is, had I shot him, he would have been dead. For what? To steal whatever he and others on his boat thought was of value on my raft? To harm me? And, if so, for what reason? It all seems so dumb and unnecessary. Thankfully, it didn't come to that and my day could continue without harm to anyone. (Except of course, possibly to me!)

About five miles out of St. Charles, as the wind started to pick up and the waves got more challenging, I was hit by two cruiser boats—fifteen minutes apart—both of which went by me seemingly without regard to the wake they created.

I have to admit I am still at a loss to understand why this happens. These boats come perilously close to me in a channel where they could easily leave enough space for both watercraft, but they made no effort to do so and no effort to trim down their wake.

Of course, the result was that for the first cruiser, I had to turn hard to port and then back to starboard to cut into their wake, and then take the opposite maneuver for the second cruiser based on their approach.

I was now two miles from my destination, and I realized I had been running the raft at well over the speed I'd intended for the last forty-five minutes—nearly eight miles per hour.

That doesn't sound fast, and it isn't, but what it did is keep the tube tops deep underwater, and I could sense that the starboard stern was running deeper into the river than it had been. I throttled back, and the tubes came up enough for me to see the spigot top above the water. I breathed a sigh of relief, thinking that was a good sign.

As I came within sight of the marina, I saw another marina about one hundred yards above it—John's Boat Harbor. That was the marina we had initially contacted, but at the time, based on the date of my arrival, they didn't have anything available. Coming out of the marina's mouth was a large cruiser, probably within two hundred feet of me, preparing to head south. On the raft were a couple of women and a guy who was the captain.

They took pictures, waved, and then inexplicably throttled up and created massive wakes that came right at me. They could have certainly gone past me and then sped up, but clearly they weren't concerned with the wake they created and its impact on my raft, or, I imagine, any other craft.

I turned the pontoon hard and fast to port in a circle and then brought the bow into the wake at about a forty-five-degree angle. I created a few new swear words that will go into my Raft Book of Curses when this trip is done! Once past this unfortunate encounter, I then proceeded to the marina I would stay at for the night.

I saw a group of people onshore waving at me. One of them, a tall, thin guy, was shouting at me. I couldn't hear but I yelled out to see if they knew where the marina's entrance was. They pointed, and I headed that direction.

Trouble lay ahead!

As I slowly motored to the marina entrance, I saw that the gas dock on my port side looked like a tidal wave had hit it and driven it up along the harbor bank. This, of course, was the gas dock I had been instructed to tie up to by the owners of the marina. That was not going to work!

At this point, I only had the kicker motor running as it helped me navigate more easily and quietly in these harbor areas. I looked at the slips in front and to the right of me and saw weeds growing in many of the empty slips, as well as full ones. In front of me, a large log was sticking up out of the water.

About the same time, I heard someone yell at me, "I wouldn't go in there; the water is pretty shallow, and you're likely to get stuck!" This was the same tall and skinny guy I had seen earlier. I looked down at my depth finder and saw it go from three feet to no feet. I put a hard stop on the motor and slowly put it in reverse.

I was incredulous. Why would the folks that owned this marina allow me to make a reservation there if it was in this condition? The tall skinny guy repeated his instructions not to enter and told me to go back upriver to the marina I had just passed, John's Boat Harbor, and slip in there. He told me he had lived on the river for forty years and this marina was too shallow for me to enter—that I likely wouldn't be able to get out the next day if I did stay there. That was all I needed to hear, so I backed out and proceeded upriver.

I could tell the raft was riding heavy again but couldn't tell how heavy, and frankly, I just needed to get tied up somewhere. I figured that even if John's Boat Harbor didn't have a place for me, I could tie up for a bit at the gas dock, drain the tube if I needed to, and then proceed a few miles down to find another place to stay. As I came into the gas dock, the tall skinny guy was there and helped me on. As soon as I got on the gas dock, I could see that I had taken on a lot more water than I'd imagined.

I told the guy I needed to get into a slip and get the water out. He literally jumped on the raft and pointed me to an empty slip. I didn't need any more encouragement. As I turned the raft around, the kicker stopped. And I couldn't get it started. I then tried the Nissan, and it wouldn't catch.

I'd finally had it. I was mad!

From boats trying to swamp me to a marina that had no business accepting my business to the tubes taking on water again, I lost my temper and cursed at nobody in particular but in a way that would have made any sailor proud!

But I had to take care of this problem, so I lifted the kicker higher out of the water and tried again, and it caught! We got into the slip, tied up the raft, and the guy helped me prime the pump and then slide it and get it into the tube, and water started flowing out!

For the next half hour of water coming out, I learned more about the helpful guy. His name was Al. In 1991, with a bunch of friends, he had built a forty-two foot long raft that was sixteen feet wide and taken it on a fifteen-day trip to New Orleans from St. Charles. I believe he said there were eleven of them on the raft and that sometimes they motored on throughout the night. He said it was the best vacation he'd ever had!

He was a delight. And so exceedingly kind to help me!

Soon we were joined by a friend of his, named Glen, and together they shared their background and knowledge of this particular marina. I told them I didn't have a reservation and explained the situation I was in and that I needed a place to dock for the night.

Al assured me that I would be fine right where I was but suggested we take a ride up and talk to Glennac, the marina owner, and make sure it was okay. I was pleased to do so and make my case that I really could use a place to tie up, even if it was the gas dock, for the night.

We walked up a steep ramp to Glen's truck, and Al and I sat on the tailgate while Glen drove us to meet Glennac. Before we got there, Al had Glen stop to introduce me to Pat, the harbor master. Al asked Pat if he thought it would be okay if I stayed in the slip. Pat thought about it for a second to make sure someone else wasn't booked in it and then said that it wouldn't be a problem. He suggested we still introduce me to Glennac and tell her the situation.

We continued on and met Glennac, who greeted us with a big smile and a warm heart and told me I was more than welcome to stay the night. I shared with her information about my trip, and she looked at me and said, "You gotta lot a balls!" which made all of us laugh.

I needed that laugh!

I gave her my business card, thanked her profusely, and we left to go back to the raft.

Before we did, though, Al told Glen to drop us off at his house. As we drove to his house, he told me he wanted me to stay there for the night and that he would give me his truck to drive back to the raft and transport the things I needed back to the house.

Amazing!

Not only did this stranger care enough to warn me out of the danger of the marina, but he jumped on my raft, no questions asked, and helped me save it from sinking into the river, and now he was going to allow a perfect stranger to stay in his house and use his truck!

This is the America I know, and the one I am meeting every day along this river. People who are kind and generous and give freely without question. I thanked Al for his generosity and went back to the raft to begin putting things back in order. I made sure that everything was ready to go for the morning and that all I would need to do was my usual morning routine: return to the raft, gas up, and go. I closed the doors, returned to Al's truck with my gear, drove back to his house, and began to camp in for the night.

I had a phone call with my brothers, Fred, Karl, and Hans, to discuss the pontoon tubes' status and the plan to have them meet me at Hoppies Marina in Kimmswick, Missouri, south of St. Louis. The plan was that one of them would hop on the raft with me and the other two would chase us and refuel us for as long as they could before they needed to return home. I was grateful to my brothers for their help and concern. There was a possibility that one of them would continue the journey down the river with me to the end.

The next morning, I woke up, collected my gear, and headed down the stairs to Al's truck, Al appeared to say good morning. He was kind enough to drive me over, and I made final preparations for the raft and thanked him again for his help. He signed one of the Spare Key House stickers that I had put on the front of the raft to thank those who had helped me. I gave him some shirts for himself and the others, and I drove over to the fuel dock and fueled up.

Before I left, I was reminded that I had lost the cap on one of the gas tanks. How I don't know, and to be honest, I don't know if it was hiding somewhere in the raft or somehow found itself in the river. In any case, I needed a new gas cap or I wouldn't be able to fill that tank with fuel. Al suggested we reach out to Pat to see if he had one. We walked up the ramp and walked over to the marina office, and sure enough, Pat had just what I needed and didn't want any money for it. Perfect!

After a few more thank you's and expressions of gratitude to Al, I boarded the SS Hail Mary and began my trek to Grafton. No sooner had I turned out of the marina than I was met by five separate tows pushing barges up the river. I quickly asked the first captain where he wanted me, and he stated, "Two whistle" (starboard to starboard). I began to make my way to that side, and with each subsequent tow, remained on their starboard side as we passed one another by.

With no locks and dams in my future that day, I had decided to run the raft between 5.8 and 6.1 miles per hour to see if that would positively affect water accumulation in the tubes.

Speed, along with weight distribution, seemed to be a key in managing the water accumulation.

The challenge of the lock and dam system was that speed is often a critical part of getting in and out of them quickly. This only compounded the entrance of water into the tubes. This along with how weight is distributed impacts the ride of the raft. As long as the top tubes, particularly at the rear of the raft, ride up and out of the water, the water that gets into them is minimal.

As I continued my journey to Grafton, I paid close attention to the details of this theory, keeping the raft at a constant speed and trying to keep its lift where I wanted it to be. The wind was picking up, as expected, but it was manageable. I found myself in between a tow and a ferry and navigated between them with minimal disruption. But then I found myself, within a couple of miles of my destination, at an awkward angle, and turned my head to see another tow pushing empty barges hard and fast upriver.

At first, I assumed the entourage was underway, and then it appeared to be sitting still, and as I got closer it was apparent that it was indeed under full power. I radioed the captain twice to no avail, so I went to the default position, port to port, and passed by without incident.

After getting past the tow, I called the marina to get some instruction on the best way to approach it, given the Mississippi and Missouri River's confluence and the problematic passages my maps showed in trying to enter the marina.

Brad, the harbor master, gave me good advice and instructions, and I proceeded downriver past the marina about a half mile, turned to my port side outside of the channel, and then went upriver to reach the marina.

As I was motoring upriver, I saw a large cruiser bearing down on me from the north. I could also see its enormous wake. He was on my left and on my right was the shoreline. The entire length of the channel we shared was narrow. His wake, the narrow channel, and my little raft reminded me of being a kid in a bathtub, sliding from side to side as the waves got higher and higher until they finally splashed out of the tub and onto the floor. Except instead of being scolded by my mom for making a soaking wet mess, I would be soaked and swamped inside my raft by the waves created by this Mississippi River version of the "Bathtub Effect"!

I got on the radio and toggled the captain. "This is the captain of the SS Hail Mary, a small homemade raft, proceeding northbound to Grafton Marina, calling the captain of the cruiser bearing down on me from the north on my port side. Anything you could do to turn down that wake would be much appreciated."

Without missing a beat, the response came back: "Captain of the small homemade raft, this is the Original Gangster, and I will trim this down before I get up on you. Have yourself a great and safe day!"

Now *that's* the way it's supposed to work on the river when it comes to this kind of encounter.

As the Original Gangster went by me, we both waved at one another, and I shouted "Thank you" although I'm sure he didn't hear a word. But I suspect my manic waving underscored my appreciation.

As I got closer to the marina, I called Brad again as the markings into the marina were, to me, a bit confusing. Plus, it was a windier than I would have liked. Brad came down to the dock and helped guide me into my slip.

With the raft tied up and secure, I thanked Brad and began to wind down for the day. I checked on the water and was pleased that less than six gallons had gotten into the tubes in the three hours I had been on the river. This seemed to confirm my belief that speed and weight distribution were critical in managing the situation.

As I had made my way to Grafton from St. Charles, I had gotten a text from Gus Gaspardo. Along with Bob Deck, one of his riverboat captains, Gus was driving down from St. Paul to Grafton to help develop a better pumping solution for the water. He said they would meet me around 3:30 p.m., and I was ecstatic!

Gus had already reached out to me weeks ago to offer to join me on the raft when I went through St. Louis. He had shared with me that he had concerns about the amount of traffic and my being able to manage through it on my own. I was very happy that Gus would spend a couple of days with me on the raft, all the way down to Kimmswick.

When I'd first reached out to Gus about planning this journey, he had offered his help and assistance immediately, despite the brutal economic pounding his company has taken from Covid-19. After that, he became one of my strongest advocates and mentors, and someone I repeatedly reached out to for help and advice. Not once did he decline to help, which made my trip more meaningful, and possible, each time.

Bob Deck is the kind of character you would hope to meet if you got to meet a riverboat captain! "Eccentric" might be too strong of a word, but he's definitely someone with the qualities to be an amazing eccentric if he ever decided to be one! He has written a book about his experience as a riverboat captain, which he gave to me before I left, and I'm still hoping to read it once I find some time this summer.

After a few hours of tidying up and doing some writing, as I was walking back to the raft, I heard a greeting behind me, and it was Bob and Gus! They were a sight for sore eyes!!!!

The three of us sat down, had a drink, and got as caught up as we could in a short period of time. After an hour or so of banter, Gus and Bob went and took a look at the raft tubes, and we talked a bit about what I thought the issue might be, what I had done to try to mitigate the situation, and their thoughts on the fix and solution.

Gus had brought a big bag of equipment and materials for a fix he had in mind. After a couple of hours, he fashioned a system designed to allow me to pump the water out from inside the cabin while I was motoring rather than waiting to find a location to tie up to and remove the water.

In theory, I should be able to use my pump and attach it to Gus's system and pull the water out in real time. But as I have learned on this raft on the river, theory and reality don't always collide in the most positive way!

Once the work was done, I moved the SS Hail Mary to a covered slip that the marina was kind enough to offer me, and then Gus, Bob, and I had a big dinner at a local pub. Bob and Gus had gotten a vacation rental for the night and offered me an opportunity to sleep there in the warmth of their place, and I readily accepted.

The next morning I was up at five o'clock and quietly slipped out to take a shower and ready the raft, then continued to try to catch up on my writing. Around 7:00 a.m. Bob and Gus appeared and we began to offload boxes and materials to offset Gus's weight on the raft. Along with the fuel, two other boxes, and some odds and ends, Gus and I provided the weight on the raft.

Before leaving, I had a radio interview to do. Gus and Bob exchanged final instructions on where we would meet Bob, who would drive Gus's truck to St. Louis, and then Gus and I got underway.

We had decided to use only the kicker motor on the way to the first lock and dam—the Mel Price lock and dam—and keep it running at about five miles per hour. The goal was to see if reduced speed and weight distribution would remedy the water situation. Our plan was also to test out the new water removal system once we got through the first lock and dam.

I admit it was nice to have Gus on the raft and have a conversation with someone. We talked about the trip, life, and how to address future challenges on my journey down the river. Gus has been on the river for forty years and has seen the Mississippi from its beginning to end many times. His experience and insight were invaluable to me. So, too, were his comforting comments like "You're doing fine" and "I'm confident you will figure it out." We came upon a few tow and barges (but nothing significant) and a couple of small boats along the way.

As we approached Mel Price lock and dam and I called the operator, we were notified that a tow pushing a barge would be pushing into the main chamber and we would need to wait.

Bummer!

The wind had picked up, and it was chilly, but the wind wasn't out of the east so I was happy for that. Gus and I puttered around for an hour or so, glancing at the lock and dam to see if we could determine the tow's progress, and chatted about the raft, speed, water, and a bunch of other things. I hadn't had too much casual banter with friends and family since I began the trip. Phone calls back home were usually to let people know I was safe, get an update on how things were at home, and tell folks that I loved and missed them. Just chatting about nothing was a luxury at that point in my journey and I was grateful for the chance to do it.

After about an hour or so, the Mel Price operator came on and instructed me to come into the chamber after the tow passed me by. I acknowledged the instructions and began to get underway.

Behind us was another boat making way to the chamber. As it got closer, I realized it was a small vessel I had met in Clinton, Iowa. It was a family of three and their dog, in a little boat they had purchased in Canada. If I remembered correctly, St. Louis was their final destination. In any case, I remembered this boat being tiny for the number of people and pets in it, and its posture on the water looked even more precarious than mine.

As we entered the chamber, it was much windier and more turbulent than any previous lock I had come into. Part of this was because of the recently departed tow. In any case, I took great care in entering as the rolling waves and wind had us bobbing around. This facility would be a floating bollard system, like Lock and Dam Number 19.

As we pulled in, I threw my rope around the bollard and Gus grabbed onto a set of stairs to try to keep us from slamming the rooftop into the side of the lock. Behind us, the family in the boat was having a tough time in the wind and rolling waves. They couldn't get tied up, and the young son who was trying to do so was not wearing a life jacket as he got perilously close to the edge of the boat. Finally he got tied up, but then their boat began to swing around. Ultimately, it ended up being turned around backward as we started to lower in the chamber.

It took far longer here than in Lock and Dam Number 19 to lower, and I don't believe it went down nearly as far. Furthermore, we had to wait a significant amount of time for the gates to open once we were down. And when they opened, we found a large tow pushing a barge preparing to enter the lock in front of us.

We motored by quickly and then got back underway. I shook my head a bit as the tow came upon us and passed close by, creating a wake that I then had to cut over to avoid the push against my port side.

As I looked behind me, the family in the boat had made it through and was cutting directly in front of the tow as it was proceeding into the lock. The family wasn't particularly courteous, and I was surprised they didn't get a stern sounding of the horn from the towboat. They continued with their relatively reckless ways by cutting in front of us as they passed us, creating a series of wakes and waves that bounced the raft around for a few hundred feet.

A little while later, we came upon another tow and stayed on its port side as we motored past an extensive fleeting area with tons of boats, tugs, tows, and barges. Within a few miles, we came upon a large sign with an arrow directing us to the channel we would take to get to the last lock and dam: Number 27.

In front of us was the family with the boat, who headed in the opposite direction of the arrow. After a few minutes, they must have realized their mistake and motored back into the correct channel. This was a narrow, narrow channel, and I asked Gus what we would do if a tow came in pushing barges.

His reply was, "Stay out of their way," which seemed like rather good advice!

We also attempted to use the pumping system that Gus had devised. Unfortunately, the electric pumps were not strong enough to pull the water up to the top of the pipes as they were currently set. The pump kept running but not drawing water; if we kept the pump running dry for too long without water it would burn out the impeller and we would have nothing but a ruined pump for our efforts.

So, as he has shown me time and time again, Gus came up with another solution: use the system he'd built but hack a small transfer pump unit to hand-pump out the water.

It worked!

Slowly the two of us removed as much water as we could get access to and managed to avoid a tow and barge that had entered the very narrow channel. We stayed on its starboard side, and as jumping carp flew by us, Gus pumped, I drove, and we finally got past it.

Not long after, we got to Lock and Dam Number 27, and I could not have been happier! I called, and the lock operator, Carol, answered and told me we could get right in and get right out. True to her word, that is what we did, but not before I had the chance to float instead of being tied up in the lock and dam. I thought it was a fitting way to end my lock and dam journey, floating in the pool despite my anxiety and fear about doing so in the past. Whether I have conquered my fear or not remains to be seen, but this much is sure: I was done with locks and dams on this river, and I was grateful!

The boat traffic increased once we had passed through Lock and Dam Number 27 and entered the river's mouth at St. Louis. We were only a few miles away from where we would tie up from the night and I was anxiously looking at the tubes. Would they be high enough above the waterline when we arrived to hand-pump them if we needed to, or would we have to improvise some other solution?

After another forty minutes, we saw the famous Arch of St. Louis and the riverboat where we would tie up for the night. The Gateway Arch Riverboats owner, a friend of Gus's, had agreed to let us stay there.

Moving toward our spot, we had to maneuver around several towboats and barges. As we approached, we saw Bob Deck waving at us. We brought the raft downriver and then made our way upriver to tie up. Even after we did so, we were dealing with the wakes of several tows pushing barges upriver; the raft bounced up and down to the rhythm of their wash.

We climbed up off the raft and greeted Bob. We also saw that the tubes looked like they were well above the waterline! The strategy of slower speed and weight distribution appeared to work for two straight days. I could not have been happier!

Once we tied in and cleaned up, we headed up to the hotel for the night—the rough waves that the SS Hail Mary would be enduring meant that sleeping on the raft would not be an option. We had a nice dinner, talked politics, and gave Bob a bunch of grief. He is a good sport and a good man. After dinner, we went our separate ways for the evening.

I had some trepidation about leaving the raft and how it would fare overnight, but there wasn't much that could be done to address this until I checked it in the morning.

As the day ended, I thought of my daughter, whose birthday was the following day, and how much I missed her. I fell asleep looking forward to continuing on the raft with Gus through St. Louis, and soon after, meeting up with my brothers. This would mean that the final half of the journey down the Mississippi River would begin in earnest.

Chapter 18
Gus, Gas, and Gadgets

As we headed out to the Gateway Arch Riverboat dock where the raft was tied to one of their riverboats the next morning, I got a glimpse of the SS Hail Mary, who was hiding most of her cabin underneath the walkway's high railing. It was nearly 8:15 a.m. and Gus, Bob, and I were about to begin the next step of the journey. From all indications, it would be a challenging trip through some of the busiest tow and barge traffic we would encounter north of Baton Rouge. As Gus had already shown me, his forty years of knowledge of the Mississippi made what I was doing seem like kid's play.

My confidence level was pretty high that morning—not because of my skills, but because I knew I could count on Gus to give me sage advice on how to navigate what I imagined to be treacherous waters.

When we got to the tie-up location, we were met by Gary, the Director of Operations for the riverboat company, and others. We made small talk and then went to survey the SS Hail Mary. She was no worse for the wear from the previous night, and the tubes appeared to have stayed at the same level they were the previous day.

As I readied the raft for departure, Gus removed water from the tubes using the new system he had installed. But despite his best efforts, we could not get water to draw up through the tubes. While we had been successful with a hand pump, the number of pumps it took to draw a gallon of water was eighty. To put that in perspective, when I drew sixty-plus gallons from one tube, that would have taken nearly 5,000 pumps of the little handle!

We both agreed that we weren't overly concerned about the water in the tubes based on our visual observation, given the short distance we had to go that day. If we continued to motor at the same pace, with the same basic weight distribution, with Gus serving as "moveable ballast," we felt confident we could reach our destination, Hoppie's Marina, in

Kimmswick without much trouble, then address the water in the tubes when we tied up.

We said our goodbyes, and Gus gave Bob some last-minute instructions on meeting us at Hoppies. By 9:00 a.m., we were underway.

Almost immediately, we knew that we were in for a ride that day.

The wind was brisk from the south and the water was choppy. The upriver traffic and the direction it was heading made it necessary for us to decide which side of the river we would ride at the outset. We decided to go to port and stay there, to see if the river traffic would keep to starboard or if we were going to spend most of the day playing Frogger. Within fifteen minutes, we were fighting big rolling waves created by the wind, the river, and the boat traffic in a confined and narrow space.

In previous situations where I had met this kind of water, the raft's nose would almost immediately dive into the water. However, I'd learned a few things about the raft by now, also thanks to Gus:

First, having fuel tanks sitting on the front starboard and the port bow had been a mistake. The combined weight of three Attwood tanks, twelve gallons apiece, was nearly three hundred pounds. That weight, including the sloshing effect of the fuel inside, had compounded any front-loading of the raft and the porpoise-ing effect it created.

Second, speed not only created issues with water gathering in the tubes but also pushed the raft farther down, and faster, into those rolling waves. Once inside a wave, the motors kept pushing down—not through—it.

Third, the capacity to "trim" the raft was nearly non-existent. The combination of the cabin structure, weight, and weight displacement, plus the Nissan's age and minimal power, left the raft with minimal trim effect. However, because of its placement on the starboard tube, the kicker motor had the power and capacity to lift the stern high enough to keep the top surface of both back tubes above the water while having little effect on any other aspect of the raft.

Fourth, and most importantly, cutting those rolling waves into quarter slices rather than slamming into the entire wave was critical.

My previous approach to rolling waves was to throttle up and slam into them with the idea that doing so would lift me up and through each wave. However, unlike scenes from the movie *The Perfect Storm*, where George Clooney, jaw clenched, meets each massive wave by pushing the throttle forward and riding it up and over, that doesn't happen with my raft. Whenever I tried to "Clooney" my way through, I found myself driving my raft deeper down into the rolling wave, resulting in water swamping the deck and coming into the cabin, at times filling the transom so full that water came up through the steering console in the aft section of the boat.

So now, faced with nonstop rolling waves and trying to avoid approaching tows, some with and some without barges, I kept my focus on cutting the rolling waves into quarters, keeping my speed constant, and turning my head back and forth so I could keep track of the traffic.

The wind was compounding every challenge, and as we got deeper into the river traffic mess, I could tell this was going to take some time to work through.

After a half hour or so of bouncing around on the port side of the river and not finding any relief from the rolling waves, Gus and I decided that trying the river's starboard side might be better for us.

Or, as Gus said, "It couldn't be any worse!"

He was right once we got there; it wasn't any worse. But it wasn't any better, either!

The ships kept coming, as did the rolling waves. Gus would intermittently sit on the raft's bow, and then as the rolling got worse and the water bouncing up got him soaking wet, he would come back into the cabin and wait out the worst of the waves.

As this continued unabated, so, too, did the traffic.

Earlier in this journey, I described encounters with lots of boats at one time as feeling like I was in the middle of a *Star Wars* battle scene with fighters from the Rebel Alliance and the Empire duking it out while I tried not to get in their way. This was just like that, except with even bigger ships and nature, too, conspiring to make the battle even scarier.

No matter where we looked, there was movement on the water, with tows going from side to side and barges coming straight up the river.

The rolling waves kept coming and coming and coming.

Several times we took some big rollers, and water hit the deck hard, but it mostly stayed out of the cabin.

I was standing the entire time, and my legs and back hurt from the tension of trying to keep cutting the rolling waves and avoiding traffic and keeping us from digging deeper into the water.

All the time, we kept the kicker motor at the same speed and the Nissan in idle, just in case we needed a burst of quick, extra speed.

The raft was moving faster than the kicker was turning. In other words, without the current, the kicker motor would have carried us along around five miles per hour. Because of the current, we were getting an additional two to three miles per hour of speed.

Gus continued to advise me to avoid the temptation to speed up to tackle the rolling waves. He kept saying we just needed to work our way carefully through them and keep our eyes on traffic. And he would keep telling me, "You're doing just fine" or "You're doing great." Whether he was lying to me or not, I chose to believe I was doing "just fine" even if I never felt that I was "doing great!"

During the two hours or so we fought this stretch of river, there was no opportunity to let down my guard. We had a constant presence of challenging and rolling waves and chop, wind, and traffic that required me to stay entirely focused on the task at hand.

Finally, we got to the end of the long stretch of river where we found ourselves at long last seeing the end of moving traffic.

Except for one last towboat that was pushing down hard in the water as it approached us, heading northbound. Aboard the tow appeared to be sediment collected from the dredging operation we could see ahead of us. We were on his port side; on our starboard side there were parked tows and barges, and the space between us was not very wide. The tow was cutting in right at us, which forced me to angle even further to starboard. Finally, he passed us by, but the enormous rolling waves he created began to wallop us.

I think these were the worst rolling waves we had dealt with, even with the massive traffic we had left behind. It took us a good five minutes to work through his rollers, but once we got through, the river ahead of us calmed down considerably. We had calm seas, warm sun, and little wind for the next half hour or so, and no river traffic.

After a half hour, though, the wind hit us hard from the south. It was perhaps the hardest straight-on south wind I had experienced on the trip so far.

Finally, ahead of us, we saw Hoppies Marina. As we approached, I could tell that this was a much different Hoppies than had been described to me as I planned the trip. The Hoppies that "was" included a gas dock with fuel for big and small boats and some other buildings that had once been in the river or on the river. Unfortunately, severe winter ice had sunk and destroyed the fuel barge that Hoppies had relied on to fuel customers for decades. More damage, including low water, had left other structures up on the riverbank, limiting the marina's capacity to dock boats and, more importantly, create a revenue stream for its operations.

Hoppies is considered by many to be a slice of Americana. Its combination of age, steel, and concrete give it a *Waterworld* meets *Mad Max* feel. As someone who isn't an expert on the river, or marine life, or how any of the marina facilities operate, I found it both comforting and unsettling in places like this. I could only imagine that it must be a hard life to work all this equipment and material into some arrangement wherein a living could be made.

In any case, the Hoppies team was allowing us to remain there through Saturday morning for free, and I could not have been more grateful.

As we approached, a man hailed us to pull up to the barge. We slowly came up and brought the raft's starboard side to the dock and tied it up. After a few more men approached and helped us, we adjusted the raft's position to accommodate a fifty-foot boat that would be arriving later that day.

We made introductions, and then Gus and Bob shared stories of Captain Bill Bowell's days with the folks who came to help us. As we got the raft ship-shape for the rest of the day, the Hoppies team went about their business.

The first thing Gus was going to do was cut down the height of the tubes he had inserted into the pontoons in Grafton. The pumps I had did not have the power to pull the water up high enough to drain it. Despite his best efforts to prime the pump, there just wasn't enough lift in the one-tenth horsepower pump, or wet vac. So Gus set about refashioning the tubes to be shorter. With the tubes shorter, the pumps didn't have to suck water up so high. While it would require me to lean out and over the back end of the raft to slide a hose into the tube to pump the water out, at least now the pumps would be able to actually remove the water. Even better, though the tube would be considerably shorter, it would still be eight inches or so higher than the existing access to the tube. This meant it would be further out of the water when the pontoon started filling up, which would give me plenty of room to slide the hose in and pump the water out without fear of river water pouring in as soon as I attempted the maneuver.

The best part of the day was learning that the starboard tube had barely eleven gallons of water in it after eleven hours of travel, and the port tube had half that amount.

That was a *huge* deal given that through St. Louis, we had hit water that kept us plowing through for nearly three hours, and that we had spent a long eight hours on the raft the day before. Keeping the pontoon as level as possible through proper weight distribution and a slower speed had given us time and space with the water being collected inside the tubes. And now with an improved way to access the tubes, without the worry of tube openings being under the waterline, my confidence in the trip's success returned.

We did some additional clean-up, charging, and wrap-up, and then went to stay in town at an inexpensive hotel for the next two nights.

It had been a fabulous day coming down through St. Louis. This much is true: I do not believe I could have gotten through it on the raft without Gus being onboard. His advice and his comforting presence, plus knowing that he was well aware of how we had to attack the river at that point, allowed me focus on the task at hand and not spend my time worrying about things I couldn't control. Thanks to Gus and his friend Bob, the SS Hail Mary continued to find hope on the river.

Chapter 19
Hoppie's The Last Fuel Stop for 250 miles

For decades, Fern and Charles "Hoppie" Hopkins and their legendary Hoppie's Marina were well known as the "last gas" on the river for boats heading south. When I first started planning my trip back in July, Gus had made clear to me that "You have to stop at Hoppie's!"

At the time, I'd nodded in the affirmative, not quite sure what a Hoppie's was or why I needed to go there. Over time I began to understand. Hoppie's served as literally the last fuel stop between Kimmswick, Missouri, and Memphis, Tennessee. A 250-mile stretch of river.

There's no easy way to get fuel, at least gasoline, along the shoreline for those miles, and if you haven't come up with a plan for others to run fuel to your boat, or if you don't have enough storage tanks to get you by, your time on the river may involve an empty gas tank and a vessel stranded on the Lower Mississippi. I, for one, had no intention of being one of those people! So when Gus told me that Hoppie's was the place I had to stop, I added it to my itinerary.

Unfortunately, some things had changed in the past few years at this famous spot. First, Charles was gone, although Fern remained firmly at the helm. I was told it was a rite of passage that Fern would come down to the barges and provide boaters proceeding southward a lesson in what they should expect. I understood that she would hold a meeting every day between 3:00 p.m. and 4:00 p.m. to describe conditions on the river, sharing information that would benefit anybody wise enough to heed her expertise. Second, Hoppie's had undergone some tough times of late. In 2018, ice sank their fuel barge, and despite efforts to raise it, the marina no longer was able to provide fuel to boaters. We had known this ahead of time and anticipated we would need to arrange for someone to take us to a gas station in town at some point.

However, the town is a short distance away, and a taxi trip and portable fuel tanks allowed Gus and Bob and me to make quick work fulfilling that need. My original plan was to spend one night at Hoppies, tied up to what essentially is a floating barge, but this turned into two nights, and because three of my brothers were joining me for the following week, for the critical stretch from Kimmswick to Memphis, the good folks at Hoppies allowed me three nights on the barge. I could not have been more grateful for that!

Hoppies is, admittedly, different from the previous marinas I had stayed at since beginning the journey. First of all, there are no amenities to speak of at the facility. You come in, you tie up, and if you need electricity, they have it. Beyond this, you are basically on your own.

The guys who operate the marina are enormously helpful. They are working to figure out how to get the place back to 100 percent operation, given the tough times they've experienced due to the loss of their capacity to provide fuel. Yet one can tell that this place is a testament to human resiliency. There can't be anything easy about running a facility for the years that this family has operated it.

Hard work has certainly been a big part of their success, but they also had to fight Mother Nature, the U.S. Army Corps of Engineers, unstable economies, and now a global pandemic. That they are open at all is confirmation of hope on the river.

Part of our reason for staying here, in addition to the original stated goal of securing adequate fuel reserves, was for Gus and Bob to show me how to literally park and anchor the raft now that access to marinas, docks, and other "easier" docking options would become limited and few and far between.

Although I experienced all sorts of crazy situations on the trip, the one that caused me the most distress was needing to figure out how to bring the raft up onto the shoreline for the night. Additionally, understanding how and where to anchor the raft if there was no obvious place to bring it to shore was another thing that was causing me sleepless nights.

I was not a boater. The raft was not a boat. It was a pontoon with a garden shed on top, two motors, and a rather pitiful mariner steering it.

Understanding how to safely bring the raft to shore, and equally if not more importantly how to get it back off the shoreline, was a skill in which I desperately needed a tutorial to ensure success.

Gus and Bob were kind enough to give it to me.

Around 10:00 a.m. on Thursday, we headed from the hotel to the marina, and within short order the three of us were on the raft and shoving off from the dock. The goal was to identify a location within a wing dam to anchor and learn how to pull up on the shoreline.

While one of the drawbacks to wing dams is the damage they can do to your vessel if you are not paying attention, the beauty of wing dams on the lower stretch of the river is that they create pools of protected water that makes it easier for boats, and rafts, to pull in between them and tie up. In other words, to bring a vessel into the shoreline for a safe place to park. Because the boat is inside the wing dam structures, it is also outside of the navigation channel and you can feel pretty confident that you will be relatively undisturbed by passing tows and barges and their accompanying wake.

That morning, we started by sizing up a wing dam option, determining its depth and fitness for me, bringing the raft into it, and then bringing the raft up onto the shoreline. With Bob and Gus on the raft's bow, we made a slow trek to the side of the river opposite of Hoppie's and began to angle the raft in between two wing dams. I kept my eye on the depth finder, making sure that there wasn't any sudden change in structure or depth underneath me, and then very slowly and cautiously proceeded to bring the tip of the raft onto a sand bar in front of me. Gus and Bob then threw the anchors into the beach from opposite ends of the raft, stuck them into the ground, and "Voila!"—I had successfully parked the raft on the beach! I could not have been happier!

Gus had assured me previously that this was not as big a deal as I was making it out to be, and he was right, as he had been so many times about so many things. The anchors kept the raft in place and only when the wind got particularly brisk did the port anchor slide through the sand.

Because of the wind, Gus suggested that we consider trying the same process on the Hoppie's side of the river, between wing dams on the channel's green buoy side. I was game, and we prepared to leave the beach. Unfortunately, for some reason, the kicker motor first refused to get into gear and go into reverse, then simply stalled out. I fired up the Nissan; however, reverse on the Nissan is pretty weak.

After a minute of rocking the motor from side to side, it finally came free and we backed out. Why the kicker didn't start and stay started, I did not know.

However, Gus offered me another vital piece of advice. He said to make sure to keep the stern, and consequently the motors, clear no matter what happened. He said that if a situation like this developed in the future, I should turn off the motors, reestablish the anchors, and catch my breath. Then reassess the problem and start over again. The fact is, if you are tied up on shore, you are safe. You may get stuck there, but better to be stuck on shore than stuck in the middle of the navigation channel with tows and barges threatening you along the way.

I finally got the kicker started again and we proceeded across the river. We then did the process pretty much all over again, except this time we chose not to bring the raft up onto the shoreline. While the water depth was sufficient for us to anchor, we didn't have a perfect point of attack on the sand beach, which would have left the raft's stern sitting in nearly ten feet of water. We did throw in anchors, and the perch we had was solid, so I felt good about what we had accomplished.

We went back to the barge at Hoppies and spent a couple of hours talking about what we had just done, life in general, the trip, and nothing at all. It was good to have a couple of hours to have a drink on the barge with Bob and Gus, enjoying their company and the nice weather.

We would be having dinner that evening with a friend of Bob and Gus, riverboat captain Michael Coyle, and his wife, Vera, who had come to the United States from Russia. As captain of the Twyla Luhr, Michael had been driving big tows and barges down the river for years. He's a big guy and has an even bigger personality. His eyes light up when he is excited, and they are always moving. His voice is difficult for me to describe but one I will never forget. He clearly loves Vera, and while I couldn't understand her very often because of her still-heavy Russian accent, he did his best to interpret. I could tell that Michael has a warmth about him and absolutely loves the river and the job he has had since he was a young man.

At dinner, we talked a bit about my trip, and Michael offered his insights based on decades of traveling the Mississippi. He offered me suggestions and warnings about places along the river, making it clear that my trip would be far more dangerous on the lower river than the upper river. But he also offered me confidence that it was doable.

As I shared with him where I was heading after Kimmswick, he offered me his cell phone number and told me to call him if ever I needed help. I could not be more appreciative because this stretch of the river was confusing to me and offered many more challenges.

We parted ways after our wonderful dinner.

I didn't know it then, but Michael's assistance would be critical to me in the weeks ahead. Gus, Bob, and I talked about him all the way back to our hotel, and they made it clear that I should take every advantage to engage with Michael between now and Baton Rouge. The trip was going to increase in intensity and danger, and someone like him could well be the difference between success and failure as well as life and death.

The next morning I got on the phone with Michael, and true to his word, he spent nearly an hour with me helping to plot out the next seven to ten days, all the way to Memphis. He and I walked through my travel plans and stops, and he helped me tweak them a bit and add some potential locations to tie up. Like Gus and Bob's knowledge of the locks and dams, his knowledge of the lower river was simply remarkable. My guess was that he probably knew upriver as well. His voice carried the confidence of his familiarity with the Mississippi along with lowkey assurances that I would be okay, and his counsel was delivered in a tone and cadence that kept me focused on every word he said.

I am honored that these three riverboat captains were willing to share their knowledge and expertise, and I very much appreciate how the information they shared with me directly impacted the trip's ultimate success.

As I waited for Fred, Hans, and Karl to get to Kimmswick, I knew that one of my younger brothers, Karl, who would join me on the raft, would be the beneficiary of the new skills I had learned and the information I had gathered from my time with this community.

Chapter 20
Karl Comes to the Rescue

My brothers got to Kimmswick around 11:30 at night after a marathon drive from the Twin Cities. Arriving tired but safe were Hans, Fred, Karl, and my niece, Matilda. The next day was going to be a long day on the river and I was anxious to get back on the SS Hail Mary.

Gus and Bob had left earlier that morning, and I couldn't get to the raft all day. I had spent most of my day rearranging my gear for about the fiftieth time, running quick errands to the store, and trying to get caught up on work. When my brothers and niece arrived, we chatted a bit about the plan for the next day, including a meeting in the lobby at 7:30 a.m. and being ready to get underway in the raft by 9:00 a.m. I knew it would be an early morning for them, given the lateness of the night, but I'd learned that trying to stick, generally, to a travel plan made sense.

With that in mind, I gave them the keys to their hotel room, wished them a good night, and off to bed everyone went.

The next morning I was up early, retracing what I felt the travel schedule would look like from Hoppie's to Memphis. The first item on the schedule for the day, my first day on the raft with Karl, was the Kaskaskia River. More specifically, a campground located on the point of an island after we turned onto the Kaskaskia River. As I reviewed the plan Michael and I had come up with, I took a photo of a sheet of paper where I had written the itinerary and texted it to Hans and Fred so they would generally know where Karl and I would be as we traveled.

About 7:15 a.m., Hans came down and I reviewed the plan with him and showed him on the chart how I thought it would work. We waited for Fred, Karl, and Matilda to get ready. Finally, we were all together, and I reviewed the travel plan for the day with everyone. We would need to grab some water before we left, and as we packed up the car, it was just about 8:00 a.m.

After a few minutes of getting the water, we arrived at Hoppie's around 8:15 a.m., where I connected with Ray, who worked the marina, and shared some information about Spare Key and who and what we were. I thanked him again for allowing me to tie up there and giving me some extra days so that my brothers could catch up to me.

We had to lug all my supplies back down to the raft, where I gave Karl a very brief tutorial on the SS Hail Mary and some of its workings. I assured him he would have plenty of time to learn what there was to learn on the raft.

About 9:00 a.m., we were ready to go. We bid farewell to Hans, Matilda, and Fred and told them we would see them next in Cape Girardeau. And we were off!

Before I go any further in this story, I want to share with readers how it was that Karl came to join me on the raft. Months earlier, when I had decided to take the trip down the river, I had envisioned going it alone. After all, how hard could it be, right?

As Hope on the River became a reality, so too did the reality of what the trip was going to involve. There was a nonstop requirement to pay attention to everything and anything. To towboats pushing and pulling barges, locks and dams, the weather, other boats, the river waves, and wakes, leaking pontoons, directions, wing dams, and a host of other obstacles I would deal with on any and every given day. These realities, coupled with my limitations and shortcomings as a mariner, kept me literally on my toes.

On the upper river, with its system of locks and dams, I had figured out how to manage my way—sometimes by accident, sometimes by luck, rarely by learned skill—without disastrous results. However, I always knew that the lower river was going to be a different beast completely. A beast that could take my life, as Captain Michael Coyle had told me repeatedly over dinner, if I wasn't prepared physically and mentally for what lay ahead.

In contemplating the lower river and the dangers associated with it, and knowing that my raft was starting to feel the effects of age, river trauma, and poor seamanship, I began to seriously question whether or not I would be able to successfully navigate the dangers on my own. The offer from Gus to accompany me through St. Louis really gave me more reason to wonder about the trip's odds of success if I continued alone.

The lower river would be more shallow, with a faster current and less opportunity to secure assistance from shore. On top of all that, I would be faced with the increasing level of commercial traffic from larger, faster, and more powerful towboats. These factors, coupled with a raft that demanded all my attention as it began to deteriorate, made me reconsider the idea that I might need an extra pair of hands.

Karl had shared with Hans that he thought the trip sounded like an adventure and he might be open to joining me at some point along the river. It had seemed to me that the right point was where we were now, in Kimmswick, as I was preparing for the last segment of my journey to Baton Rouge.

Like me, Karl had no experience with boats, the river, navigation, etc. So on the last part of this trip, we would learn together. But more than that was the dynamic of two middle-age men, who happened to be brothers, taking this dangerous journey together. Karl and I come from the same family and we love one another, but we could not be more different in how we think, live our lives, and react to the world around us.

I called Karl and shared with him where I was at mentally on the trip and what I thought it was going to take physically to complete it. I told him that if he was up for an adventure, I would consider it a privilege to have him join me.

His response was "Erich, I'm committed to helping you make the trip a success!" And that is how Karl came to join me on this adventure of a lifetime.

I had decided we would use the kicker motor most of the day, and since our travel schedule called for us to go about forty miles, I felt pretty confident that we would reach our destination with plenty of daylight left. The goal was Kaskaskia, Illinois, but I also had the city of Chester as a backup about another ten miles down the river if, for some reason, our plans changed. I tried not to spend all my time educating Karl on everything about the raft. I figured things would eventually make sense, so I tried to answer questions he had and then enjoy the ride.

We had a fair amount of wind, mostly from the south, which meant we were fighting to keep the raft moving forward at a decent speed, making the trip a bit of a challenge. No matter how often we tried to build up some speed, we would turn directly into the south wind and it would cause the raft to be sluggish, which required me to throttle up a bit to keep us on pace. The longer the day went on, the stronger the wind got, which made it also pretty chilly as it was mostly overcast and already a bit cold out.

About ten miles or so into the trip we encountered our first tow—actually, two of them.

The first was a massive structure. I couldn't tell if it was moving or not and, to be honest, I didn't even know if it was a barge or a tow. For the longest time we simply thought it was a dock that another tow with barges was moored to. However, as we got closer we saw that it was two tows, one pushing something I hadn't seen before—blades for windmill propellers! The height of this barge was simply colossal, and I am still trying to find someone who might be able to tell me how tall it was. I have to believe it was at least the height of a twenty-story office building.

Barely above it was the tow tower that was pushing this structure up the river. Directly behind this tow was a traditional tow pushing about fifteen barges up the river. We decided to stay on the starboard side of both of them and as we passed, their rolling wake gave us quite a ride. I used the technique that Gus taught me: quarter the wake and not take it on directly.

Still, it was a bumpy right for a while and Karl got a quick introduction to some of the rollers I had been dealing with since the beginning of my journey. Once through this stretch, we continued onward, encountering a few more tows here and there and a couple of small fishing boats, but nothing too ornery.

The wind continued to push hard against us, and I have to admit a stout south wind can kind of knock the energy out of you after a while. There was really no way to block it when underway without creating a sail effect on the raft. So except for a warm coat, hat, and gloves, there isn't a lot of protection against it.

As we came around a bend, we both looked at the navigation charts. We felt we were getting close to the mouth of the Kaskaskia and, to be honest, I was looking for some obvious sign of the turn. Why I thought there would be sign saying "*Kaskaskia River-Turn Here!*" I do not know, but there isn't and there wasn't.

Soon we saw some people standing and milling around the port side bank of the Mississippi, and according to our navigation charts, the mouth of the Kaskaskia should have been near the area where they were standing. The other clue was seeing some picnic tables on an island that was jutting out a bit into the river.

Karl remarked, "I think that's the mouth of the river right there." and pointed to an inlet just beyond the point of the island. He was right. We began to turn out of the navigation channel and into what was clearly was the mouth of the Kaskaskia. There, much closer than I imagined, was the Kaskaskia Lock and Dam! Now, the plan was not to lock through and go further upriver. It was simply to turn the raft to port and slide it up on the shoreline and tie up for the night.

Which is exactly what we did. With not much effort we got onto the shoreline and Karl jumped off and threw the anchors into the water.

The problem was, I didn't feel particularly comfortable with how close we were to the Mississippi River channel, which couldn't have been more than fifty yards from the mouth of the Kaskaskia River. I assumed that northbound and southbound tows would create significant wake and cause the raft, at a minimum, to do a lot of rolling around, and at worse dislodge us from our location. The Kaskaskia current was virtually nonexistent where we were, but the rollers from the tows on the Mississippi would change that in a hurry.

I suggested to Karl that we untie and move several yards further along the river on that shoreline and tie into a protected area that was kind of an elbow. This maneuver would also bring us closer to the entrance of the lock—although, as I have learned, these are not nearly as close as one thinks they are. Still, I wanted to be sure that where we were planning to tie up made sense, and I decided to call Michael Coyle to confirm this with him. He assured me that were in the right location but then suggested we call the lock and dam operator and ask them if they had any advice on the best places to tie up. I hadn't even thought of that, but it was a great idea!

So I found the phone number in my *Quimby's* and called it, and after a couple rings a man answered. I explained the situation and the trip and asked if he had any advice on the best place to tie up on the island.

Without missing a beat he said, "Well, why don't you just tie up to my dock. After all, a barge might miss the turn on the Mississippi River and come crashing into you where you're trying to park now."

Um, what?

Yeah, I hadn't thought of that, but after looking back at how close the mouth of the Kaskaskia was to the turn off the Mississippi for a northbound tow, it made perfect sense!

I readily accepted the offer and after some coaching on the phone and shouting over the top of the lock, Karl and I found an extraordinarily convenient place where there were cleats attached to a kind of concrete walkway on the starboard side of the entrance to the lock. We quickly tied up and I scooted over to where the gentleman who ran the lock was to thank him for his kindness.

His name was Charles, and the only request he had was that we not climb a very tall steel ladder attached to a concrete wall. He said that if we fell, we would fall right into the water and then likely go over the dam.

No further message was needed to convince me that we wouldn't be climbing the ladder!

I thanked him again, and at his request told him I would call him on the radio on channel 14 in ten minutes to give him details about my trip and the raft so that he could enter it into his records.

Walking back to the raft, I laughed out loud at our good fortune and luck. While I have confidence that we would have been just fine on the shoreline, the fact that we would be tied up securely to a concrete wall for the night was absolutely a treat.

Every single time I needed something like that to happen, it happened, and I knew it was because there were good people in the world willing to lend a hand.

I called Michael and shared the news with him. He was delighted at our good fortune and wished us a safe and restful evening.

Karl and I got everything straightened up, got the windows in, and started to figure out how our bed layout was going to work. After a bit, we had a plan and then just kind of hung out and revisited the day. I was glad that his first night on the raft would be something a bit easier than being tied up on the shoreline. About an hour or so after we tied up, I got a call from Hans. He said he, Fred, and Matilda were at the lock and dam and wanted to get us some beer! I chuckled and said I didn't think that was going to be possible unless they could get Charles to let them in. Unfortunately, the lock office was closed for the day and they weren't going to be able to access the lock platform to even wave at us.

After about twenty minutes of shouting into the air, blowing the air horn, and trying to orient them to where we were, it was decided that we probably weren't going to see one another that night.

They headed to Cape Girardeau and Karl and I hunkered down for the night. It was chilly and soon I was grabbing my orange hunting coat to snuggle further into the sleeping bag.

Unfortunately, besides the chill of the night, there was also a constant gurgling sound, and then every once in a while what sounded like a gulping sound from the river. I was worried that what I was hearing was water slowly being sucked into the pontoon. So I would get up, shine my phone light onto the tubes, and assure myself that they were safely out of harm's way. Yet within a few minutes I would be awakened again by the same sound. It was a fitful sleep and at around 4:30 a.m., after Lord knows how many times I had gotten up, Karl looked over and inquired, "Um, what exactly does 'first light' mean?"

He was referring to my plan for us to be ready to leave at first light, and I assume he was thinking that I thought 4:30 was first light.

I assured him that it wasn't, and we both tried to grab a couple more winks of sleep.

By about 5:30 a.m. I was up and made us coffee as we prepared the raft for departure. As it got closer to daylight, we were pretty much ready to go. However, I wanted to try to radio and see if there was any tow traffic entering the channel near the mouth of the Kaskaskia.

Michael had suggested I do this, given the fact that the channel was bracketed on both ends by pretty sharp bends, which made it nearly impossible to see approaching tows. Furthermore, if they were making turns in the bend, it was going to have an impact on our ability to proceed safely forward.

After several inquiries without any answer, we slowly and cautiously got underway. As we peaked the nose of the raft out into the Mississippi River channel, Karl looked both ways as far as he could. Once we were satisfied we couldn't see anything, we got ourselves into the channel and underway.

The plan for the day was a sixty-two-mile journey to Cape Girardeau. The reason for the early departure was that we were hoping to arrive around 3:00 p.m. to take advantage of the opportunity to meet the mayor and to garner some media attention. A man named John McGowan had reached out to me on August 17 with this email:

Dear Mr. Mische,
I read the Star Tribune article of your trip down the Mississippi. Up until March, my entire career has been in social sector serving nonprofits in an administrative capacity.

For the last 15 years I have resided in Cape Girardeau, Missouri. A potential stop on your way downstream. As a sleepy Mark Twain town it may not be a lucrative one. Our NPOs are down between 30 and 40% on revenue.

However, I believe that my media connections for both radio and TV may prove helpful in getting the word out about your trip. Potentially, without making a stop.

If there is anything I may do to assist you in your endeavors, please don't hesitate to ask.

I had immediately responded with gratitude and told him I would love to take him up on his offer.

As Karl and I proceeded, the wind was behind us from the north at around ten to twenty miles per hour, which I hoped would help assist us in creating some speed. Again I had decided to travel mostly on the kicker motor, with a plan to turn the Nissan on every hour or so to let it idle, and that we would also begin regularly removing water from the tubes.

After some trial and error, Gus had perfected the system that would allow Karl and me to remove water in real time from the tubes. In other words, to remove water as we were underway and under power. The key was to prime the pump by holding the tube that would be in the pontoon to draw the water up in the river. Then, when water began to come out the other side of the garden hose, to pinch the hose with water it in and slide the tube into the pontoon. We tried it out multiple times in Kimmswick and it worked, but the real test would be as we were actually traveling.

We tried it and sure enough, it worked perfectly and like a charm in both pontoons! We didn't draw much water and I told Karl I thought that was a good sign. Once we got a system down this would work perfectly!

As we went along further, I had decided we would try to keep our speed up to around eight or nine miles per hour. That would help get us to Cape Girardeau in the timeframe we were hoping for, and if we could keep bailing water in real time I felt that we would afford to take this approach. Furthermore, the strong north wind was helping us pick up another mile or two per hour in the faster moving current.

Every hour or so Karl and I would drag the extension cord to the back of the raft and plug it into the generator, and then I would lean back and remove the cap from the first pontoon.

He would take over steering and then with the tube stuck in the water and the hose end in my other hand, Karl would plug in the pump and I would wait until it primed. Once it was primed, I would crimp the hose and then stick the tube into the pontoon and wait for a second, and then water would flow! Each time we did this, for both pontoons, it usually produced a gallon or two of water, and often not even that amount.

We continued to try to run the raft so that the rear end of the pontoons did not have water running over the top of them. And each time we followed up with the water removal plan, it resulted in very little water being drawn out. We continued this pattern and kept our speed up, but we also began running into more and more tows.

Not only that, but the size of the tows was increasing, as well.

Furthermore, Michael had given me a list of different bends on this stretch of the river and encouraged me to check in via radio before we entered to see if there was any northbound traffic we should be aware of.

Dutifully, each time we did this.

Unfortunately, not every time did we get a response.

On that day, we ran into eight tows pushing barges as well as a large dredger and what I believe was a fuel barge. We also went through two different sections of the river where tows were "fleeting" barges and causing a ruckus with the water.

Throughout the day, with the tows that did not respond to radio calls, I stayed on their port side—one whistle, port to port. Each time we had to contend with pretty intense rolling waves, and at one point I told Karl that it reminded me of a section of the river in St. Louis that Gus and I went through. However, Karl and I continued to make good time despite the river traffic.

The weather, particularly the sun, made infrequent visits during the day, and the wind continue to be extraordinarily strong. Most of the time it was at our back or near our back. But from time to time, based on where we were traveling with the bends in the river, we would run smack into it, particularly if it was blowing from the northwest.

We also faced a new challenge, or at least it seemed new, of strong cross currents in the water. As we came into one particular bend, I could see what appeared to be two different streams of water going in different directions. In addition, large whirlpools were swirling around, and I could see that the water here was nearly sixty feet deep. In starting to come around the bend, I suddenly could hear both the Nissan and the kicker (which I had running in the event we came across a tow in this confined area) make sounds as though they weren't grabbing any water.

The raft itself suddenly felt as though it had no power.

Then the wind caught us.

This was enormously unnerving.

I wasn't quite sure exactly what to do. I trimmed both motors down so that they dug deeper into the water and throttled up. Soon the raft picked up and started moving but I could feel the whirlpool effect starting to try to turn us.

I did not like this. So I throttled hard on both motors and as I did, I could feel the back slide to the right and the front slide to the left and then get hit again by wind.

I said a few curse words and throttled back down. That seemed to do the trick and got us moving. I then slid the raft further to the starboard side of the channel and away from the churning mess that we had come through, which seemed to be mostly situated on the port side of the channel.

This happened to us once again further down the river, but thankfully the second time around it was less intense and there was much less time involved. As time went on, we encountered more tows and more roller waves and endured more bouncing like a bobber on the ocean. But we were still making good time, and soon I was able to text John McGowan to say I thought we would arrive somewhere around 2:30 p.m.

My other two brothers and Matilda had already connected with John, and the plan was that we would all meet at the Kidd's Fuel Barge, where we would tie up. As we got to within an hour of the final destination, we ran into a situation which, again, was new to me, but about which I had been warned by Michael Coyle to be prepared for.

In front of us was a tow on a sharp bend that literally looked like it was doing a U-turn in the middle of the bend. It was clear that we wouldn't be able to proceed forward until it was done with its maneuver. While we waited for it to do whatever it was doing, Karl and I emptied the water from the pontoons. I transferred fuel from a tank into the Nissan so we would have total power when we came into Cape Girardeau, and otherwise we proceeded slowly forward.

Finally, the action the tow was taking was complete and it was obvious it was now making its way south into the channel in the same direction that we were going. Now the problem was, how do I pass it and on what side?

As I was getting ready to radio the captain of this southbound vessel, I spied in front of it on its port side barges suddenly coming into view around the bend of the river.

Pretty soon we saw more and more and more.

Finally, it was apparent that this tow had forty-two barges it was pushing upriver!

Yikes!

I got on the radio and toggled 13 and said, "This is the captain of the pleasure boat that is currently southbound behind a tow that is southbound, now seeing a northbound tow proceeding in our direction. Would either captain of the vessels I mentioned have advice on how I should proceed?"

A voice came on the radio and told me to get on the ship's port side.

Problem is, did the voice come from the southbound or the northbound tow?

So, I radioed again and asked, and then received confirmation that I was to stay on the port side of the southbound tow. As we did that, I began to motor ahead of the southbound tow, guessing that it was going to stay put until the northbound vessel got past it.

Of course, I was wrong!

Not very long after I began my maneuver, I could tell that he was proceeding forward. In judging the angle between where he was, where I was, and where the navigation channel was, I couldn't tell what exactly I was supposed to do. Additionally, I was running out of space between the shoreline and my raft as a huge sand bar was starting to jut out into the space between the shoreline and the navigation channel.

If I kept on this path I was going to run aground.

Yet if I got back into the navigation channel I was convinced the tow would run me aground. I got back on the radio and simply said, "This is the captain of the southbound pleasure boat that the southbound tow has already assisted with directions. I have to tell you I am at a loss as to what I should be doing right now in terms of where you are and where I am. I need some advice."

Calmly he directed me to get closer to the red buoys on the navigation channel and keep them on my outside but stay close to them. He said as long as I did that I should be fine.

With that in mind, I proceeded forward. However, as I looked at the depth finder, I could see that the water was getting shallower and shallower. Karl reminded me of the sand bar and suggested that we were running out of deep water.

He was right, and pretty soon I saw that the depth finder was showing only three feet of water. That did it. I turned the raft directly toward the channel and kept my eye on the southbound tow. Almost immediately the water got deeper and as soon as I got within a foot or two inside the channel, I turned hard to port and began my journey back down the river toward Cape Girardeau.

At this point we needed to figure out where Kidd's Fuel Barge was and keep our eye on the southbound tow. John McGowan had sent me a photo of the barge, so Karl and I tried to eyeball the shoreline to see if we could figure it out. At about the same time we spotted it, and Karl was fairly sure he saw Fred and Hans.

As we came toward the barge, it was very windy from the north and I was concerned about which approach I should make. I told Karl I wanted to try to approach from upriver and see if we couldn't finesse it onto the dock.

That was a dumb decision.

First, it was just Karl and me at the moment, and coming in from the upriver side was not only going to involve a fast-moving current, but also the wind. Trying to throttle down and slide the raft onto the side of the barge was going to be difficult for someone who didn't really know how to drive a boat!

Second, Hans and Fred, for the moment, were on the opposite side of a gate that was locked and wouldn't be the extra set of hands that we needed to literally grab the raft and bring it to the barge. Almost immediately I regretted my decision as I came in fast and had to slide the kicker into reverse to keep from slamming into the barge. In the meantime, I nearly got Karl smashed into the side of the barge. I cursed.

I reversed hard and the raft barely moved. At this point I knew I needed to take a breath and refocus the angle of the motors in a way that would turn the nose of the raft back down river and allow me to throttle up, then turn to port and get back into the river so I could turn it and come back upriver.

I could see Fred and Hans climbing around the locked gate and clambering onto the fuel barge.

I told Karl we would now approach from the downriver side and that he would need to throw Hans the rope from the bow on the port side and let him grab it and quickly tie up. I came upriver and started to angle the raft toward the middle of the barge with the idea that I would slide it further up as the current slid me into the side of the barge.

With some effort, that is pretty much how it worked, and soon Fred and Hans and Karl had us safely tied up the barge.

Whew!

Soon we were joined by Mayor Bob Fox, John McGowan, Melissa Stickel of the Community Partnership of SEMO, two television reporters, a public radio station, and Matilda.

After doing some interviews about the trip and Spare Key, pulling water out of the tubes, and buttoning up the raft for the night, we proceeded up a steep ramp and then to a hotel that Melissa Stickel had arranged.

The only challenge, for the moment, was that John had mentioned that the fuel barge was going to need us to leave at 7:30 the next morning for a couple hours while a boat came and fueled up. I was trying to determine if that was going to be feasible or if it would just make more sense to take off the next morning and head to our next stop, which was Cairo, Illinois.

To be honest, I was beat. It had been a long day. While it wasn't a crazy day in terms of specific challenges or crisis, it had worn me out. So I made the decision that we would spend two nights at Kidd's Fuel Barge, even if it meant I had to get up early the next morning and move the raft for a couple hours. With that decision made, we proceeded to our hotel for the night.

Once again the kindness of strangers who became friends was a remarkable reminder that people are good in this county. It's a reminder that people are looking for hope but they are also bringing hope to others.

On our second day I got up early, did some writing and was picked up by John and we had a great lunch at the Pilot House. Karl got in a run, and I spent some time refueling the raft with Hans before he, Fred, and Matilda went further down the road to meet us in Hickman, Kentucky. That evening Karl and I hunkered down for an early bedtime and I reviewed our travel plans for the day ahead.

The next morning as my brother Karl and I prepared to leave Cape Girardeau for Cairo, we did so after two full days of being in beautiful city, with wonderful people having given us their kindness in ways we will never forget. We left Cape Girardeau, as we have left every community that has welcomed us with open arms and kindness, with the understanding that no matter where we have been we have found hope on the river.

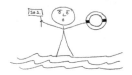

Chapter 21
Prepare to Abandon Ship

It was a crisp and cool but clear morning in Cape Girardeau. Karl and I woke up, and the plan was to walk to the raft at 7:00 a.m. and depart at around 8:00 a.m. I grabbed some coffee and then we headed toward Kidd's Fuel Barge, where the raft had been tied up for the past two days.

I had purchased a little canvas wagon in town and was now using it to bring my luggage and computer bag to the raft. I figured that it might come in handy in future stops, as we would be tied up in places that might be a mile or two's walk from gas and food, so being able to wheel things back and forth would be useful.

As we approached the raft, a guy with a mask and three dogs came up. I asked if I could take a picture of his dogs, and he agreed and then said, "It's John!" I looked again and sure enough, it was John McGowan, who had been and so remarkably helpful in planning our trip and our accommodations in Cape Girardeau.

At lunch the previous day I shared with him that I tried to take pictures of dogs in each town I stopped at and send them to Owen, Maisie, and Mary-Helen, so he decided to bring his dogs over so I would be able to do just that!

As I chatted briefly with John, Karl brought our things down to the raft. It was cold, so I was eager to make sure that we started the motors and gave them plenty of time to warm up. I told John I would try to come right back but needed to get things prepped on the raft. Unfortunately, in the time it took for me to do that, he had to go to work. I cannot emphasize enough how grateful I am to folks like John.

People who began as strangers will become lifelong friends of mine because of Hope on the River.

Karl and I got the raft ready. I started and tended to the motors. He got the pump prepared to drain the pontoons. Our process may not

209

have looked pretty, but it was efficient and got the pump primed into the pontoon so that each of us could return to our respective places on the raft and continue along our way.

After draining the pontoons, we put away the acrylic signs, made sure charts, maps, and digital equipment were ready and working, including the radios and depth finder, and got underway. The plan was to travel to Cairo, Illinois, and tie up at an island location called Angelo's Towhead, with the following day being a relatively short jaunt to Hickman. Travel distance would be a bit over fifty-one miles, and we felt pretty confident that we would be able to make good time and get to Angelo's Towhead with plenty of daylight to spare.

As we got underway, the wind was not particularly strong but the temperature was still brisk. We began with only the kicker motor going, and I planned to try to get into the channel and hope the current would bring us up to about eight miles per hour.

Travel that day would be filled with the many sharp bends in the river that Michael Coyle had given me a heads-up about. He emphasized that we should avoid, at all costs, any towboats that were attempting to maneuver inside of river bends in a sort of U-turn that would have us caught between the shoreline and the rear engine of the towboat. The areas he warned me about were marked on my navigation charts and I intended to pay awfully close attention to them, per his instructions!

The day seemed perfect for travel, and our plans were pretty well marked out. As with most things on the trip, nothing was ever quite what it seemed later in the day! The travel was pretty unremarkable at first, other than the water being relatively calm and without a lot of towboat traffic. We did encounter a couple of tows here and there, but generally speaking we were able to get by them without much trouble.

Even in the bend areas that Michael had warned me about there weren't tremendous problems, and we certainly didn't find ourselves in a situation where towboats were doing U-turns.

As we got to within ten miles of Cairo, we began to talk about whether we should just continue to Hickman or stick with our plan to tie into Angelo Towhead. In this same stretch, we came upon a couple of towboats in a relatively narrow channel bend, accompanied by more deep water, rapid currents, and what I can only describe as the small but aggressive whirlpools that I had dealt with the previous day.

This lower level of the Mississippi runs much faster than the river above the locks and dams. Sometimes it would catch me off guard so quickly that we were suddenly going three to five miles faster than just a blink of an eye ago. And in some of these bends, the water current was so fast and the whirlpools so ubiquitous that, coupled with wind, we had to fight to keep the raft going straight.

We found ourselves in one situation within a couple of miles from the turn-off to Angelo's Towhead, where a tow was running upriver and the only location for us to pass him was on his starboard side. Unfortunately, there wasn't much room between him and the shoreline, so we ran through some rough wakes for several minutes until we were able to get back underway at our original speed.

We found ourselves in another situation after this where three towboats were coming at us simultaneously. The first two were nearly right on top of one another, and in this situation, we were told to stay on the port side of the towboats.

Again, there was truly little room between us, the shoreline, and the towboats. The roll and the wake were intense, and I struggled to keep us cutting into the wake the right way without getting too close to the vessels.

In situations like this, I needed to move closer to the vessels in order to be able to have room to turn back toward the shoreline to cut the wake. If I didn't, I ran out of room on the raft's starboard side and ran the risk of hitting shallow water and submerged obstacles nearer the shore. After finally getting through this, we at least knew we wouldn't face another significant bend until sometime after we got past Cairo.

Soon afterwards, Karl and I decided that we would indeed continue to Hickman and stay there, especially since I had earlier in the day spoken with the Coast Guard based in Hickman, who suggested I talk to the captain of the ferry about tying up. When I reached Captain Jeremy, he readily agreed that I could tie up to his ferry barge and it wouldn't be a problem. Given a choice between that and being able to leave the raft and perhaps get into town or staying tied up on an island for the evening in the raft, we chose the former. Besides, as I told Karl, it was only a short seventeen miles. We would get to Hickman with plenty of light to spare in the late afternoon.

At about the same time, Fred texted me and asked what our plans were, and I shared with him that we were going straight to Hickman rather than Cairo. He asked me how long that would be, and I said we should arrive there between 4:30 p.m. and 5:00 p.m.

Unfortunately, as I would discover about twenty minutes later, I had made a significant miscalculation.

I have never been particularly good at math. Today was a perfect example of why! As I looked again at the map, and then at the numbers I had calculated in terms of total miles, something didn't add up. The distance on my map looked a lot further than seventeen miles. In fact, it looked twice as far as what I had told Fred and Karl.

I reworked the numbers and, to my horror, it was clear we were more than thirty miles from Hickman. Based on our current speed, it would be closer to 6:00 p.m. before we got there. I triple-checked my math and sure enough, my math deficiency was now painfully obvious.

I was both angry and embarrassed. Karl was annoyed, and rightfully so. It meant more time out on the river and would potentially put us into a situation where it would be getting dark before we could dock for the day. We both decided to stick with the Hickman plan, though, and figured if I throttled up the motors to get us going around nine or ten miles per hour, and we vigilantly cleared water from the tubes every hour, we should still get to Hickman with plenty of light on our side.

What we didn't take into account was that twenty of those thirty miles were going to be some of the craziest, heaviest towboat traffic I had seen, second only to St. Louis on the journey.

In fact, as we were passing Angelo's Towhead, we came upon the confluence of the Ohio and the Mississippi rivers. There were barges as far as the eye could see up the Ohio River.

But they were behind us, and that was good.

Unfortunately, what was in front of us was exactly the same, and all these vessels seemed to be moving in a relatively chaotic dance motion.

And a lot of them were moving toward us!

Our plan to move quickly through the water was also being thwarted because we were no longer in tight channels that helped keep our speed up while also blocking the wind. Rather, we found ourselves in vast pools of water where the wind was getting choppier as it picked up. When all this was combined with the churn caused by towboats, we were slowing down.

There isn't as much current in these large bodies of water, so you end up relying solely on your motor power. The problem with that is if a south wind is added to the equation with the chop and the waves, there's not much you can do to make the raft move faster than eight miles per hour.

If I hadn't been wrong on my Hickman calculation, that still would have gotten us into the harbor with daylight to spare—just barely.

But at this pace, it was going to be well past sunset before we got there.

I had given both Hans and Fred a heads-up about my mistake. I asked if they might talk to Captain Jeremy in Hickman when they arrived to make sure they could convey to me how I was to make it to his location—especially since I would be coming in hot and with daylight fading.

As we continued on our way, we continued to encounter massive numbers of towboats—some moving upriver—others moving across it—and others looking like they were getting ready to pull away from the shoreline at any moment. At one point, a towboat came on the radio and warned another towboat that there was a "floating school bus with a guy with binoculars" who was "proceeding south and you should be aware of it!"

Karl and I both laughed, and I got on the radio and toggled back: "This is the floating school bus speaking to the northbound towboat respectfully looking for guidance on how we should pass one another."

He came back on with a smile in his voice and said, "If the school bus is talking to the Charlotte, I would advise two whistles—starboard to starboard."

I complied with this guidance, and we passed without incident.

At this point, Karl and I decided that we should clean the water out of the pontoons. I also decided to replenish the fuel in the kicker motor and the Nissan for the final stretch to Hickman. If we were going to run hot, I wanted to make sure I didn't end up running out of fuel in either one.

Unfortunately, we were still not out of the land of a million towboats and barges. After we finally managed to get through the current section of the river, we turned right and saw another massive forest of towboats and barges on our port side.

However, we didn't see any moving—yet—so at this point I floored the motors, and we both agreed that we would shorten our interval to every half hour to drain the pontoons.

Sadly, the large pool, the waves, and the wind continued to keep our speed down to less than eight miles per hour. No matter how much I trimmed the motors or changed the pitch of each motor's pace, I couldn't get the raft to go much faster. My heart sank as I continued to run calculations showing us getting in later, and the sunset getting closer to happening before we arrived at the harbor.

At about 5:15, Fred texted me that he and Hans had connected at the Hickman Ferry with Captain Jeremy and had a plan. They tried to send me a video and an explanation of where I would need to turn when I got there, but I was too overwhelmed with the situation to focus much on it.

We had just passed through the last of the big water and were now back in a channel. It was starting to get darker, and we had difficulty trying to identify where the channel turned.

Although we finally figured it out, we also once again found ourselves with a towboat coming upriver in the rapidly fading light. We were able to squeeze by it but then came upon another, and then one more, before the channel finally rounded the bend to the right again.

It was about this time that I realized it had been longer than we had planned to remove water from the tubes. However, we both knew that daylight was burning and slowing down wasn't going to help our cause much. Besides, we both felt confident that we had been doing a good job keeping the water out. Even with some of our high speed, the water volume had been pretty minimal, and if we got to Hickman quickly, we would have plenty of wiggle room to drain the pontoons.

At about mile marker 930, near-disaster almost struck.

As Karl and I were coming out of a bend with Wolf Island Bar on our port side, we happened upon something called Moore Island Dikes. I saw two towboats making their way towards us. It was clear that my only option at that point was to go port to port. However, there was definitely no room on my starboard side to venture beyond the green buoys.

Suddenly, in front of me was a giant, swirling, massive whirlpool. Simultaneously, the water dropped to a point where my depth finder wasn't correctly calculating the depth. I could feel us being pulled and pushed forward, from eight miles an hour to nearly fifteen miles an hour. Worse yet, I could feel the starboard bow start to be grabbed by the whirlpool and the raft beginning to get sucked into its motion.

I turned the raft to port, just enough to get out of the whirlpool, yet within thirty seconds of getting past that situation, I suddenly found myself fighting the largest roller waves and wakes I had experienced so far on this trip.

The towboat to my port side was not only creating its own massive wake, but the swirling waters powered by the current were making it all even worse. I could not find any relief, and the rolling waves kept coming—kept getting bigger—and we kept moving faster into them. I cut the motors except for a slight forward motion on the kicker so that I would have some ability to steer the raft. But even still, I was moving forward at ten to twelve miles per hour, and the raft kept digging deeper into the waves and driving down into the river.

I tried to cut them diagonally—I tried to find a place to move further to my starboard—but it was too shallow, and I could see rocks that would be the final resting place of the raft if I did that.

I was desperate, near panic, and feeling the situation rapidly spinning out of control. I was no longer in charge of the raft. The river was, and I thought that our trip, if not our lives, had come to an end.

At this point, I told Karl to grab the inflatable raft and one of the life preserver rings, and as calmly as I could, with a lump in my throat and my legs shaking, I said, "Let's just make sure we're ready if we need to get off the raft or it starts to go down." Water rushed up over the bow, pouring in the cabin and washing away an empty gas can and anything else that wasn't firmly tied down.

How we made it through that situation, I do not know. I hope it was a lot of luck, a little bit of learned knowledge, and the morning prayers I said before departure each day that conspired to see us through the carnage.

While the second towboat created its own challenges, we were finally able to navigate to the channel's red buoy side and get out of the way of the constant beat of waves and wake. I suggested to Karl that we probably needed to tend to the pontoons, given the beating.

Karl, however, suggested, and rightly so, "Why don't we get the hell out of this channel before we get nailed by another set of towboats in here!"

He didn't have to tell me twice. I reset the trim of the motors, tried to synch their speed, and got the raft up to a nice 10.5 miles per hour.

The upside to the nasty episode was that we hadn't lost any speed during the encounter. On the contrary, I was able to glance at my depth finder a couple of times and happened to see that our speed through all of this stayed well above eleven miles per hour. That was undoubtedly going to help us get moving a bit faster to our ultimate destination.

We continued to pick up speed, and then, with about thirty minutes of daylight left and a towboat in front of us a mile or two away, I connected again with Hans to run through our arrival plans.

Again, I was pretty frazzled, and trying to understand what he was saying was not working all too well. That plus the fact he told me there were now three more towboats running our way; this was about enough to make Karl and me want to scream!

Finally, I could see one of the landmarks Hans had been talking about ahead, and my spirits picked up a bit. It was, however, getting darker and darker.

As I looked at my watch, I knew we were going to see the sunset before we got to the turn-off to Hickman Harbor—the only question was how dark was it going to get before we arrived and would the lack of light make it impossible for us to know our location.

We had to stay port to port to the towboats proceeding north, and then I realized that my depth finder kept showing that we were only in about two and a half feet of water. I checked the navigation guide on my iPad, which showed that we should easily be in twenty feet of water.

This was a problem. I had towboats coming my way; I had to stay in the lane I was in, which was uncomfortably close to the shoreline, and my depth finder was showing me one thing while my other device was showing me another. I decided to believe that it was deeper than what my depth finder told me and continued to press on.

At this point, we had been able to get our speed up to about twelve miles per hour, and we were making relatively quick work of the distance between us and the harbor.

I got on the phone with Hans, and we talked about where he was and that he had his headlights on. He had told me this earlier, but I couldn't figure out which were his headlights and which were lights from other structures on the shore.

But as I got closer, I could figure out his lights.

He advised me to turn in at the harbor entrance and come directly toward the lights. As I began to do that, I realized that the towboat that had been ahead of me was now stopped and appeared to be directly in front of the harbor entrance.

That wouldn't work.

I called the towboat captain on the radio, and he told me to pass port to port—or at least I think that's what he said. Also, he told me he was backing up, or nearly stopped, and that I should pass him and get into the harbor.

At this point, the sun was gone. My ability to perceive distance and objects was deteriorating rapidly as daylight diminished. It also occurred to me that passing him on his port side would require me to go around his back, and if he was in fact backing up, that was a terrible idea!

So I got back on the radio and asked him to reconfirm his guidance.

He told me to pass on his starboard and proceed in front of him when I'd traveled enough distance, and then turn into the harbor.

This I could readily agree to!

As I continued to throttle to get past him while darkness fell, Hans and I continued to talk. He told me to angle toward his car lights.

I also still had to keep my eye on the towboat because, even though I was sure he was stopped, as he had indicated he was or would be, I didn't want to suddenly find out that he had changed his mind or that I had misheard something.

Finally, with enough distance past him on his starboard and with enough space separating his bow from the raft, I turned sharply into the harbor.

There, Hans was waving his hands frantically in the light from the surrounding vessels and shoreline. I turned off the Nissan and used the kicker motor to go toward him, and we also saw Fred and Matilda.

We got tied up. We drained the tubes. We were delighted that little water had gotten into either of them despite the hard running of the last hour and a half. I thanked God for getting Karl and me there safely and for my brothers and niece being there to meet us.

We grabbed our gear. We buttoned up the raft. Proceeded to Hans's car and then drove into town for dinner and an evening at a hotel. We would stay two nights in Hickman. The second night would be spent on the raft.

All told, we had been on the SS Hail Mary for nearly eleven hours that day. We had traveled eighty-four miles. We had almost abandoned the raft in high seas and made our way under a spit of darkness.

I was exhausted and exhilarated. I was grateful for my brothers— the one on the raft and the two who were there to greet the us—and was reminded again of my good fortune to come from a big family of people who have never hesitated to help one another.

If any day made me feel like it was time to stop the trip, though, that was the one.

I could handle the leaking pontoons. The cold nights. The cranky motors. Even locks and dams, fast water, whirlpools, flying carp, and a raft that made the smallest waves feel like whitecaps. But the massive rolling waves challenged me to my core. It made me question my decision to be out on the river. And it quite literally scared me, to the point of trembling, when I got into my hotel room.

I was nervous about the remainder of the trip ahead of us. That day had been a brutal reminder that the Mississippi River, with all its beauty and majesty, could just as quickly kill you as charm you.

I was prepared to give two months of my life to the trip. Not to give my life. But as I prepared for bed, I knew I was committed to seeing the trip through to its end.

Chapter 22
Hurricane Delta Comes to Play

The next morning, we got to the raft about 10:30 a.m. and began to prepare to return our clothes, electronics, and extra fuel to the raft. I had interviews with three different media outlets scheduled thanks to a member of the Hope on the River media team, Mary Jane Rodes with RunSwitch PR—a Louisville, Kentucky-based public relations firm. They were invaluable in getting us great publicity during the short time we were in Kentucky, and I cannot thank Mary Jane enough for her efforts!

When we arrived at the ferry barge, our friend Captain Jeremy and another person were there. I had not met Jeremey the night before because of the late hour of our arrival but now had a chance to thank him for his kindness personally. However, before I could do that, as I was stepping onto the ferry there was a space between the concrete drive-way and the ferry of about three feet of shoreline. As I stepped onto the shoreline my right foot began to sink deep into the mud. I quickly pulled it up and out and got onto the ferry, but my foot was already covered with thick dark mud from the river.

Because of the low water on the river, the Dorena-Hickman Ferry was not currently transporting vehicles to the other side. They still would take the ferry out to run over to the other side for their errands, but it was parked for the time being except for those runs.

Meanwhile, the ramp that designed to allow vehicles to board the ferry wasn't long enough to reach the shoreline because of the low water, so there was about three feet of space between dry land and the ferry. I, of course, hadn't looked at those three feet and went right into the mud!

Oh well, it would dry eventually and come off!

So I chatted with Jeremy, and Karl began to load our stuff back onto the raft.

Fred, Hans, and Matilda went into town to get gas for the raft, and

Jeremey said he and his shipmate needed to take the ferry to the other side to deliver some paperwork.

It occurred to me a few minutes later that with the ferry gone there was no easy way for me to get the fuel from Fred, Hans, and Matilda when they returned.

The only path to reach them was now going to be walking directly to them onto the shore, where there was all sorts of mud! So this time, thinking ahead, I removed my shoes and socks and slowly began to walk my way up the shoreline. Of course, I found myself stepping in the wrong place, and both feet went down into the sucking mud right up to the bottom of my knees!

Behind me, some young guy working on a barge was laughing at my predicament. I suppose it was kind of funny watching me try to get myself out of the mess and then proceed to grab the gas from Hans, turn around, and nearly go right back into the mud!

For the next half hour, we built a makeshift bridge from the dry part of the shore over the mud and onto the ferry barge that we were now tied to. Logs, branches, cement blocks, and chunks of wood were deployed, and soon we had something Karl and I could walk across if we stayed low and took our time.

We didn't have much to do that day except speak with a few people and wait for the morning, so Karl spent time reading and I charged up the powerpack and did some raft errands. At 2:30 p.m., a young reporter from public radio station WKMS, Liam Niemeyer, came to do an interview. We spent about an hour together. I showed him the raft and how it worked; he took some photos and we were done. He sent me his story the next day, which did an excellent job recounting our trip up to this point. At about 3:30, a reporter named Shelley Byrne from *The Waterways Journal* came for an interview. As we began to walk toward the makeshift bridge, she unfortunately took a step in the direction of the ground that wasn't as solid as we thought, and *boom*, her left foot went straight into the mud. As I grabbed her hand to keep her from going face-first into it, her right foot became stuck as well!

Ugh!

We were able to get her out and on more solid footing, and then I went and retrieved her shoes from the deep muck.

We decided to finish the interview from the ramp, and then I had Karl take a few photos on the raft for her story. We said our goodbyes and I jumped back on the raft for a Zoom call with WPSD-TV, which was short and sweet.

After the interview was done, Jeremy came by and gave me a lift into town to pick up fuel and food, and along the way I did a Zoom call with the Spare Key team of Abby, Alexia, and Sarah, to talk about the last leg of the trip from Memphis to Baton Rouge.

The three of them, along with Kristi, had been keeping busy with all sorts of Spare Key projects, including the Lend Smart Mortgage Mike Lust Golf Tournament, as well as helping to steer the Hope on the River trip to its successful conclusion. They are a great team, and Spare Key and I are fortunate to have them making sure we can continue to have the privilege to help families "bounce and not break."

Jeremey brought me back to the raft, and then had to reposition the ferry so that workers the next day could attempt to lengthen the ramp further so the ferry could do its work once again. He signed one of my Spare Key houses and wished us the best of luck!

Karl and I hit the sack, planning for a quick departure at first light.

We had realized at this point that now that we were traveling the Lower Mississippi, we could plan our itinerary to make better time. The current was faster here than on the upper river, and there were no locks and dams to create havoc with the travel schedule. And of course, because Gus and Bob Deck had "fixed" the problem with the water coming into the pontoons, the raft was not slowed down by this as much.

Typically, above the locks and dams, I had been limited to about six to eight miles per hour or else I would find myself looking desperately for a place to tie up before the end of the day so I could drain the pontoons. Generally speaking, I would only power up both motors if I needed to get into a lock ahead of commercial traffic, get out of a lock while preventing protracted entanglement with the churn at the exit, or get past the wake of a towboat as soon as I could.

Now, especially since Karl was on the raft with me, we could add another ten, twenty, or even thirty miles of travel a day to the schedule. The two of us, working together, had a system for removing the water every hour or so when we were at high speed. High speed was mostly around ten to twelve miles per hour, except when we hit some of the areas of the river where the current was much stronger and faster, and then we got the raft upward of fifteen miles per hour. The SS Hail Mary didn't steer as well at speeds above thirteen miles per hour, so we had to pay careful attention to where we were in the channel and try to be easy on the steering wheel, plus throttle down if necessary.

Our next goal was to get to New Madrid, Missouri—roughly thirty-three miles downriver—and after that to Caruthersville—about thirty-eight miles away. However, projected rain and Hurricane Delta required us to re-evaluate this plan. Although I had reached someone in New Madrid who said we could tie up to their harbor dock, we weren't entirely sure how that would work given the lack of places to stay other than the raft. If heavy rains were going to fall, I didn't want us to be on the raft but at a hotel or some other close-by, dry and safe location.

To that end, I had reached out to the mayor of Caruthersville and asked if the city had any safe and secure place where I could tie up the raft for a few days and wait out the rain. She responded promptly and we chatted by phone. She indicated that she had spoken to the head of the community port authority, who suggested that I tie up along the river at Reynold's Park.

Based on the conversation, I understood that there would be a chain we could tie the raft to, and the hotel I had spotted near Reynold's Park appeared to only be a few blocks away.

With that information and the promise of a safe and secure location, Karl and I decided we would make way directly to Caruthersville from Hickman—roughly seventy-one miles.

That morning, we went through our routine and had a cup of coffee while waiting for first light to appear. Finally, at 6:52 a.m., we felt it was light enough to get underway!

The day's seventy-one miles were going to be accomplished at as high a speed as possible. Our travel weather was also supposed to be pleasant, with light winds and warm enough, hopefully, that we wouldn't have to wear coats.

We encountered several towboats pushing upriver throughout the day, but we also found ourselves now dealing with towboats pushing downriver. The approach to passing them required the same degree of caution and communication. So far, the difference was that passing a southbound towboat didn't come with the same amount of wake and churn as when we passed a northbound towboat. The biggest challenge with passing the southbound towboat was getting up enough speed to get by them as quickly as possible. When passing them, usually on the green buoy side of the channel, the front end of the barge they were with would get uncomfortably close. We hugged the buoys as tightly as we could without compromising the safety of the raft or the occupants!

About seven hours or so later, we were within an hour of Caruthersville and began to talk about how we would execute the tie-up to the shoreline. I was getting a bit more anxious the closer we got because the mayor had told me previously that she would not be available to assist us with directions. For some reason, I had neglected to ask her if there would be a point of contact if we ran into a snag.

That was dumb. I am usually pretty careful to make sure I have identified a second party to connect with if the first person I spoke with wouldn't be available. This would soon become the problem I was worried about as we came upon Caruthersville and saw Reynold's Park on our starboard side. The park is located between a grain elevator and a riverboat casino.

The shoreline was all rock, and there were three concrete ramps. One was obviously the existing boat ramp. The other two were ramps of some kind that were no longer being used. However, as we slowly circled, I could not for the life of me see a conspicuous place where we could tie up. What I saw were the ramps and a *lot* of rocks on the shoreline.

I thought I saw a hopeful sign in that the rocks seemed to drop straight down into the river. Meaning that perhaps if we had to tie up to them, we wouldn't have the pontoons scraping onto sharp rocks overnight. Yet this was not working out as I had hoped, and most certainly wasn't going to work out for three nights as we had envisioned.

Finally, I suggested to Karl that we nose the raft onto one of the ramps and put out the anchors, to see if that would work.

He was dubious. I don't blame him. I was, too, but at the moment I felt we needed to at least see if this approach was doable.

We nosed in carefully, and soon we were tied up successfully.

However, I could tell that with our butt sticking out into the river, and the water pouring over the top of the pontoons, this was not a viable solution for one night—much less three!

We pulled off and continued to circle and contemplate our options.

In the meantime, I called city hall, which gave me the number to the individual at the port authority who had said we could tie up to a chain on the riverbank.

There was no answer.

I finally called the police department and sheriff's department, and the dispatcher said she would send someone down to give us a hand. I thought that someone who knew this section of the river would come down and immediately say, "Hey, this is what you need to do!" and that made me feel a bit better about our current predicament.

The truth is, we had plenty of daylight to figure out our options, but the ones we saw in front of us at the moment didn't seem optimal.

I had also called Captain Terry from Wepfer Marine who I had met via phone in Hickman, Kentucky as I was looking for additional places to tie-up as I travelled down the river, to see if he had any suggestions for Caruthersville. Shortly he put me in contact with Phillip, a local captain from the Wepfer facility in the area. He was nice but indicated he didn't

believe they had anything available, so suggested we head to Cotton-
wood, about thirteen miles downriver, and tie up at a barge they had in
that area. I added this to my mental checklist, but I didn't think another
two hours out on the river, fighting towboats at what was now nearly
4:30 p.m., was a good plan for us.

A few minutes later, an officer showed up above the shoreline. He
sat in the car, and I expected he would call me. After watching him for
five minutes, and no phone call came, I contacted the dispatcher again
and asked if this was, indeed, the officer she was going to send down. It
was, and she connected me directly with him.

I didn't catch his name, but after I had asked him if he had any
advice, his response indicated he wasn't inclined to offer much help other
than to warn me several times not to block the boat ramp.

That wasn't going to help, so I thanked him for his time and hung
up.

At this point, we decided to travel downstream about one hundred
yards to the riverboat casino and see if there was any favorable shoreline
in that spot where we could beach the raft for the night. I also called the
general manager, who, while polite and understanding, reminded me
that since 9/11, boats were not allowed to tie up on a riverboat casino.
This was unfortunate, because it would have been an ideal solution!

The manager sent out his security director to see if he could walk us
through any options from the shore. However, the closer we looked at the
riverbank, and the more we talked with him, the less confident I became
that this shoreline was a good option. Low water meant there was far too
great a chance we would ground the raft before we could safely tie up,
and the receding water revealed any number of downed trees that were
dangerous threats to the raft.

Our options diminishing, I called Gus and told him of our predicament and our situation in relation to the shoreline. I shared information
about its rocky nature at Reynold's Park and asked if he thought it was
wise to try to tie up there.

He said as long as we went in slow with our nose and kept the port
side to the shore, we should likely be okay.

So that is what we did.

Slowly, very slowly, we approached the shoreline. As we got to it,
Karl carefully jumped out and secured an anchor on the port bow side.

He then took the other anchor and secured it to the middle side of
the shoreline.

He then took a line I had tied to the rear of the raft and tied it to a
tree.

As we looked at the situation, we also took some comfort in the fact that passing towboat traffic seemed to go at low speeds in the area generally. They were far enough out that the wake they created wasn't as tumultuous here as it had been in other locations.

We took the fenders from the raft's starboard side and tied them to the port side to add extra protection from the rocky riverbank. We then drained the pontoons and packed up the basic necessities we would need for the night.

Before we left the raft, I got a text from Gus, who said he had spoken with Lee Nelson of Upper River Services. Gus had shared with Lee the challenge we were facing from weather and, most urgently, the situation in Caruthersville.

Lee told me to text him, and I did. He told me that he was working on a plan and that we should anticipate heading to Osceola, Arkansas, the next day to a property owned by Wepfer Marine. I was thrilled to hear this news!

I told Lee to keep me updated and then let Karl know that we would be staying only one night in Caruthersville and proceeding to Osceola—sixty miles away—in the morning.

Both of us then carefully made our way up the rocky terrain, trying not to fall. If we had, we would have gotten some nasty bruises and cuts. If we fell on our head, even worse! Finally, we heaved our gear up on top of one of the ramps, and I took a last look at the raft and took some pictures.

As I said to Karl, we were safe onshore. All we could do was hope that the location where we'd put the raft, and how we had tied it, would be sufficient to keep it in good condition until the next morning.

After grabbing our gear up, we ran into a city employee who said the mayor had let her know we were coming and that she would be happy to drive us anywhere we needed to go, and that we should use the rec center to shower. We thanked her and the mayor for their kindness but let her know we had booked a room at the nearby hotel.

Her reaction to hearing the place where we were staying was not reassuring! Without coming right out and suggesting we not stay there, she strongly suggested we stay somewhere else.

And when we got there, I have to say I don't blame her!

I had had to use two different travel sites to book rooms at this location. I'd booked what was billed as a king-size room with a couch through both sites. I figured Karl would sleep on the bed and I would sleep on the couch. Both were preferable to sleeping on the cots on the raft.

Before we got into the hotel, I could tell from the windows that it was a tough place. Some had curtains. Some had things that were made to look like curtains. Others had shreds of curtains. I sighed when I saw several handwritten signs on the front doors, including strict demands not to loiter, etc.

When I walked in, the lobby smelled of stale smoke.

Then a man and a woman appeared behind the lobby counter and asked what I wanted. As politely as I could muster, knowing that this was not a place that would have worked for three nights for us and would only need to work for one night, I let them know I had booked a room online.

The woman then informed me that she didn't know if they had any rooms because she was pretty sure she had rented the last one out to someone earlier in the day. I reminded her that the room should have already been booked online, so she would need to have a room for me. Both she and the man behind the counter went back and forth about what rooms they had. One had a door they couldn't open. Another had a door they couldn't close. The queen suite had a shower that didn't work, and it was a smoking room.

Back and forth they went and I finally, again as politely as I could, asked if they had a room that even had a single bed in it that wasn't a smoking room. Surprisingly, and for whatever reason, they had been remiss in knowing that they did, indeed, have that kind of room, but for only one night. I said we would take it, and as soon as I could get them to complete the reservation, Karl and I quickly made our way to the room through the dank corridor of this hotel.

Stale cigarette smoke was everywhere. Handwritten signs were everywhere, threatening to call the police. Fire employees. And kick residents out of the hotel if they propped doors open.

This was less a hotel/motel than a boarding house, and not a particularly nice one.

We got into the room, and it was about as bad as expected. It stunk. And not just of cigarette smoke; it reeked of a room that people had tried to make not stink. Two stick air fresheners had dried out but were still sitting on a desk and the sink, just another indicator that this was a place where things may have, indeed, come to die!

We decided to take a quick walk to a convenience store to get some things, and Karl wanted to grab his cot from the raft.

Once back, we settled in for the night, but not before Karl realized that the sink had a hole in the pipe so that when you ran the water, it poured onto the carpet.

Yes, morning couldn't come soon enough! When it did, Karl and I were awake way too early. We had planned to get up and be on the raft by 6:00 a.m. to be ready to go by first light.

As it was, we were both up around 4:00 and couldn't get back to sleep. Finally, at 5:30, we made a break for the raft quickly and quietly.

In the dark, we made our way down the rocky shoreline even more carefully. As we climbed onto the raft, it seemed none the worse for wear. I turned on the lights, and we started to put things in place to be prepared to drain the pontoons and then at first light get underway. I made us some coffee, and as we waited for daylight, the raft would occasionally rock from side to side and seem to be scraping on something.

That made me extremely nervous. I tried to use one of the push-poles to hold it steady as a couple of towboats came by. Karl reminded me that it had been doing this all night while we were gone, and he was right—if anything bad was going to happen, it likely already had!

Soon it was light enough to drain the pontoons. We did so, and I told Karl I wanted to get off the shoreline and just sit in the river until it was more light than dark and we could get underway. We went about figuring out how to get off the shoreline and proceeded slowly.

Of course, as I was holding the front of the raft while Karl untied the rear line, I slipped. My leg went into the river, and my right hand came down hard on the rocks. It hurt like heck, but my pride was hurt more than anything else. I came up with a few more words to be added to the Raft Book of Curses, and Karl quickly pushed us out far enough for me to feel safe starting the motors and slowly backing away from the riverbank.

As luck, bad luck, would have it, two massive towboats had just started to pass the channel we were heading into. One south, the other north.

So, we had to wait at least until the northbound towboat got far enough past for us to then get in behind the southbound towboat. When it did, we powered up, and I radioed the captain of the southbound tow, who told us to go past him on his starboard side.

We throttled up as quickly as we could and did just that.

The day was warm, and the wind was calm, and we were going fast. I had been warned that there would be a great deal of river traffic today, and both Karl and I felt that being off the river sooner rather than later would be the smart move.

An hour into the trip, we did our thing with the pump and the pontoon and then throttled back up. We ran into a couple more southbound towboats and followed the same procedure as before. About halfway into that day's trip, we came upon a northbound tow on a bend that hadn't been on my navigation app. It was pushing fast and hard, and it was full. I could see the rollers behind it, and they were huge!

We would pass on its starboard side. Unfortunately, as we passed, we would be on the inside of a bend, which would then require us to shoot straight into a massive and wide pool of water on the river. The waves from the wake were huge, and pretty soon I was bobbing and weaving as slowly as I could through the violent water. Because I was in the bend, I couldn't do much for several hundred yards but ride it out. Finally, I was able to get back into the navigation channel and cut the waves more effectively since I had more room to spare from the shoreline. However, this barge must have been pushing for a while because the waves were relentless.

Finally, I was able to cut back across the channel again to the opposite side from where the barge had been pushing and get a reprieve. At this point, we got back to nearly calm water, throttled up hard, and got underway. As we continued, we came upon another southbound towboat.

This one was pushing fast, and when I radioed the captain to ask for advice on how to pass him, he chuckled and told me to wait until I got closer.

Karl laughed, too.

This had happened the previous day when I had asked a captain where I should pass, and he'd laughed and said to wait until I got closer.

The reason for the mirth is that I wasn't nearly as close to those ships as I thought I was.

Furthermore, the raft isn't really that fast. It took me a lot longer to get close to them than I expected, and my guess is that the advice the captain gave me likely would change based upon where we both were at that time.

Finally, we got close enough and it was apparent I would need to try to pass on the green. However, no matter how hard I pushed the raft, a boat on my port side was not slacking off and was going just as fast as I was. Finally, after a half hour of this and knowing that a bridge was coming up and only one of us could go through at a time, plus knowing we hadn't de-watered the pontoons recently, we slowed down and let it go by and proceeded taking water out of the pontoons.

Soon we were back underway at full speed.

We still needed to get past the towboat, and finally we got back on his port side. The water was like glass and there was no wind. It took a good twenty minutes, but we eventually got past him far enough to get back over to the center of the channel and proceed.

When we were one and a half miles away from mile marker 875, I texted James Myric from Wepfer Marine, who would be our point of contact when we arrived to tie up. Lee Nelson had been able to secure a commitment from the owners to allow us to tie up at their facility and wait out the effects of Hurricane Delta.

Our Caruthersville plan had been a flop. There would have been no way for us to be tied up there for three days. The raft would have eventually suffered some damage, and we likely would have found the trip's future compromised as a result.

James gave me directions on where to turn into their facility, and a phone number and radio channel to give them a heads-up when we were closer. Based on my navigation app, we had only one more towboat to reckon with, and sure enough, a northbound tow, a noticeably big one, was coming toward us. I radioed the captain, who told me to come by on his port side, and we did. With a brief interval of rolling wake wave, we were back underway at top speed.

At about mile marker 873 we turned the corner and got walloped with high wind. This had been in the forecasts I had seen, but it wasn't supposed to be at this speed until a couple of hours later.

There wasn't much we could do but get through it.

I then radioed James and reconfirmed where we were meeting him. We were to take a right turn into a chute at mile marker 875 and proceed up the channel for a half mile to where we would tie up. We cut into the chute and slowly motored up the channel past massive empty barges. I joked with Karl, saying, "Look, the enemy!"

We got to a towboat and I radioed James again, and there he was at a low floating dock as we pulled up. James was a young guy, thirty-nine, who had worked for Wepfer in Osceola for nearly twenty years. He works hard, knows what he is doing, and is responsible for its operations.

Within a half hour we had tied up, emptied water, and buttoned up the raft for the impending rain, and then James drove us to our hotel. He is another example of a good guy who goes out of his way to help people. That he was willing to help us out with this situation, give us a ride to a hotel, and be available while we were there is simply another illustration of how kind people were in all the places I had traveled.

James dropped us off at our hotel, and Karl and I settled in. We made a quick trip to Walmart, driven by a de facto cabdriver named

Perry, who was retired from twenty-six years of painting farm buildings. I bid Karl good night and we retreated to our rooms.

It had been a long day, but a good day. We were safe from Hurricane Delta, secured in a dry location for the next few days, and ready to rest up for another long haul down the mighty Mississippi River!

Chapter 23
Walking in Memphis

I admit I felt a bit rusty when faced with the end of our three-day stay in Osceola and the beginning of our trip to Memphis, which would be followed by our final leg to Baton Rouge. I was eager to get back on the SS Hail Mary and proceed the roughly fifty miles to Memphis, but I was also somewhat anxious about what the river would look like after days of rain and the remnants of Hurricane Delta.

Karl and I got picked up at 7:00 a.m. by a young man named Dalton, who worked for Wepfer Marine. The good folks at Wepfer, both the owners and those who work for the company, were extraordinarily generous in supporting us with the trip! I cannot begin to thank them enough for their generosity, or to thank Lee Nelson of Upper River Services for the kindness and courtesy he extended to Spare Key and me from the beginning of the journey. Lee and Wepfer came to our aid at a critical stage in the trip, when I was beginning to wonder if we had an end game that would enable us to reach our destination.

After a short drive from the hotel, we got out of the truck, thanked Dalton for the ride, and got the SS Hail Mary ready for departure. I was pleased to see that she was no worse for the wear after several days of heavy rain and wind. We checked the water in the pontoons, and it was minimal. We mixed and loaded up our fuel, and within an hour we were ready to depart. As we did so, a Wepfer towboat was beginning some fleeting, and we passed them by and waved our thanks for the safe harbor to the captain and Dalton, who was onboard as a deckhand.

As we entered the river, a southbound towboat was in front of us, and, thanks to the guidance of the captain, in short order we were past him and on our way to Memphis. The wind was stout, as I expected it to be, however it began to get even gustier the farther we went. I had initially planned for this to be a "leisurely" trip down the river at nine miles per hour, but the combination of the current and wind had me pushing the raft upwards of ten miles per hour.

About two and a half hours into the trip, we came upon a south-bound tow called Rusty Zellar and began the process of trying to pass it—first, at his direction, on the port side.

However, as we began to set up that trajectory, a northbound tow-boat appeared in front of us, slightly to our starboard.

Before encountering the Rusty Zellar, I had been able to contact Michael Coyle, the captain of the Twyla Luhr, whom I had met while in Kimmswick. He told me that he and several other towboats were waiting for the passage of the Zellar before they, too, would begin again to head north. Initially, he indicated that the northbound towboat, the Charles Southern, would likely stay put until both the SS Hail Mary and the Zellar got past.

However, it was clear that the raft wasn't making enough speed to pull past the Zellar. A combination of wind, heavy waves, and the slow current made me rely on my boat motor skills—which, as you all know, are lacking! We could barely keep the raft at nine miles an hour, and that wasn't going to get me past the Zellar, which was keeping pace on my port side.

Suddenly it was clear that the Charles Southern was most definitely underway. At this point, I radioed the Zellar again and asked the captain how he wanted me to proceed. From the Charles Southern's angle, it almost looked like I would be passing on its port side—one whistle—but it would be a very narrow passage, and it would bring me directly into the churn of its engine.

I wasn't looking forward to that.

Nor was I looking forward to the answer from the Zellar, whose captain said, "Why don't you all just run right in between the two of us?"

As has been my practice from the beginning, I heeded his advice and, as usual, it was the right advice. Thankfully because the Southern had just gotten underway, there was little current and chop from his engine.

That, however, was going to change quickly.

No sooner had we rounded the bend, the Zellar off to my port side, than I saw three northbound towboats on my starboard side.

The second of those towboats was the Twyla Luhr, the ship Michael Coyle was captaining. He texted me and radioed me on channel 72 to pass them on the starboard—two whistles—and to keep on running as hard and fast as I could, since the Zellar was nipping at my tail now on the port side.

As I looked ahead of us, the water seemed like it was alive. The combination of the current in this particular area, with the three massive towboats keeping their engines going, had created a mess of water that, along with the wind, made the raft hit waves like they were made of sand.

Each wave hit hard, and I wasn't getting much speed. Suddenly, as I looked to my right, I could see the first of the towboats that were waiting for the Zellar to pass begin to get underway!

That was going to create even more of a mess.

Nothing I could do at this point would get us going faster. I tried trimming the motors—which on a good, calm-water day barely works, and on this day did virtually nothing. I could tell that the pontoon's rear was riding low in the water, which meant we would need to begin bailing water out of the tubes soon.

Unfortunately, Michael also informed me that after we got by these three northbound towboats and the Zeller, there was another large towboat, the Martha Lynn, making its way ahead of me through an enormously narrow and fast current bend. He warned me not to meet them in that bend and that once we got by him to call the captain of that vessel on channel 13 and coordinate our encounter ahead.

As we passed the Twyla Luhr, Michael came out and waved and took some pictures. Once we got past him, he texted, "Good Luck! And call anytime!"

I am so grateful for his help!

Finally, because the Martha Lynn was coming upriver, we made some distance from the Zellar, which had to slow down to let the Lynn get by it before it could enter the bend we were soon to head into.

I reached the Martha Lynn captain, who informed me to come by on his port side—one whistle—and with trepidation, I got closer to him. I was genuinely concerned that I would get into that beginning of that bend, and his engines would have ripped up the water so much that there would be massive waves.

Thankfully, for whatever reason, the water was relatively calm, though fast, in this turn.

Karl and I got into position and started the process of removing water. I figured that since we had spent a lot of running time in the water (we had left port early that morning), along with the terribly choppy and rough condition of the water we had been in, the starboard tube was going to have plenty to drain out.

However, even after twenty minutes, the pump was still pushing water out of the hose.

That concerned me.

I wondered if we had somehow, finally, ruptured the pontoon.

As the water continued to pour out, I grabbed a pump I had bought back in Kimmswick.

I am a redundancy guy and always want a backup to my backup. In this case, I had the two one-tenth horsepower pumps that had been dependable. But since we were still pulling water, I was concerned we might be losing the fight with the water coming into the tube.

The backup-backup pump was a self-priming pump that had a half horsepower motor attached to it. I had no idea if it would work. Ever since purchasing it, my plan had been to try it out when we tied up, but I kept forgetting. Now I was hoping that it would hastily remove the water that the other pump was having trouble vacating.

As soon as I dropped the hose into the tube, the water began pouring out of its other end. Within ten minutes, it sputtered, signifying that the tube was now free of reachable water. I quickly did the same with the port tube, which had little water.

I told Karl that out of an abundance of caution, we should remove water from the starboard pontoon every thirty minutes, just to make sure that we didn't find ourselves in a situation with a tube that had split open. We removed nearly forty gallons of water—320 pounds—and that made me think about earlier days in which I would desperately pull out over sixty gallons of water when I was able to get the raft tied up.

Fortunately, subsequent pumping of the tube reassured us that we probably had been dealing with a situation in which the rough water and speed had combined to put more water in the tube than usual.

Each time we pumped, we found a relatively small amount of water in the pontoon.

Once past the Martha Lynn, we only encountered one other towboat. It was about ten miles out of Memphis, and it cut across the navigation channel to a dredging station and was out of our way long before we arrived upon the scene.

With about an hour and a half to go to reach port in Memphis, the wind became simply ferocious. It was pushing us around like a weather bully on steroids, and neither Karl nor I were enjoying it much. The wind created swells on the water and waves that keep punching the front of the raft. This, coupled with some menacing clouds, had me searching for a safe haven shoreline in case we found ourselves stuck with a thunderstorm or worse wind. We continued to push, and finally, about forty-five minutes before we reached Memphis, we got a reprieve from the wind—our course and its direction were finally with harmony, which allowed us to motor forward.

Our arrival at the Memphis Yacht Club was uneventful and pretty easy. We pulled in, refueled our gas cans, and tied up for the next two nights. A local newspaper arrived and we spent some time being interviewing about the trip thus far. The plan was that in two days we would begin our trek to Helena, Arkansas, and ports beyond. We were optimistic that we would continue to find Hope on the River.

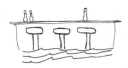

Chapter 24
A Guy Walks Into a Raft

Karl and I enjoyed a couple days of nice weather in Memphis. We had good conditions for an important task: replacing the half of the shed roof that had ripped off somewhere between Cape Girardeau and Hickman! Because he is younger, and I am not, Karl opted to climb onto the roof to help secure the new material that Wendy, Paul, and ASI Signage Innovations were kind enough to ship to us in Memphis. Within a half hour, we were able to get the roof replaced without Karl falling into the river! Again I am reminded that there is no way the trip would have happened without Wendy and her support. I am enormously grateful for all of it!

Karl then took off to explore Memphis. I spent the next few hours on the raft tidying up, doing some videos for Spare Key to use for marketing, making some Happy Birthday Facebook videos for friends of mine, and generally just catching my breath. A few hours later, I finished my errands at the raft and began the forty-five-minute trek to our hotel by foot. (The previous day, after our arrival, we had gotten a ride from the reporter with the *Daily Memphian*.) Once back at the hotel, I did some more work, checked in quickly with Karl and with home, and then decided to call it an early night.

Although we had planned to get a taxi or a ride service back to the raft the next morning, given how nice the weather was, Karl suggested that we walk. I am glad we did. It was a lovely day, and I appreciated the pleasant stroll.

When he had set out the day before, Karl had taken the folding wagon I'd purchased in Cape Girardeau to help us cart fuel to the raft, so luckily we had something to put our two stout bags of equipment, clothes, and other stuff in for the long walk back to the raft. We planned to begin walking at 5:00 a.m. and be ready to get on the river by first light. So I set my alarm for 4:00 a.m., but as has been the case for some time now,

I was usually up by 3:00 a.m. I've never needed a lot of sleep, which is good because whether I go to bed at 8:00 p.m. or midnight, I am usually awake by three o'clock in the morning these days!

Karl and I connected that next morning at 5:00 a.m. and began our walk from the hotel to the raft. It was already muggy and warm, and the brisk walk only made it warmer. By the time we reached the raft, we were soaked with sweat, but we made it there by 6:00 a.m., which was our goal.

We got the raft ready to go, and at about 6:50 slowly proceeded down the harbor channel to get into the main channel of the Mississippi. As soon as we began to throttle up, I knew that the Nissan wasn't working quite right. It seemed sluggish and wouldn't give me the power I was used to getting from it in the early days of working my way down the river. I had replaced its fuel filter the day before, just like I had done back in Keokuk, Iowa, when the Nissan began to sputter and stall out. When I'd looked at the fuel filter recently, I had seen that there was sediment in it. Fortunately, I had been smart enough to grab a few extra filters when doing errands.

However, I hadn't replaced the spark plugs as I'd planned to. I figured that as long as the fuel filter was new, the plugs I'd put in while in Keokuk would be okay; after all, they weren't even two months old! But the farther we went, the more difficult the Nissan got. We had to travel seventy-two miles to Helena, and our goal was to get there with plenty of daylight left.

As I tried to get more power, the Nissan kept sputtering and throttling down.

Finally, I told Karl that he should drive while I quickly replaced the spark plugs. It took me about two minutes to do this. I restarted the Nissan and, amazingly, she came back to life!

I was delighted! We were back in business.

However, as we went along, we encountered more and more northbound traffic and not very much southbound traffic. We found ourselves dealing with the aftermath of several rolling waves created by the towboats in narrow channels, but other than that, things seemed to be going just fine.

About three hours out from Helena, the Nissan started to act up again. It kept sputtering and, while not stopping, would barely run. I was at a loss. I texted several people I had come to rely on for things like the motor and asked them for their opinion. Each of them believed it was the fuel line.

If *only* I had brought an extra fuel line! That was my mistake! Unfortunately, I lacked an extra fuel line, so I had few options.

Eventually, I grabbed our folding chair and, while Karl drove, I continued to press the fuel bulb periodically to keep fuel moving into the motor. That seemed to work, and so for the next couple of hours, that is essentially what I did to keep the Nissan running.

In addition, I swapped out the fuel tank at the suggestion of another one of my friends to see if that would make any difference. It seemed to help temporarily but didn't permanently fix the problem. We encountered some additional towboats and had to battle our way through their waves. Finally, we found ourselves within an hour of Helena Harbor.

I placed a call to Terry Ferebee, who is with Helena Marine Service, and introduced myself. He told me that the plan would be for us to tie the raft to a barge at the end of the harbor, barely half a mile off the navigation channel but in slack water.

Slack water is precisely what it sounds like—slack. It's water off the channel in a harbor or some other protected area that is as still as you can imagine. While we wouldn't be able to get into town, we would be safe for the night off the channel, and we could stretch our legs on the barge.

We arrived at the barge and were quickly tied up. Karl and I then went about the business of cleaning up the raft and preparing it for the next day.

The issue of the Nissan motor, though, was concerning to me.

While it was conceivable that I could have muddled my way through the upper river above the locks and dams with just the kicker motor, it was a virtual impossibility for someone with my skills, or lack thereof, on this raft to make it to Baton Rouge with only the kicker motor. My concern was that it was the fuel pump that was failing, and even if it wasn't, that I didn't have access to anywhere that could replace the fuel line to see if it was indeed the problem.

I spoke with Lee Nelson again, who continued to be absolutely invaluable in finding us safe places to dock during that last stretch of the trip and ensuring our safe arrival to Baton Rouge. We both agreed that without two motors, the likelihood of me completing the trip was pretty slim. I shared with him our plan, which was to motor seventy-eight miles to Rosedale Harbor, Mississippi, and that if early on the Nissan wasn't performing at the level it needed to, we would turn back around, tie up, and see where things went from there.

Shortly after Lee and I hung up, I got a call from Terry Ferebee, who said, "Hey, Lee said you have a motor problem. What's up?"

I tried my best to explain the situation given my limited knowledge of anything mechanical. He then put me on speakerphone with a mechanic by the name of Tim that worked for him, and they asked me a number of questions.

Finally, Terry said, "You know what, why don't you move your raft to the boat ramp right across the harbor and Tim will come over and meet you and take a look at the motor."

Amazing! And so unexpected. So kind. So generous.

A pickup appeared a short time later and Terry emerged, along with Tim. Karl jumped off the raft and tied it up to the pickup truck, and Tim, without so much as an introduction, was soon on the raft and then at the back of the raft eyeing up the Nissan!

You could tell that he knew his way around motors—big and small.

He ended up running back to his shop and picking up some parts, and just as we were ready to lose the last of the daylight, he and I took the raft out to the river and made sure the motor was working.

It seemed to work just perfectly!

In the dark, we made our way back to the boat ramp. I thanked Tim, and then Terry who had shown up again, and we then slowly made our way back to the barge.

I was overwhelmed by their kindness. There was no reason for them to extend themselves further than they already had done by allowing us to take up space in their harbor. Tim had spent two hours working on the motor and could not have astonished me more with his skill and determination.

Karl and I eventually tried to get to sleep around 9:00 p.m. Both of us were up early to get the raft ready for travel to Rosedale Harbor.

I won't lie. I had a restless night, thinking the trip might have finally lost its last luck. I knew that traveling seventy-eight miles with only the kicker motor wasn't going to work. Even at its best, I could get the kicker to eight or nine miles per hour by itself. But having to deal with towboats and wind and anything other surprises would mean we wouldn't get to Rosedale Harbor until dark.

The raft isn't made for the dark, even though we had to do it in Hickman. And, even then, it was only for about fifteen minutes, and we still had enough navigable light. If I couldn't get to Rosedale Harbor, I wouldn't be able to get to any of the other places we needed to get to in order to reach Baton Rouge.

So when we set out for Rosedale at 7:00 a.m., I was apprehensive. It didn't help matters that within a couple of minutes of moving out of

Helena Harbor and onto the main channel, I throttled up the Nissan and she immediately sputtered.

"That's not a good sign!" I said to myself.

Pretty soon, however, I got the raft up to about ten miles per hour, and that was going to be our speed as long as we could keep it up.

Within an hour, though, we were already starting to see what our day would look like.

Two northbound towboats were running in a narrow channel, tearing it up and creating oceanlike waves. One I saw, the other I didn't see until we were already committed to entering the channel that both towboats had been running in hard and fast. The situation, and the layout, were nearly identical to the situation we faced going into Hickman.

However, this was worse.

As the second towboat went by on my port side, it was painfully clear that this was a perilous situation. The words "low water levels," "two towboats churning up the river," "a fast-running current," and "my raft" should never be used together in the same sentence.

Yet on that day, they were.

The first waves were uncomfortable but manageable.

The second waves, however, were unimaginable.

We were literally surrounded by waves, and I could not find a way out.

Suddenly we were lifted on a massive wave, which then proceeded to fling us deep down into the river. Water poured into the cabin. The pontoon's front door, the one that had the logo of the Padelford on it, was closed until the next wave ripped open, tearing off one of the hinges and knocking the Padelford sign out of its frame.

I could not figure a way out of this. As I looked to my right, it felt as though we were literally underneath the top of the river.

With nowhere to go except to keep going, that is what we did.

One wave held us aloft and then drove us into the next one, over and over again.

I cannot believe that the towboat could have even seen us in this maelstrom of waves if they were watching. How far we might have been from the river bottom at times, I don't know, but the very thought that we were close enough to have stayed down there chills my bones.

Eventually, we made it through far enough to deal with merely uncomfortable waves, and then, finally, mercifully, we got to calm water.

I was sweating and my entire body hurt.

The tension was exhausting.

As I had tried to do ever since Gus and I went through this in St. Louis, I throttled down and worked the waves as patiently as I could. I looked for calm water and wove my way toward it at slow speed. The entire time I did this, every muscle in my body was tensed. I kept my mind entirely focused on the waves and made sure that I was seeing as much as I could in front of me and around me to find a place where calmer water seemed evident.

I gave Karl the wheel and went about removing water from the tubes and trying to figure out what had just happened and how I could avoid it in the future. The challenge was that when our navigation app didn't work in identifying where river traffic was, we often found ourselves encountering towboats—and I do mean, plural—in narrow bends in the river. How long those tows had been in the bend, chewing up the river, only they knew. And when we got there, the residue of their efforts tossed us around like a beach ball.

I considered the option of simply waiting and letting them pass and then giving their wake enough time to settle and calm down. Unfortunately, because my depth finder was no longer reliable in telling me depths, I was reluctant to go too far outside of the navigation channel. However, I decided I might have to take that risk on these last days of the trip.

This time, we had gotten lucky. Or maybe luck, combined with the knowledge that I had to take a slow and deliberate approach through the rolling waves, is what saved us.

We weren't in a hurry. While we currently anticipated getting to Baton Rouge on October 21, I was not willing to put my brother or myself at risk because of a date. If we had to take another day or two to get there safely, then that is what we would do.

We were enormously grateful that Tim's work on the motor seemed to have done the trick as we continued. It ran smoothly all day, but also gave us speed when we needed speed. Once we got to the next town in which we could get off the raft, I planned to find a replacement fuel line. Until then, we were grateful for the fix that Tim had created.

About an hour out of Rosedale Harbor, I called Steve Couey with a company called Jantran. He and Jantran would be helping us out with a place to stay when we arrived in Rosedale Harbor. Steve and I chatted a bit, and he told me that we would be tying up to one of their towboats, the Riverton, when we arrived. I was grateful for this kindness because it would mean we would be off the river's main channel. We would still have enough daylight left to catch our breath.

To get into Rosedale Harbor, you have to go about a quarter mile past a patch of land between the river and the harbor entrance. We had had a north wind accompanying us the last few miles, and it had helped push us along. Unfortunately, that same north wind was now working against us as I turned the raft back upriver. Along with the powerful current, the wind had us moving about two miles per hour even with both motors pushing at full throttle.

The farther into the harbor we got, the harder the wind blew. I was exhausted, and I think Karl was, too, after our encounters with nearly two dozen towboats on that stretch of the river that day.

When we saw the Riverton, I called Steve again, and he and I talked about tie-up options. Eventually, we settled on tying our starboard side to the port side of this north-facing towboat.

Several apprentice deckhands came down to help us, and I got to meet Steve in person.

I thanked him profusely for his generosity and for allowing us to be tied up at a safe location overnight. Then he added to his generosity, inviting us to stay in the crew's quarters, enjoy a meal with some of their apprentice deckhands, and if necessary, use their shower facilities. None of which was expected, all of which was enormously appreciated.

It had been a tough day. Eighty miles. Towboats. Huge roller waves. But we had made it safe and sound, and I was grateful to God and those who'd cared for us in Helena, and those caring for us that night in Rosedale Harbor.

Karl and I planned to leave the next day between 8:00 a.m., and 9:00 a.m., as our trip to Greenville, Mississippi, would only be forty-eight miles. We would need to mix some additional two-stroke fuel, refill the kicker motor, and get the raft prepared for travel down the river. As on every other day, we had spent twenty-four hours finding Hope on the River—over and over again.

Chapter 25
Fast and Furious

Our friends at Rosedale Harbor had taken good care of us. Fed us. Given us a warm place to sleep and a safe perch for the SS Hail Mary alongside the Riverton. As we got ready to leave the next morning, we spent extra time preparing our fuel and ensuring that our trip to Greenville would be as uneventful as possible. The trip would be "brief," and we were eager to take advantage of it.

The plan for Greenville was to tie up slightly off the channel on the left descending bank, then find a hotel in town and refuel. As we got closer to our destination, I become somewhat obsessed with checking the fuel supply. We had continued to chew up far more fuel than I anticipated with the Nissan, and that was in large part because we had been running both the Nissan and the Mercury at full speed.

When I think of the days where I had naively thought I could venture down the Mississippi with nothing more than a rudder and a long pole, I chuckle to myself. Even after I was disabused of this notion, I still thought I could make the trip with only the Nissan. After that latest bout with the Nissan, which Tim had fixed in Helena, I was even more grateful that I'd listened to people who were, and are, much smarter than I am about the river.

While I understand how people who have the skill and ability to kayak and canoe down the river can do it and avoid the type of tow traffic we faced, I still think that would be an undertaking much more challenging than mine. At least they would have the benefit of being able to ride up along the shoreline without the worry of shallow water, enabling them to avoid the power of the towboats and their barges. But the thought of making that journey, particularly on the lower river, without two motors makes me shiver.

We decided to run the motors hard on our trip to Greenville. Our goal was to get there early enough to get fuel, get some food and water, and prepare the raft for the next day, when we would travel to Lake Providence, Louisiana, and sleep on the raft. Thanks to Lee Nelson and the industry and the companies that stepped forward to support us, we only had several more "short" trips between Greenville and Vicksburg—after which we would travel seventy-two miles to Vidalia, Louisiana.

We made good speed after leaving Rosedale Harbor, though try as we might we continued to wrestle with northbound towboat traffic. It wasn't as challenging as previous days, but we found ourselves having to throttle down and slowly work our way through roller waves that were as tall as the raft.

I remember talking with Rob, a young guy who several years ago, along with a friend, built a raft using plastic barrels and took this same journey. He told me that he had a system for calculating which towboats were the ones they needed to stay away from based on looking at the number of rollers they kicked up behind them.

The further we went down the river, the more I paid attention to those rollers. The difference, though, is that while I didn't have a set date to be off the river, we couldn't afford to dillydally too long waiting for towboats to get by us and for their wake to subside.

As we came within five miles of Greenville, I could see the FindA-Ship app showing a seemingly endless series of northbound tows between us and where we needed to tie up for the night. Furthermore, the path we needed to follow would require us to cut from the right descending bank (the green side of the channel) to the left descending bank (the channel's red side).

As we began our final turn in the bend before the Greenville location, I saw three massive northbound towboats pushing empty barges hard up the river. Unfortunately, although the channel they were occupying may have had enough room for both of us according to my navigation charts, it meant that we would be competing for space in a shallow channel amid increasingly heavy waves.

I couldn't take the risk of battling all those towboats.

To that end, I decided to stay outside the green buoys and run as hard as I could at an angle that would allow me to bypass the churn they were creating, and then angle sharply over to the Greenville dock where we would be tying up for the night. Generally speaking, this isn't something I would do. The odds of running in shallow water, hitting a submerged tree, rocks, or some other obstacle, was very real. However, I was hoping that the raft's motor and transom would draft high enough up in the water for that not to happen.

In a case of brotherly miscommunication, Karl reminded me that I was well outside the navigation channel and running the risk of hitting shallow water and grounding the raft. He gave me a look of disapproval because he knew that running in shallow water was usually something we would never do.

I did a lousy job trying to explain to him my strategy and my hope that our draft was enough that we wouldn't find ourselves coming up on something so shallow to stop us in our tracks.

Finally, we both got on the same page and were able to locate precisely where we were going to pull in.

The dock we needed to tie up on was less than a football field's length off the main navigation channel. To get to it, we had to cross the strong current of the channel and then turn left into water that formed an eddy pool next to the dock.

To be honest, I didn't quite understand the approach to the dock, and my first attempt had us nearly smashing into it. After a few more tries, we finally were able to tie up. However, the bollards we tied up to were several feet above the raft and required us to be creative as to how we would climb up to the dock from the raft.

Despite the relatively short trip, Karl and I were exhausted from the final thirty-five minutes of racing outside the channel to get to this location. Thankfully, we were soon tied up safely with full fuel tanks and headed to our hotel.

The plan, originally, was to purchase a replacement fuel line for the raft. However, we both just needed rest and decided that we would rely on the skill of Tim the Mechanic from Helena Harbor to get us to our next stop safely.

As we prepared to say good night, Karl and I decided we wouldn't need to get underway until nine o'clock the next morning given the short distance to Lake Providence. We had arrived early at this location, and we felt that if we left at nine we could probably get to Lake Providence in plenty of time to avoid nightfall. It had been a long day traveling a short distance, and we were both glad to be tied up safely in Greenville.

Chapter 26
Learning to Play the Yazoo

The plan that morning was to get a ride at 7:30 a.m. from our hotel to the Greenville dock and then prep the raft for departure. Alas, as is the case with the industry that never sleeps, issues with fleets of towboats came up unexpectedly and our anticipated ride didn't arrive. While we weren't given the reason for the towboat trouble, we assumed, and rightly so, that it took precedence over our travel plans. Commercial business comes before a goofy guy and his brother on a raft on the river.

And, with that, we patiently waited for a ride to pick us up. Ultimately, the person who managed the facility where our raft was tied up, Richard Word, came and returned us to the dock where we he gave us a case of drinking water for the trip. We thanked him for his thoughtfulness and went about getting the raft ready.

As I looked out behind us, there was a vast channel and a towboat working its way north.

The question was, could we prepare the raft soon enough to get out of our perch before the tow got so close that we had to wait, or should we make a run for it right away?

We worked quickly and finally got ourselves untied.

As we began to back out and turn the raft around, I got on the radio and asked the northbound tow captain whether we should wait for him to come by or proceed forward.

He suggested that we would be going faster south than he would be going north, so it might make sense for us to make a break for it.

So, with teeth clenched, we did.

Running hard in situations like this means a race to try to get past the engine wake of the towboat before the waves hit us. In this case, we got lucky and we were able to run through the outside left channel far enough to get past his wild roller wake.

About a half mile into the trip, Karl looked at me and remarked that we had left a folding chair we purchased in Greenville at our hotel! Along with a case of Diet Coke we had bought the night before!

I shook my head and muttered, "Figures." We continued along our way.

Our destination that day was Lake Providence, and I was pleased to receive a text from Gabe Gattle, the owner of Terrell River Services there, who had extended the offer for us to tie up in the harbor to one of the barges where they worked. The alternative would have been to tie up to a tree along the shoreline, so I was immensely grateful. We would spend that night on the raft and the following night in Vicksburg, where we would have the benefit of refueling and staying in a hotel.

Our journey from Greenville to Lake Providence seemed to be a blur of past travel days.

Perhaps it was the river's current and the fact that we were now getting to the point where putting distance between ourselves and our last stop, and trying to get closer to our final stop, had become the foremost priority.

The river began to blur together for me in a series of bends, followed by a series of northbound towboats, followed by massive roller waves and the sense of relief that we had made it through.

I knew that my focus was becoming a challenge, and I had to work hard at it. I was tired, worn out, grateful beyond measure for the help we had gotten, and aware that we were now in more desolate and unforgiving areas. The water was shallow and the bends were narrow, and despite our best efforts and the power of technology, we were struggling to avoid northbound tows. When we encountered them, I did my best to time our entry into channels in hopes of getting through their wake sooner rather than later. Sometimes it worked. Sometimes it didn't.

On that particular day, we found wider channels but no less shallow water. We hit some towboat wakes hard, and the nail-biting commenced. But we persisted until we got through and could continue down the river.

A few miles from our destination, Karl and I began looking closely at the chart and the shoreline. We were supposed to contact Mickey, the captain of the MV Kim King, which was part of the Terrell River Service fleet, and he would instruct us how to tie up at their facility.

We did precisely that, but there's an interesting dynamic that comes into play when someone like me, who has never been on the river, talks to people who have spent their entire life working on the Mississippi. What they consider to be directions are barely comprehensible to me. It is not because they aren't talking sense, but because I simply don't understand their river language. For example, the captain made some reference to calling the dredging operator at the harbor's opening and asking him to stop dredging before we arrived, and then to head right up to the harbor until we got to the end of it.

As Karl and I got closer to where the navigation chart and map told us we needed to turn right, we couldn't understand the shoreline or where there could possibly be an entrance to a harbor.

Worse, the entrance location, according to our charts, was now being threatened by a northbound towboat encroaching on our space in the channel and seemingly threatening to block our way in.

The closer we got to where the charts were telling us should be an opening, the less it looked like there was. All the while, I was nervously eying the northbound tow, which wasn't slowing down and getting closer and closer to us.

Finally, with a sense of relief, I said to Karl, "I see it. I can see the opening to the harbor." There was no way this was visible to the untrained eye of someone traveling southbound on the river. Without the navigation aids, we would have gone right past it and then have to work our way back up the river—a difficult task given the powerful currents.

Thankfully, the dredger that we were supposed to call and ask to stop dredging had completed its work for the day, and we were able to turn right up the harbor and proceed.

In front of us was a towboat moving ahead, so I got on the radio and asked for Mickey. He told us, "I'm in the Kim King ahead of you, just follow me in!"

And that is what we did.

Slowly, as his towboat pushed a single empty barge up the harbor, we followed behind him. This was a slack water harbor, so we took our time, and as we did, I emptied the water from the tubes.

We passed multiple towboats whose crews and captains saw us and waved. Many did give us odd and bemused looks as they watched our little raft making its way up the harbor.

About fifteen minutes later, we approached the end of the harbor and the Kim King turned to starboard. Mickey explained that we wouldn't be tying up to his barge but to a submerged barge that lay half on the shoreline.

We slowly eased the raft alongside this barge on the port side and tied up. I waved my thanks to Mickey and we began to get organized for the rest of the day and evening. We had arrived around 2:00 p.m., so we had plenty of sunlight and heat to enjoy. Because there was no power at this location, we decided to start the generator and plug in all our electronics for use the next day.

As the day's sun began to fade, the weather cooled considerably, and we decided to put the raft windows up. In addition, the way the raft was positioned, we were dealing with a breeze coming in from the aft, so we had to place some plastic and cardboard on the windows to keep it out of the cabin.

The next morning I woke to what felt like a storm of lights as towboats began moving early. As I got up, I saw one towboat pushing a barge seemingly right at us. When Karl got up, we both watched as the barge moved closer, and we both wondered if they saw us. We were getting ready to give them a shout.

Eventually, the barge slid past us and traveled closer against the shoreline about one hundred feet in front of us. We weren't quite sure what was happening, but by that time, we were getting the raft ready for the morning's run to Vicksburg.

Soon we were ready, but we had a new problem: the barge that had slid into the shore had tied up with its towboat's stern backed up into the channel that we needed to get through to exit the harbor.

There was a deckhand on this barge, and I yelled up to the guy and asked if there would be enough room between the towboat and the shoreline for us to fit through. Unfortunately, he said he didn't think there was, as there was a beached pontoon behind them. Worse still, he said they were waiting to load an excavator and that wouldn't happen until it was full daylight.

We had planned to start for Vicksburg at first decent light. This was going to cause a problem with that plan.

But there wasn't much we could do about it and would have to wait. And so we waited.

First light came, and there didn't seem to be any movement of an excavator.

Suddenly, the loudspeaker from the towboat blared, and the captain suggested I walk over to his barge and take a peek to see if I thought we could sneak through. The barge we were tied to had a ladder we could climb down, so I did that and then climbed up onto the barge that was waiting for the excavator.

I walked back and took a look, chatting a bit with the towboat captain, Gary. We both agreed that there seemed to be about fifteen feet of width between the rear of the barge and the pontoon on the other side—plenty of room for me to get through as long as the water was deep enough.

I thanked him for allowing me to take a look and said we would get underway. As I walked towards the end of his barge, he came back on the loudspeaker and said, "I love the Norwegian accent!"

I laughed and gave him a thumbs-up. There's something particularly amusing about my Minnesota accent getting called out by a guy with the Louisiana accent. I gave Karl a thumbs-up too and got back on the raft, and away we went between the pontoon and the towboat, with a wave to Captain Gary.

Coming out of the harbor onto the river channel, Karl and I looked both ways to make sure we weren't going to be surprised by towboats going north or south. We had fifty miles to travel, and my hope was that it would go smoothly. I could tell we would have some wind, but I hoped we wouldn't have a lot of northbound traffic. We would have the opportunity to stay at a hotel that night in Vicksburg and be well rested for the long trip to Vidalia the next day.

As we proceeded, the wind got a bit wilder but not too crazy, and we were making surprisingly good time. I knew the challenge for us over the next few days would be whether or not the Nissan would keep performing at the level it had been since Tim fixed it, and if the weather would continue to hold.

About fifteen miles out from Vicksburg, we started hitting choppier water. As has been our practice, I dutifully removed the water from the pontoon. I had also begun the practice of topping off both gas tanks every other time I removed water. Since we had gotten the Nissan repaired, I'd quit switching out gas tanks and simply transferred fuel as we traveled under power with a transfer pump. I didn't want to tempt fate by using a different gas tank and removing the fuel line in case that would some way or another disrupt the flow of fuel to the Nissan.

I also had continued the practice of keeping the fuel tank gas cap connected pretty loosely to the Nissan. The Attwood tanks we had were great for storing fuel, but I didn't think they did a good job of venting, and that created a suction that made it difficult for fuel to flow through the line.

As we came around a bend, I could feel a harsh wind, and the water was enormously choppy. A warning signal in my head kept sounding and I wasn't quite sure why.

About fifteen minutes into the bend, the warning signal suddenly became clear—it had been quite a while since I had cleaned out the tubes, and we had been not only running in hard water, but we had to get past two northbound tows and had been battling their wake and waves for a significant amount of time.

I looked out the back, and the starboard tube pipe that Gus had installed was underwater!

This was *bad*.

It meant that the pontoon had collected so much water that it had broken the "safety zone," which Gus installed using an eight-inch pipe that was supposed to always stick high enough out of the water to ensure that we never found ourselves on the water without the ability to pull water from the tube.

Karl and I were both in the back of the boat at this point—he was driving, and I was looking anxiously at the sinking starboard pontoon. I told him to jump up front and see if that would take enough weight off the back to have the tube come up to where we needed it to be.

It didn't.

I stopped the motors, hoping that the lack of movement would allow the tube to come back up.

Nope.

In fact, the choppy water made it worse.

Whether it was real or imagined, I could feel the back of the raft slipping further under the water.

I turned off the kicker motor and then got the Nissan back under power and trimmed it down so it would try to push the rear back up.

This seemed to work enough to get the tube up out of the water a couple of inches.

The question now was, when Karl came back to take the wheel, would our collective weight push it back down?

I had Karl come back and push the throttle up to half speed.

He did, and the tube stayed up at the same level, giving me an inch of space between the water and the tube to get the pump inside it.

I moved quickly and hoped against hope that the pump wasn't going to have an issue.

I slid the pump tube inside the pontoon and the water began to flow.

My relief was palpable, but my concern now was whether or not the pump would be able to get water out faster than whatever water was coming in. Minutes passed, and the water continued to pour out of the other side of the pump, and I couldn't see whether we were making any progress.

Finally, I could see a slight improvement on the starboard side as the raft platform began to lift out of the water slowly.

Eventually, it became apparent that the pontoon was rising, and eighty gallons of water later the pump coughed, signaling that the water was cleared. I said a prayer of gratitude and proceeded to clear the port tube, which had a fair amount of water but not nearly as much as the starboard tube.

I told Karl that I would clear the tubes every twenty minutes until we got to Vicksburg to make sure that something other than my failure to remember to do this wasn't creating a problem for us.

We were both exhausted but grateful that we had averted disaster. The problem was, we had been so far out on the river that I don't know if we would have been able to make it to shore before the raft would have slid under the water at starboard.

Thankfully, for now, that wasn't going to be a problem.

Soon we were within three miles of Vicksburg Harbor, but as we came around the bend, we ran smack dab into a ton of northbound towboats with massive barge formations and one southbound towboat not far ahead of us.

To get to the harbor would require us to exit the Mississippi River navigation channel and travel three miles north up the Yazoo River. That entrance was on the left descending bank, and we were going to need to cut across the river from where we were. That wasn't going to happen as long as the northbound tows were sitting there waiting to get underway.

So I radioed the southbound towboat and asked the captain for some guidance. I told him we were going to exit eventually at the Yazoo River.

He came back on the radio and suggested we slide in behind him and follow him to the exit. He indicated he would be going directly past the Yazoo River entrance and that being behind him would keep us safe from any northbound towboats.

I wasn't going to argue with that logic!

So we slowed down and settled in behind him.

As we slowly made our way towards the Yazoo River exit, Karl and I once again tried to make sense of where the entrance to the river was based on our charts. Finally, the southbound towboat began to turn its bow into the river's bend to our right, which opened up an angle for us to get by on his port side.

As we came by him, suddenly the Yazoo River entrance became evident and we began to turn the raft left, into the channel.

What I had failed to take into account when we turned in was that we were now going *upriver*, which meant against the current. The three miles we had to go up the channel to get to where we were tying up for the night would take a while at four miles per hour. So we hunkered down as both motors worked hard against the current to get us up the Yazoo River.

Our trip out of here would be much faster in the morning, but for now, it was going to take more time than we had anticipated. Eventually, we came around a slight bend into the Vicksburg Harbor, and the current became less intense, allowing us to make a bit better time.

Then we saw our perch for the night—the Teresia Towboat and one of its deckhands, Billy Hatten.

He hailed us over, and soon we were tied up alongside the Teresia and secure. We made our introductions and then began to offload what we would need for the night and, most importantly, our fuel tanks. I didn't want to leave Vicksburg without all our tanks filled and our power packs and other equipment fully charged. Our good fortune was that the Teresia had external power that allowed us to plug in everything we needed to charge.

Because it wasn't looking like rain, we chose not to put up the windows for the night and opted to get off the raft and go to our hotel as soon as possible.

The Teresia was tied to an extensive series of barges along the shoreline, requiring us to climb up about ten feet to get on the barges before we could walk up to Billy's truck and get to dry land.

Crossing the barges there was like walking an obstacle course. Beyond the equipment that was on the barges, there was about a one-hundred-foot section that had a walking path only three feet wide, and on one side was a twenty-foot drop directly into the river!

So with our hands full of fuel cans, my computer bag, and Karl's backpack, we walked slowly and carefully through this maze of steel cables, open hatches, and other equipment. The plan was to get Karl checked into the hotel and then Billy and I would get the fuel cans filled and bring them back down to the raft. Getting the fuel back to the raft in daylight, given the obstacle course we just walked through, would be much more preferable than doing it at 5:30 in the morning, in the dark!

We dropped Karl off, then Billy and I took care of our fuel at the gas station. When we got back to the barges, it became clear that this was going to be an adventure, getting fully filled gas tanks down a steep hill, across the barge obstacle course, along the length of a narrow trail that had a steep drop into the river, and then ten feet down onto the raft.

We found a workable wheelbarrow that helped to get the tanks down onto the barge and then about fifty feet forward until we had to physically grab them and lug each of them to the top of the barge near the raft.

If anybody thinks I didn't get a workout on the river, they should have seen me that day. I was soaked with sweat and exhausted, but we finally got the tanks onto the raft. Because I was there already and didn't want to deal with it in the morning, I told Billy I wanted to get the fuel mixed before we left for the night.

Soon we were back in Billy's truck and on my way to the hotel. He could not have been kinder and more patient with the two idiots on a raft on the river! Billy served in the Army for nearly thirty years before he retired, and for the past five years had been on the river on a towboat. I learned that he was working on getting his captain's license. Billy is proud of his family, his kids, and his new life on the river—another example of someone who has served America in so many different ways.

We got to the hotel and agreed that we would meet the next morning at 5:30 and head back to the raft.

Vicksburg, Mississippi, is a city with a rich history, but as has been the case with nearly every stop, the amount of time I had to tour was pretty limited. Once I arrived at a location, got the raft cleaned up and ready for the next day, and then communicated to folks who needed to hear from me that I was safe or followed up on other communications, I was tired and just wanted to relax. I hope to return with Owen in the future and spend a few days exploring this colorful and historically important river town.

Chapter 27
A Towboat Army Attacks

The next morning, Karl and I met Billy at the hotel entrance and soon we were back at the raft. It would be a long haul to Vidalia, and I wanted to be sure that we were making our way down the Yazoo as soon as there was enough light to do so safely. We figured that by the time we got to the mouth of the Yazoo, it would be light enough for us to throttle up into the river channel. The raft was ready, and all we needed was daylight, which arrived soon enough.

At about 6:45 a.m., we thanked Billy for his help, shoved off the Teresia, and began our trip down the Yazoo. Our departure was, in fact, much faster than our arrival, and soon enough, we got into the navigation channel. We were going to tie up that day along the channel at a family-owned business called Vidalia Dock.

If we could keep our speed to around ten miles an hour, I hoped that we would pull into the dock around 2:00 p.m., give or take a half-hour or so. So away we went!

Much of this stretch of the trip didn't have much to distinguish it, other than that it was unremarkable for any challenges. The current was fast, the wind was pretty subdued, and we were making great time.

About ten miles shy of our destination, I was pleased to see that we were poised to arrive early, and I was just about to comment to Karl that fortune favored us that day.

And then it hit.

Hard.

The last stretch of river was not only fast, but narrow, and the north-bound towboats that had been waiting for southbound towboats to get past them were now itching to go. They continued to chew up the river channel during the time they waited, and the shallow water, coupled with the narrow channel, was a petri dish of rolling waves and wakes.

We entered this stretch and the first northbound towboat's wake hit us. But it was the one right after it that hit us harder. There was nowhere to hide in this space, and we had to work hard to navigate through their rolling wake and the subsequent waves they created.

I throttled down the Nissan and kept it on idle while I kept the kicker barely moving us forward. It was brutal in this location, but finally we got through it.

As I quickly cleared the pontoon of water, Karl shouted that two more towboats were making their way toward us. This was crazy!

This bend went on for several miles, and it got no wider, and there was nowhere for us to hang out and wait for them to get by us. So we went through the same process of being trapped in roiling waves, and this time the waves were even worse because now it was multiplied by the previous two towboats that had been where these towboats were now heading.

The waves got higher, and I had to deliberately avoid looking to my left or right to see just how nasty the waves had become. I knew myself well enough to know that had I seen the deluge, I would probably have lost focus on what I had to do, which was to slowly work through this mess.

Finally, we got through that section of the bend.

But before we got fully through this bend, we encountered another half dozen towboats, and each time we found ourselves flailing around the wakes and waves that they created.

And then the river opened up in front of us—big and wide and welcoming! But to get there, I had to get through the last two towboats that were moving fast and with empty barges. The last towboat shoved massive amounts of water into the raft and soaked us. I gulped as I saw one last massive wave coming right at us. For some reason, I decided to turn the raft away from it and throttled hard.

Surprisingly, the maneuver worked, and the massive wave went by us harmlessly, and we were able to throttle up quickly to get to calmer and safer water. As we came around the bend, which would lead us to Vidalia Dock, I emptied the tubes so we wouldn't be full when we tied up.

Soon we found a towboat in front of us attached to a barge. At the captain's instruction, we swung around and then came back up the river to tuck in between the barge and the shoreline. This would protect us from river traffic overnight, and when we tied up, we greeted the captain, Michael.

The barge top was about ten feet above the raft's deck, so we had to climb up to get there. Additionally, there would be no power that night, so we needed to charge things with the generator and bring mission-critical equipment that needed charging to the hotel.

I wanted to make sure that we went and thanked Sarah Calhoun with Vidalia Dock for allowing us to tie up there, and despite Karl and I being exhausted, it was important for us to meet her in person and say to say thank you.

As we prepared to get in Michael's truck to go up to the Vidalia Dock office, a woman came down and began taking pictures of the raft. I shouted out, "Are you Sarah?"

"No, I am Sarah's mom, Carla!" she answered. I thanked her for being there and for helping us, and we headed up to the office.

When we got there, Sarah came out with her grandmother, who had started the company over sixty years earlier, along with several employees and other family members. Then Carla came up, and Karl and I explained Spare Key's mission and the purpose of the raft trip and thanked them profusely for their kindness.

Sarah said she had gotten a call from Lee Nelson that we needed help and was more than happy to offer support. This recurring theme over the past week or so, from companies that have better things to do than deal with an idiot on a raft, filled me with gratitude. They had work to do—important work moving material, equipment, and food, plus creating jobs for thousands of people—and here I was on a raft trying to raise money to save Spare Key.

But it was Spare Key's mission that they wanted to support, which is why so many had been steadfast in their willingness to do what they could to make sure our trip down the river concluded successfully.

We thanked Sarah and her family a million times over and then got back into Michael's truck and dropped Karl off at the hotel, and then Michael and I went to do three things: Get fuel, get fuel lines, and get me a bottle of desperately needed scotch after the last ten miles of our trip to Vidalia Dock!

The fuel lines were backups in case the Nissan had issues between Vidalia and Baton Rouge. Lee Nelson had worked tirelessly to find us a fuel line that would replace what was on the Nissan, but to no avail. So the backup plan was to have the materials needed to make a new one if we found ourselves needing one.

Unfortunately, I didn't know what the dimensions were of the fuel line, and to be honest, I didn't want to tempt fate by removing the fuel line from the motor and the fuel tank. So when we got to the marine store, I asked the owner to give me one of each fuel line dimension he thought we would need—which ended up being three fuel lines.

With the lines, the fuel bulb, and clamps in hand, Michael and I completed the other two tasks, and eventually he dropped me off at the hotel.

Like others I have met, Michael has a long history on this river, and in this case, with Vidalia Dock. He had worked there for twenty-five years and was grateful for the life he had been able to create because of the work he was fortunate enough to do. He was proud of the life he had built and only too happy to help us on our journey.

Our hotel was a five-minute walk from the raft, so we wouldn't need a pickup in the morning. Karl and I agreed we would meet in the lobby at 5:45 a.m. to head out to Old River Lock, where we were hoping to be able to tie up near the lock and dam for the evening. Old River Lock was sixty miles from Vidalia Dock and we wanted to be on the river as early as possible so that when we got there, we could figure out our various options.

We got the raft ready, and at about 7:10 a.m. Michael emerged from the towboat and helped untie us, and soon we were on our way.

The day was clear and sunny with no wind. I was grateful for that, and we kicked it into gear. Soon we were making twelve miles an hour down the swift current.

About forty-five minutes into the trip, we entered a long bend that would take us to the left descending shoreline. As I peeked ahead, I saw something that troubled me—a slowly descending fog that was starting to fall in front of us. While the sun was burning through the haze, it wasn't high enough in the sky yet to be burning off this fog.

Soon we were at the bend entrance, and suddenly the red buoy in front of us disappeared into the fog. We had one stop before Baton Rouge. We had come all this way. I was anxious to complete the trip.

But I would not make the mistake of taking us into the fog and traveling blind. I told Karl I was going to turn back around and get out of the falling fog and wait. We had been making good time, so it was frustrating that we would need to stall our forward progress, but I didn't regret it.

During my entire time on the Upper Mississippi River, there was only a single day when the weather started to deteriorate and clouds began to fall, jeopardizing the visibility. Eventually, I got lucky and it cleared.

This fog was not going to clear soon and getting caught in it would be worse than being caught in the darkness. Wandering around in the fog, not knowing where we were or where towboats and barges might be, was simply dangerous.

We chugged around outside the fog for 45 minutes, and then red buoys began to peek through, so we carefully motored forward. Before we entered the channel, I got on the radio and asked if there were any northbound towboats. I got an answer from the Southern Belle captain, who indicated that he was northbound but currently tied up on the left ascending shoreline.

As we headed south, I saw his towboat safely moored to our right and confirmed that it was him with a radio call. Once he confirmed his location, Karl and I continued to proceed down the river bend, but then the fog swallowed up the entrance in front of us again.

I told Karl we couldn't go any further until that fog burned off.

That decision was reaffirmed when I got a text from Lee Nelson, watching the traffic on his computer in St. Paul, Minnesota, telling me that a northbound towboat was now making its way toward us and, equally important, a southbound towboat was also making its way toward us.

I knew that sitting out in the middle of the channel between two towboats was an idiotic place to be. So, I called the Southern Belle towboat captain and asked if we could slide in behind him and wait for this confluence to clear out. He came back on and invited us to tie up to the side of his ship, and that is exactly what we did.

Captain Derek and his crew came out and asked if we needed anything: a shower, food, anything. They wanted to know everything about our trip, Spare Key, and us. They could not have been kinder, and it was another reminder that anytime we needed help, and hope, there was someone there to give it.

About twenty minutes later, the fog began to clear. I looked upriver at the towboat still working to enter the bend, which would meet us on the straightaway. I looked at my iPad app and saw that the northbound towboat was still a few miles down the river.

I thought about it and figured if we got ahead of the southbound towboat, it might slow down the northbound towboat and make our journey easier. So we untied and quickly throttled into the channel and proceeded south.

A few miles down the river, the northbound towboat appeared and thankfully had slowed down enough for us to get by without having to deal with significant roller wakes and waves. The fog continued, much less dense, for another five miles and then finally entirely burned off the river.

Finally, we could get up to full speed. We went as quickly as we could to make up for lost time and get to Old River Lock as soon as possible. Hours later, with what may have been the easiest section of travel we had experienced on the river except for the fog, we arrived at our destination and tied up. One night left before we would be in Baton Rouge.

Chapter 28
Hope Discovered

I didn't sleep much that night since we were preparing for our trip to Baton Rouge. But we spent our last night on the SS Hail Mary safe from mosquitos, the warm evening allowing us to keep the screens exposed.

I got up in the morning and made coffee, and then we made sure the raft was as ready as we had ever gotten it. It would be sixty-nine miles from our current location to the entrance of an area where there was a pronounced bend. According to the map, we would then have a mile trip up the channel to a ramp where we would remove the raft from the river.

As daylight broke, we made our way onto the river. The weather could not have been more perfect. There was no haze. No fog. No wind. Just the river. Our raft. And our final destination.

As we continued on our way to Baton Rouge, I deliberately didn't think about anything other than getting there. I knew there would be time in the future for me to share my thoughts about the trip and the journey with those of you reading this book. But at that moment, I wanted to stay focused on making sure we reached our destination safely and securely.

The day before, I had been filled with anxiety because I had thought I miscalculated the amount of two-stroke oil we would need to complete the trip. A friend provided us with additional oil at Old River Lock, and my concern was abated. Also the day before, our battery pump, the best one we had, that worked the fastest, had stopped working. In my haste to fix it, I had stripped the head of a screw to access the pump's impeller. A friend stepped up and helped fix the screw, so I could make the repair to the pump, and it was now working.

We were enjoying smooth sailing, and the few northbound towboats we encountered were on wide channels that allowed us to remain far away from their wake.

About twenty miles out from Baton Rouge, I checked in with Jeff Beahen, who would be meeting us with a trailer, and ZDave, a connection of Lee Nelson's, who would be assisting with getting the raft out of the river. I confirmed we were running fast and that it was likely we would arrive well ahead of our initial estimate of 3:00 p.m.

As we rounded a bend, we found ourselves behind two southbound towboats moving fast. I decided to stay behind them and use them to cover any potential northbound traffic we might encounter. This was one of the best decisions I made on the trip, as their speed matched ours, and when we finally found ourselves dealing with a northbound towboat, we were ready.

I began to pass the southbound towboats, staying on their port side. I went fast but couldn't get going fast enough to pass them both. We finally got past the first one and began to pass the next. Suddenly, a northbound tow appeared, heading toward the narrow part of the channel we needed to get through. Thankfully, because we had run so close to the southbound towboats, he hadn't had time to throttle up his engines enough to create the chaos of waves behind him. Soon we were past him with relatively little wake to contend with and were now ten miles from Baton Rouge.

I was now getting texts from friends wishing us well as they watched our journey on our Facebook livestream. They were excited, and I am sure, relieved. A few of them made it clear that they hadn't given me much chance of surviving the trip at all. Still, I stayed focused on getting to the end, not letting myself dwell on memories of the trip. We weren't done yet, and that was my goal.

About seven miles out, we came upon two northbound towboats—the last two I could see on the app before we got to Baton Rouge. They were one right after another, and the first one passed us on wide water. The second one, though, was making its way through a tremendously narrow section of the river, and I could see its huge rollers churning up the water. I decided to slow way down and wait until it got through and out into the wider river. It cost us about fifteen minutes, but as soon as I saw he had cleared the channel, I throttled up. By the time we got to where he had chewed up the channel, the amount of commotion was pretty minimal.

We now had four miles to go. One last northbound towboat showed up on the app, but we passed him by quickly, and he was tiny. Now, two miles to go, and as we turned into the final bend, we saw a wide section of the river and both shorelines filled with towboats and barges. And, in front of us, a towboat making way north. Just a single towboat. We would need to descend left to get to the turn, and as I anticipated passing him on the left, I also saw that there were northbound towboats coming up behind him. It wouldn't work for me to be on the left side, so I decided to stick to his port side.

We got by the towboat, but the wind and waves in this channel reminded me of the section of St. Louis where I had to deal with increasingly higher waves and nonstop towboat and barge traffic coming from all directions.

We were now a mile out from the exit, and once again we found ourselves not able to determine the location of the entrance to our turn. After a few fitful moments and cross-referencing our maps, charts, and digital devices, we found the spot on the Lower Mississippi River chart. The problem now, though, was a nonstop stream of northbound tows clogging up the left side of the river, which was where the passageway to the channel was that we needed to enter.

We nervously continued downriver, frantically searching for the entrance and hoping we hadn't passed it, which would require us to turn around and try to power our way back up the river, against the current, to find it.

Finally, there were only two towboats in our way, but the entrance for us to get into the channel was still not obvious.

I radioed the towboats and asked them if what lay between the two of them was the entrance to the channel. They confirmed it, and I began to make my way there. Finally, I could see the entrance, but I could also see massive roller waves approaching us from the nonstop churn of those northbound towboats. This wasn't going to be easy!

We hit the waves, which were some of the largest we had encountered on the river, and we were less than a football field's length away from calm water. It would be just our luck that after nearly two thousand miles, two months, and ten states, the trip would end less than a half-mile from our destination, lost to the last waves of towboats right outside of Baton Rouge!

My decision to stay focused on the trip until its true end served me well at this point. As Karl and I and the raft bounced violently up and down on the river and water poured into the front half of the raft, I saw two last waves coming at us from starboard. For only the second time on the trip, I decided to throttle hard and turn away from the waves in the hope I could avoid being driven to the bottom of the river. And for the second time, it worked. The waves passed by us harmlessly, and we slid off the last wave into the entrance of the bend to Baton Rouge Harbor and off the Mississippi River.

And then the Nissan died. It literally died. It stopped working, and I laughed out loud.

Tim the Mechanic had promised me this: the Nissan would get us to Baton Rouge but he made no promise of it getting us any further. He was right. We had made it to Baton Rouge.

And while the Nissan had stopped working the moment we got off the Mississippi, I was able to coax it back to life to work with the kicker and get us up the channel. Now the only remaining anxiety I had was the condition of the boat ramp. Finally, there to our right was a boat ramp and two people at the end of it, a pickup truck with a trailer above them. We had arrived!

Now we just needed to get the raft off the river.

Rob Powell, ZDave, Steve Reardon, and Jeff Beahen greeted us at the base of the ramp, and we slide the raft onto the trailer. It took a few minutes to get it positioned right, but finally we had it secured and out of the water and at the top of the ramp.

We were off the river.

We were off the raft.

The journey's end had arrived.

I had gone looking for Hope on the River.

I had found it along every mile I traveled. And, in making this journey, I had nearly completed Spare Key's three-year journey of registering our nonprofit in every single state in America, which allowed us to serve families anywhere in the country.

Hope on the River would soon become Hope Across America.

Epilogue

The final act of my Hope on the River journey was to complete Spare Key's final state registration in Baton Rouge. Karl and I stuck around the city for a couple days and through the weekend, with a plan to meet with the Louisiana Secretary of State on Monday, finalize the paperwork, and begin our less hazardous journey back home to Minnesota.

On Monday morning, as soon as the office opened, I walked in, completed the paperwork with the front desk staff, and did a quick photo op with secretary of state, R. Kyle Ardoin. With a bunch of thank you's from me and a bunch of congratulations from them, I took my leave, got back in our rental car, and Karl and I began our trip back to Minnesota.

The journey of Hope on the River was complete. We were safely off the water. The SS Hail Mary had been sold to ZDave, and my mission on the river was done.

Over the next two days, Karl and I drove through rain and weathered the close confines of brothers who had already spent too much time with each other! In my family of nine kids, in our "old age" we have an unwritten rule when it comes to big family gatherings: all of us are just fine together for about four hours. After that we start getting on one another's nerves. That's the great thing about big families. Each of us would give the shirt off our back for the others. But put us in the same room—or raft—for more than four hours and things start to get a little salty.

Karl and I had used up our four-hour time limit and more! We would both be glad to be back in the "normal" confines of our lives.

The success of this trip had always been in doubt, and no more so than when I found myself on the Lower Mississippi River. I am convinced that without Karl, my effort would have failed. I would likely have had to call it quits because of the difficulty of preventing a leaking pontoon raft from sinking, avoiding being capsized, and steering clear of destruction by towboat with only myself to navigate the river.

More importantly, I could have very well perished on my own if I had not had the good sense to get off the river if things got too dangerous. As it was, and as it is, Karl was the necessary addition of the first mate that I needed to complete the trip successfully. Period. Thank you, Karl.

We arrived back in the Twin Cities, and we hugged, and Karl went off to continue his life without me and my raft and the river.

I walked into my house and hugged my wife for a long, long time. More than anything else that I had missed, I missed her and being in the same airspace with her.

My dog, Sailor, and I caught up, too. She didn't bite me, and that was a good thing.

Eventually, I reconnected with Owen and Maisie, and over the next several days with other friends and family. I reached out to my mom to assure her that Karl and I had, indeed, survived the trip and she could quit worrying about two of her nine children.

The transition from a great adventure to the day-to-day routine of a "normal" life was interesting. I had spent nearly every waking moment from early July to the final day of my trip almost four months later eating, breathing, sleeping, planning, preparing, and executing this effort. It consumed me from morning until night, and for the nearly two months I spent on the raft it was my reason for being.

Then, almost as quickly as it had begun, it was done.

We had achieved or exceeded nearly all of our goals.

We wanted to reach Louisiana and do the paperwork that would allow Spare Key to be able to serve families in all fifty states.

Done.

We wanted to raise at least $250,000 in donations.

Done.

We wanted to raise our organization's profile and bring the attention of tens of thousands of people to our mission and our www.helpmebounce.org online platform.

Done.

I wanted to survive the trip and return home in one piece.

Done.

Done, done, done, and done!

As I write this epilogue in preparation for the publication of this book, I have revisited nearly every single mile and minute of my trip. I can close my eyes and remember each day in different ways. The mornings I prepared, the hours standing until my legs ached, the wonder of the new things I saw, the joy of reaching my destination alive, and the privilege of meeting strangers who became my friends.

I have been asked repeatedly about what surprised me the most about the trip.

My honest answer: Everything!

There's not a single part of any element of this adventure that wasn't new to me. I am in awe of all of it. In awe of the people who made it possible. In awe of the Mississippi River. In awe of the God who watched over me but didn't make it easy for me.

I look at the life I have lived as a series of adventures. This has been added to that list. God willing, it won't be the last one for me, or for Spare Key. Any success I have had in my life hasn't happened because I was the smartest or most talented person in the room. I remain a person with a C minus intellect who possesses nothing unique other than my DNA.

What I do have, I think, and what has allowed me to achieve any successes is a clear sense of purpose and determination. That purpose and determination has allowed me to overcome all my many limitations and do what others might decide wasn't worth the effort, or that they felt they weren't capable of doing.

It never occurred to me that I couldn't put the trip together or that it wouldn't be successful.

Once on the river, I may have doubted my skills and judgment, but I never doubted my resolve in getting to the end.

Every day, I reminded myself of what I was doing, why I was doing it, and that as long as the raft floated and the motors started, I had every chance of success.

I took this trip at fifty-seven years of age. I boarded the raft carrying more weight on my body than I cared to and ended the trip carrying a lot less. In the days, weeks, and months since the trip, I have regained much of what I lost. And maybe a bit more!

But I was reminded of the value and importance of taking care of oneself in this life. I'm no athlete, yet I have run seven marathons and done a lot of longer and shorter running and cross-country ski races in between. I did these things not because I expected to win; I did them because I could. And I could because after spending twenty years of my life smoking cigarettes and drinking too much and abusing my body, I made wiser choices later in life that allow me to do any of the things I want to do or decide to try to do.

Like taking a homemade raft down a river.

The simple act of being able to kneel, bend over, carry eighty-gallon cans of gasoline across a dock, across a barge, and down a ladder were all a part of this journey's effort. Standing for eight hours a day, steering the raft, holding onto a rope thrown over the wall of a lock, and grabbing onto the side of a dock to keep from crashing into it all required some level of physical effort. I am immensely grateful that I could do these things that we take for granted in life when not on a raft on the Mississippi River, and for knowing that these things were essential for my life on the river.

Taking a raft down the Mississippi was never on my bucket list. But it's now in the bucket.

There are still things on my bucket list, and I imagine, and I hope, there will be things added to the list that I haven't even thought about yet. I hate the idea that there will ever be a time in my life that I don't say to someone, "I have an idea!"

I went down the river to raise money and awareness for Spare Key during a global pandemic. I was looking for hope.

But I was also doing my part to bring hope to others. I know that I found hope in the people I met; only those I met will be able to say whether I brought it to them.

With our www.*helpmebounce.org* platform, Spare Key will continue to do its work and seek new ways to help even more families across America who are facing a medical crisis avoid adding a financial crisis to their lives. There is no shortage of people who need help in this country as they struggle to navigate medical disasters that chew up their savings, force them from their homes, take them away from their jobs, and all too often undermine their future. My job, and that of everyone at Spare Key, including our Board of Directors, is to do all we can, whatever we can and wherever we can, to help those families "bounce and not break."

My trip along that river of hope wasn't the end of Spare Key's journey or, for that matter, my own. By the time you read this, I may already be on another adventure to help Spare Key and the families we are committed to serving. Maybe a mountain to climb, a country to traverse, or a race to run is in my future. Perhaps there will be something I haven't even thought of yet that will rival the adventure I have shared with you in this book.

This much is true: I traveled 1,700 miles, over two months and ten states, on a leaky pontoon with a garden shed on top down one of the most powerful rivers in the world. Despite flying fish that hit my raft like missiles, oceanlike waves and wakes, monster towboats and my own shortcomings as a mariner, I lived to share my tale.

I found Hope on the River, and in doing so, Spare Key is now able to share Hope Across America.